Volume 31

# INFLUENCE OF FUNDING ON ADVANCES IN LIBRARIANSHIP

Advances in
# Librarianship

Volume 31

# INFLUENCE OF FUNDING ON ADVANCES IN LIBRARIANSHIP

## Advances in
# Librarianship

Edited by
## Danuta A. Nitecki

Associate University Librarian
Yale University Library
New Haven
Connecticut, USA

and

## Eileen G. Abels

Professor
Drexel University
College of Information Science and Technology
Philadelphia, Pennsylvania, USA

Emerald

United Kingdom • North America • Japan
India • Malaysia • China

Emerald Group Publishing Limited
Howard House, Wagon Lane, Bingley BD16 1WA, UK

First edition 2008

**Reprints and permission service**
Contact: booksandseries@emeraldinsight.com

**British Library Cataloguing in Publication Data**
A catalogue record for this book is available from the British Library

ISBN: 978-1-84855-372-9
ISSN: 0065-2830

Awarded in recognition of
Emerald's production
department's adherence to
quality systems and processes
when preparing scholarly
journals for print

INVESTOR IN PEOPLE

# Contents

# A Review of Research Related to Management of Corporate Libraries   93

## James M. Matarazzo and Toby Pearlstein

# Alternative Funding for Public Libraries: Trends, Sources, and the Heated Arguments that Surround It   115

## Denise E. Agosto

# From Foundation to Federal Funding: The Impact of Grants on Education for Library and Information Science   141

## Linda C. Smith

# Contributors

*Numbers in parantheses indicate the pages on which the author's contributions begin.*

**Denise E. Agosto** (115), College of Information Science and Technology, Drexel University, Philadelphia, PA, USA

**Songphan Choemprayong** (37), School of Information and Library Science, University of North Carolina at Chapel Hill, Chapel Hill, NC, USA

**Lori Eakin** (37), School of Information and Library Science, University of North Carolina at Chapel Hill, Chapel Hill, NC, USA

**Trudi Bellardo Hahn** (1), College of Information Studies, University of Maryland, College Park, MD, USA

**James M. Matarazzo** (93), Graduate School of Library and Information Science, Simmons College, Boston, MA, USA

**Toby Pearlstein** (93), Global Information Services, Bain & Company, Inc., Boston, MA, USA (Retired)

**Jeffrey Pomerantz** (37), School of Information and Library Science, University of North Carolina at Chapel Hill, Chapel Hill, NC, USA

**Linda C. Smith** (141), Graduate School of Library and Information Science, University of Illinois at Urbana-Champaign, Champaign, IL, USA

# Preface

What influence do funders have on advances in librarianship? The idea to devote this 31st volume of *Advances in Librarianship* to this question arose from a conversation between the co-editors during which they wondered if the library and information science (LIS) professions were influenced in similar ways as other disciplines reportedly are by the agencies and foundations that fund research in their fields. The notion of the influence of funding is not new. Mangan (1999) notes that the focus of the American Association of University Professors' meeting held in May 1999 was on the influence of corporate funding on medical academic research. The increase in corporate funding is due at least in part to a decline in government funding, the author notes that often with this type of funding, "the sponsors decide what will be studied, how the research will be conducted, and how and whether the findings will be published" (p. 14). Approaching the same notion from a different perspective, Goldfarb (2008) tracked the academic output of 221 academic researchers who had received funding from the NASA aerospace engineering program in 1981 in order to explore whether research with specific usable outcomes has a negative impact on scholarly publication. Overall the findings of this study support previous studies that concluded that academic research efforts in the United States are responsive to social and technological needs. Further, Goldfarb notes that commercial outputs of research, such as those that result in NASA type studies, complement academic output.

The editors' conversation led to framing a volume that would address the influence of research funding on advances in libraries and librarianship from two perspectives: funding agents and specific initiatives. Through a collection of chapters, the editors hoped to address several questions. Do the agendas of those agencies and foundations that fund research in the profession shape the topics of sponsored inquiry and methodologies used to gather evidence for research that advances libraries and librarianship? What are the trends in the questions funded, in the areas of librarianship supported, and perhaps of greatest interest, in the impact funders have made on our understanding of libraries, librarianship, and solving problems that face them? In this volume, authors were invited to explore what areas of the profession and professional inquiries have been supported by individual government and private agencies, professional associations, foundations, and individual philanthropists. By examining what funding sources have supported, questions about the nature of influence they have on advances in librarianship would be explored.

The traditions of *Advances in Librarianship* offer an appropriate forum to explore these questions through a collection of in-depth reviews of the literature and practice on different perspectives related to the theme. The series aims to present a variety of aspects of the field of librarianship through the publication of critical articles and surveys, based on the published literature, research in progress, and current developments, relating to all segments of the profession and related topics. Contributing authors are encouraged to address provocative and stimulating topics that will ensure that trends are identified and research results of interest are made available quickly in a rapidly changing profession.

In identifying authors for this volume, the editors found a very favorable response to the theme and at the same time, a hesitancy to tackle preparing a chapter, given the challenges of the topic. There does not seem to be a body of literature about the influence of funding on LIS research, nor is there an expressed concern that the profession's advancement may be influenced by external funding agendas. This volume may be the first to fill this void. Although the editors were disappointed that numerous potential authors declined their invitation to join this exploration, they are very pleased to present the five excellent chapters that comprise this 31st volume in the *Advances in Librarianship* series.

Trudi Hahn opens the volume with Chapter 1 in which she presents a comprehensive overview of federal government sources of funding for research in library and information science. From her review of the literature and conversations with key personnel initiated through personal contacts, she concludes that each of the few agencies funding LIS research have mission-defined agendas to advance research in specific areas such as biomedical needs (NLM), science and technology (NSF), the humanities (NEH), and service to the communities of learners who use libraries and museums (IMLS). Yet none exhaust the funds available to issue grants because there is a shortage of excellent proposals. The federal government agencies are perceived to be malleable and open to good research ideas, thereby supporting the theme that researchers set the agenda for advances in librarianship that occur through research. Hahn ends her chapter with a helpful summary of advice from the literature and private contacts for preparing a successful research grant proposal.

Focusing on the history of the digital library in Chapter 2, Jeff Pomerantz, Songphan Choemprayong, and Lori Eakin offer an insightful look at the funding support for what is currently the most active area of research and development in libraries. The development of the digital library and its multitude of activities require large sums of money, funding which has come initially from two major contributors and more recently from individual institutions. The authors identify the Institute of Museum and Library Services (IMLS) as having "single-handedly greatly expanded the amount of cultural heritage materials available online" and the Andrew J. Mellon Foundation as extending its support of educational and cultural heritage to provide major funding for development of the digital library. Pomerantz and his colleagues also discuss the commingled relationships of funding agency missions, the opportunities and agendas for building and maintaining the digital library, and changes in librarianship. Based on a thorough review of the literature and knowledge of research projects, the authors also suggest gaps in the body of publications which suggest future research topics.

The next two chapters look at the volume's theme from the perspectives of two types of institutions—corporate and public libraries. In Chapter 3, James Matarazzo and Toby Pearlstein argue that research trends relevant to corporate librarians are less affected by sources of funding than by pragmatism. Little applied research has been published that offers the managers of corporate libraries evidence helpful to them in decision-making or for promotion and advocacy of their libraries. Such librarians, including ones with advanced training, seldom have time or institutional support to engage in conducting research. The authors reviewed the erratic influence of professional associations, particularly the Special Library Association (SLA), in formulating and funding research agendas focusing on corporate and other special libraries. Changes in the SLAs scholarly communication vehicles and grant resources have resulted in an uneven and weak record of influential research trends affecting corporate libraries in North America. In contrast, the authors reviewed trends in Australia, United Kingdom, and New Zealand to identify a greater productivity of research studies and compilation of data to address the corporate library managers' need to value the impact of their libraries. Funding and research leadership provided by professional associations and government institutions in these countries may either be the result of environments already committed to managerial accountability or may be key contributors to fostering evidence-based decision-making among corporate librarians. Matarazzo and Pearlstein do not suggest the direction of influence, but by highlighting several successful research activities, they have supported a suspected relationship between research funding agendas and managerial practices in the corporate library sector.

In Chapter 4, Denise Agosto examines alternative funding sources for public libraries through a systematic review of a decade of LIS literature and a case study of one (West Chester, PA) public library. She illustrates the lack of consistent trends among public libraries regarding the extent of government support each receives, where nearly equal percentages of libraries showed increased support, as did reductions, but all are faced with challenges to sustain essential operations or to grow to meet changing user demands. Supported by detailed evidence from her literature review, Agosto presents well the controversy over the potential interests held by fiscal supporters (such as corporate foundations or business marketing programs) from whom public libraries accept needed financial resources, and the potential challenge these interests make to the public library's mission to provide free and unbiased access to information and related services to its citizenry. She leaves open the question of how commercial and philanthropic interests might be shaping advances in public librarianship, but suggests that the answer is not simple or necessarily universal.

The final volume chapter, written by Linda Smith, turns to questions about the impact of funding on the education of the library (and information science) profession. Smith describes three periods of substantial investments in educational programs, beginning with those made by the Carnegie Corporation in the 1920s and 1930s, followed by the programs funded by the United States. Office of Education in the 1960s and 1970s, and concluding with the present decade's contributions made by the IMLS. The first period resulted in the establishment of graduate education programs within libraries and universities, and initial surveys of educational needs that set the core curricula and competency requirements to prepare professionals to both manage libraries and engage in research of questions about information use and library activities. During the second period, federal and foundation funds were provided to defray the costs of training both for students and schools of library education; reports and renewed interest were produced in the profession's research agendas, its identified and continued development. Most recently, substantial federal funds again have been offered to recruit and prepare the next generation of professionals who will be responsible for continuing the principles of assuring free access to information as a fundamental principle of a democratic society. Smith presents a thoroughly documented case without articulating a conclusion about the extent of influence of funding sources on advances in librarianship. A handful of major foundations and federal funds have supported the development of a library profession through support for graduate education and research since the 1890s, and with the start of the 21st century have channeled resources to address challenges of creating a diverse profession (particularly to reflect the ethnic makeup of the populations served), and developing skills in applying information and network technologies. Smith also presents evidence that although several of the pioneer educational programs have been closed within individual universities, current funding agendas have fostered continuation of the profession's research and development within an environment characterized by both collaboration among institutions and outcome-based accountability.

Reflecting on the original questions posed to this volume's contributing authors, the editors suggest that indeed relationships exist between the sources of funding for the profession and advances in librarianship. Historically, the formation of the librarian profession, through designing and offering a common core preparation and developed skills, as well as encouraging systematic inquiry to form a researched body of knowledge, were advances that may not have occurred or at least not as quickly if not for the provision of grants and resources by key social minded foundations and philanthropists such as Carnegie, H. W. Wilson, and Kellogg, and the federal government in its commitment to support of libraries as a public good. Such acknowledgement of the role of librarianship in advancing the democratic principles of access to information and lifelong learning continue among foundation and government support today. Key funders, such as the Andrew H. Mellon Foundation and IMLS have provided invaluable support to advance the digital library, even though it has not been among their mission objectives. Advances in libraries as service organizations have also been the result of both government and private funding of specific interests such as biomedical and humanities research, as well as access to computers and associated electronic information sources among disadvantaged populations. Although questions are raised on occasion about the motivation of commercial interests funding libraries, contributions from foundations associated with Microsoft, Target, and WalMart, for example, seem to require little more than public relations acknowledgment in exchange for significant grants to support library operations. In this volume only corporate and public libraries were examined in depth and clearly the latter have seen advancement of their ability to meet better their social mission with financial support from funders, while the particular type of special library has benefited from association support, but in minor ways. In general, the authors who addressed the topic of research funding, suggest that agendas are set by LIS researchers rather than by those providing the funds. The profession has not taken full advantage of seeking funds available for research, and may be advised that a developing trend is that awards are granted for well-prepared proposals, with favor to those planning outcome-based assessment and explorations undertaken in collaboration with shared expertise from different organizations.

This volume is by no means a comprehensive review of the topic of the influences of funding on advances in librarianship. It poses the question and several excellent explorations have offered some insights that suggest several funding opportunities exist for those engaged in research or managing new initiatives to lead future advances in the librarianship. Any success that this volume might bring, especially to encourage further conversation about this interesting foundation for advancing the profession and its areas of inquiry, should be attributed to the eight authors who prepared the content chapters of this volume. As editors, we assume responsibility for any oversights in addressing the topic that result from our unsuccessful attempts to commit contributions from prospective authors we had invited to prepare chapters on other perspectives on the topic. Appreciation is once again extended to the following dedicated members of the Editorial Board for the generous guidance they offered authors in preparing their drafts and the volume editors in pursuing the topic: Cheryl McCarthy, Professor, Graduate School of Library and Information Studies, University of Rhode Island; Mary Jean Pavelsek, International Business Librarian, New York University Libraries; Nancy Roderer, Director of Welch Medical Library, Johns Hopkins University; and Robert A. Seal, Dean of Libraries, Loyola University Chicago. We began preparation of this volume with Elsevier, but during our final stages of preparing the manuscript, we learned that this series, *Advances in Librarianship*, has been sold to Emerald Publishing. We look forward to finalizing this, our last volume as editors, with the new publisher's staff but wish to specially thank Zoe LaRoche for her continued assistance, first with Elsevier and through the transition to Emerald.

## References

Goldfarb, B. (2008). The effect of government contracting on academic research: Does the source of funding affect scientific output?. *Research Policy* 37, 41–58.
Mangan, K.S. (1999). Medical professors see threat in corporate influence on research. *Chronicle of Higher Education* 45(39), A14(2).

# Federal Support for Library and Information Science Research

Trudi Bellardo Hahn

College of Information Studies, University of Maryland, College Park, MD, USA

## Abstract

The US Federal government is a potential source of support for advancing Library and Information Science (LIS) through funding experimentation, innovation, and demonstration. Most agencies are not as much interested in advancing the research front in LIS as they are in LIS contributions that advance other fields. The full potential of federal funding to impact LIS is far from realized. LIS researchers should be aware of each agency's mission as well as the types of research that each one supports. Many people contribute to research agendas but the most influential are researchers themselves. Becoming more successful in winning grants will require researchers to become better grant writers and to collaborate with people outside LIS.

## I. Introduction

### A. Scope and Method

This overview is aimed at new and aspiring investigators—academic researchers or practitioners—in the field of library and information science (LIS) who want to compete successfully for federal monies in the form of grants or contracts in order to do original research, develop innovative or model programs, or initiate new types of services. It also is intended to assist those who wish to know how the field can be advanced and how federal funding can be used to solve problems in the LIS field. Digital library research and development has been an important target area of federal funding for well over 10 years, but it will not be covered in depth here because it is covered in another chapter in this volume.

It must be admitted up front that it is extremely difficult if not impossible to determine exactly how much federal support goes to LIS research. The primary reason is that the field's boundaries are highly porous and ever shifting. Further, in this day and age, nearly every researcher and practitioner who wants

INFLUENCE OF FUNDING ON ADVANCES IN LIBRARIANSHIP
ADVANCES IN LIBRARIANSHIP, VOL. 31
© 2008 by Emerald Group Publishing Limited
ISSN: 0065-2830
DOI: 10.1016/S0065-2830(08)31001-0

to mount a project of any size has to find collaborators—other information institutions (archives, museums, K-12 schools, religious groups, community organizations, hospitals, local businesses, or other), specialists in other skill sets (such as statistics, computer programming, demographics, or graphics), or researchers from other disciplines—say, geography, psychology, biotechnology, or computer science, to name but a few. One thing that is immediately apparent from examining studies funded at the federal level is that partnerships and interdisciplinary collaborations are important. However, if someone other than an LIS researcher is the principal investigator on a project or study, the LIS role may be difficult to determine.

This overview begins with an historical review from the literature going back nearly 25 years. Then the focus is narrowed to roughly the past 8–10 years, depending on the agency. Excluded from the scope are the E-rate program (discounted telecommunications rates for schools and libraries) and other federal programs that do not give grants directly but instead funnel federal appropriations to states or regional jurisdictions for local distribution. A large number of federal agencies have awarded some sort of grant or contract to an LIS researcher, but the emphasis in this review is on the few that have provided the bulk of the federal grant support for LIS.

In addition to searching the published literature, I scanned the web sites of the agencies who provide major funding for LIS, conducted interviews with agency program officers and researchers who have received grants, consulted *Bowker Annual* from 1998 to 2007 for descriptions of particular programs, searched Grants.gov by broad topic areas for funding opportunities, and where appropriate, reviewed Congressional budget requests or appropriations justifications, Congressional testimony, and news releases from recent years.

## B. Research Questions

Overall, this chapter addresses funding for research, development, and demonstration projects involving a range of topics subsumed under the diverse field of LIS. The main focus is on projects involving all types of libraries and the clients they serve, as well as information science research that advances knowledge in the field related to information retrieval, databases, access, bibliographic control, collaboration through networks, management of libraries and information services, and other key areas.

The particular questions addressed are:

- Which agencies have provided the most support for LIS research?
- Who is shaping research agendas—federal agencies, or individual researchers (top-down or bottom-up)? How are research agendas currently being set? What external/environmental factors are driving research and development (R&D) priorities?

- What specific initiatives have been supported? Overall, during the past 9–10 years, what have been the trends in topics and issues?
- Which initiatives are currently at the top of federal agencies' funding agendas?
- To what extent are federal agencies having an impact on our understanding of libraries, librarianship, information science, and on solving the problems facing the field?
- How can the LIS field garner a larger portion of federal research and demonstration funds?

## II. History of Funding for LIS: Pre-1998

In attempting to sum up funding in the LIS field during the period 1964–1984, Fitzgibbons (1984, pp. 537–538) discovered that "literature searches on funding for research on librarianship were not very productive" and that "information on funding for research is scattered as well as scarce." She found *Bowker Annual* articles helpful, as well as the *ALA Yearbook*, which was last published in 1990. Fitzgibbons noted also that "trying to draw clear, clean lines between research on the one hand, and development and demonstration on the other" was complicated (p. 541). In 1984, there were four major research funding agencies for LIS, three of which were governmental: The Department of Education HEA (Higher Education Act) Title II-B programs, the National Science Foundation (NSF) Division of Information Science and Technology program, the National Library of Medicine (NLM) extramural program, and the Council on Library Resources. Of this group, the NLM program is the only government grant program of interest to LIS still operating today. Fitzgibbons struggled, especially with NSF and NLM, to assess when any given funded study was within the field of library and information science. Examining the grants these two agencies awarded, she discovered either through the titles or the researcher's affiliation (whether associated with an ALA-accredited LIS program) that "many of the projects funded by these two agencies were not related to librarianship but were in the areas of computer science, engineering, theoretical mathematics, medicine and so on" (pp. 543–544). The "and so on" disciplines have expanded greatly since 1984, but the situation remains the same today: most of the funding from these agencies goes to researchers who are *not* affiliated with LIS schools. Among Fitzgibbons' recommendations was for professional organizations and scholars in each area of the field to establish research agendas and to help secure more federal dollars for LIS research.

The part of NSF today that is most closely aligned with the broad field of LIS is the Directorate for Computer and Information Science and Engineering (CISE). It was formed just two years after Fitzgibbons' article. Bamford and Brownstein (1986, p. 449) noted that the new Directorate was "directed to fundamental understanding of information and information processes ..." However, the specific focus was to be on computing and communication technologies. Bamford and Brownstein called for inter-disciplinary collaboration, but the disciplines they had in mind were computer and cognitive scientists, electronics engineers, and mathematicians. Many of the researchers in these fields identified or aligned themselves with information science. Their home affiliations, however, were seldom in LIS programs; they were associated with other disciplines such as computer science and engineering.

The state of LIS research in 1990 was poor, according to Hernon *et al.* (1990). They described it as fragmented, non-cumulative, generally weak, and dealing with trivial problems. LIS researchers used "descriptive rather than inferential statistical techniques" (p. 215). Hernon *et al.* claimed that part of the overall problem was poor academic preparation among those most likely to conduct research—academic librarians and LIS faculty. They also felt that the discipline of LIS itself needed a clearer definition, and that practitioners in the field needed to help the researchers to articulate significant researchable problems.

Altman (1991) assessed the funding prospects for LIS research and painted a similarly dreary picture. The lack of focus and definition in LIS had allowed researchers from other disciplines to grab "a larger and larger share of federal funded research grants" (p. 114). Even as the size of the federal budget for research had been growing quite dramatically during the 1980s, LIS researchers' share was getting progressively smaller and smaller. Among the examples she cited was the NLM, which awarded 174 grants during the 1980s, but only 15 (11.6%) of them were to library researchers (either practitioners or LIS faculty). The situation at NSF during the same period was "even more dismal"—library-oriented researchers won only 3.63% of the grants awarded by the Division of Information Science and Technology.

Altman attributed the decline to the fact that NLM and NSF had broadened their definitions of information to "embrace a wide variety of approaches" (p. 120), which leaned more toward engineering and computation. In addition the competition for funding had dramatically increased and was becoming "formidable." Many of the proposals at NLM for example, were coming from physicians with a lot of knowledge about computers (some held both MD and PhD degrees) and thus the sophistication of their proposals was high.

Altman and Brown (1991) also examined NSF's support of information research and noted that it had evolved from its earlier mission begun in 1950, which was to improve publication, indexing, and dissemination of scientific and technical documents. While designers of computer systems and programmers, as well as linguists, had been involved in these projects, researchers and developers from the library and information center world had been major players. By the late 1970s however, the boundaries of what was considered information research were blurring and the projects funded were becoming more diverse. Throughout the 1970s and 1980s the names and missions of NSF divisions changed frequently. While it might have been true that the NSF was providing the largest amount of funding for library/ information research of all the federal agencies, it was becoming increasingly difficult for LIS researchers themselves to compete with computer scientists and engineers for that funding. Altman (1993, p. 274) noted that NSF research dollars "for library-affiliated researchers slid from a high of 21.55 percent in 1979 to zero by 1991."

Altman's explanation (1993) for the precipitous decline in NSF funding for LIS research was that LIS faculty were not under the same pressures as faculty researchers in other disciplines such as computer science, electrical engineering, economics, and psychology, where bringing in research money is a prime criterion for promotion and tenure. She also speculated that since the 1980s LIS researchers have left the major developments and advancements in the field to R&D staff in companies in the rapidly growing information industry. As further evidence of the disengagement of LIS researchers from this federal funding agency, she cited the American Society for Information Science (ASIS) 1992 conference, which featured 85 information science experts. Of these 85, only one had received an NSF grant in the past 13 years and that individual was not affiliated with any LIS organization.

Meanwhile, at the Office of Library Programs (OLP) in the US Department of Education (USDE), which had been the prime source of LIS funding and leadership in LIS research since 1965, the budget was shrinking, not expanding as it was at NLM and NSF (Mathews, 1991). Federal dollars for LIS research had declined dramatically from 1967 to 1976 ($20 million) to the period 1977–1989 (only $5.9 million). Because OLP's budget was so tight, Mathews recommended an assessment that would identify the areas of LIS with the greatest need for funding. Mathews pointed out that, as libraries of all types across the country were facing budget crises, they needed data from research to improve their chances for success in competing for local dollars. However, most practitioners were not trained or otherwise inclined to utilize research or to become involved in setting research agendas. Mathews asked: "Are the results of research making their way into the hands of library practitioners?" (p. 45).

White (1994/1995) thought not. Practicing librarians are part of the problem, White asserted, if they have no interest in the research publications and research conference programs in their own field. The small size of the LIS research community also meant that it did not have enough clout to negotiate with federal agencies, especially with NSF and NLM, on priorities or agendas for funding. The only reason, White argued, that NSF or NLM would be interested in funding LIS research would be not to further knowledge or solve problems through innovation and testing in the LIS field, but rather to solve the problems of other groups such as scientists and engineers. He did not take comfort in the fact that the USDE was supposed to be funding LIS, since he believed that the education community did not regard librarians and library researchers as being on the same level as education researchers. In fact, he said, professional educators think "there is really nothing for libraries to research" (1994/1995, p. 30).

According to White, federal funding had been available in earlier decades under the rubric of science information research, which allowed research libraries and LIS education programs to study phenomena and issues that would help them make better operational decisions. Those opportunities, however, had been eliminated. They were "replaced by mathematical and sociological studies undertaken by individuals with neither a background nor interest in libraries" (1994/1995, p. 30).

White's opinion about practicing librarians having little or no interest in research was reinforced in a recent news item published in *American Libraries* that described increased federal support to help local libraries serve their communities better, but it mentioned nothing about research grant monies becoming available (Stone, 2006).

In a major report about library research in the period 1983–1997 (Libraries for the Future, 1998) were several key points about federal funding patterns:

- Total federal support for library research has averaged less than $275,000 per year,
- Federal funding for library research peaked in 1987, and
- While other types of research funding have declined, federal funding in specific research areas such as digital library planning has increased.

Klassen (1997) reported that in 1996, USDE Library Programs funded only three research and demonstration projects, for $1 million each. The three grants went to the Shoah Foundation for digitizing videotapes of Holocaust survivor stories, the National Museum of Women in the Arts for creating an archive of women artists' materials, and a multi-state consortium of libraries for building a system architecture for library catalogs, bibliographic databases, and other Internet resources.

## III. Institute of Museum and Library Services (IMLS)

### A. Establishment of a New Agency

Even as readers in the LIS community were digesting Klassen's 1997 report, the planning for a new independent federal grant-making agency to replace the USDE Library Programs had already begun. The 1998 *Bowker Annual* featured the first entry for the Institute of Museum and Library Services (IMLS) (Frankel, 1998). The USDE programs along with the programs from the Institute of Museum Services had been consolidated into a single program in 1996, and by 1998 the new agency was dispensing dollars.

About 90% of the money was targeted for a new program under the Library Services & Technology Act (LSTA), which replaced the Library Services & Construction Act (LSCA), which had earlier replaced the Library Services Act (LSA), inaugurated 40 years earlier. Continuing the tradition of LSCA and LSA, the funds were to be funneled to states to be administered on a local level. LSTA was to support building or enhancing electronic networks, sharing of resources through consortia, acquiring telecommunications technologies, and targeting library services to persons having difficulty using a library or to underserved urban and rural communities. Between 1998 and 2006, IMLS channeled $1,339,418,000 to the states under the LSTA. However, this overview will focus on the much smaller program called the National Leadership Grants (NLG), and evidence of direct federal funding for research studies and demonstration projects.

Frankel (1998) announced that guidelines for the NLG would emphasize education and training in LIS, preservation projects, and model projects of cooperation between libraries and museums. NLG would support "applied research and demonstration efforts that emphasize access to improved library and information sources" (p. 304). The word "applied" was key—IMLS did not intend to compete with NSF or NLM in funding basic research unless the project could serve as a model to be adopted by other libraries, information networks, and related organizations.

Also in the 1998 *Bowker Annual*, Dunn (1998) reported on the last Research and Demonstration program grants that USDE had awarded the previous year. In 1997, USDE spent $5 million—partly on three projects; the remaining funds were used to support the Department of Education's America Reads Challenge. In that same year the new head of IMLS, Diane

Frankel (1997) declared that librarians were surprised and pleased to have their federal funding program moved out from under the USDE umbrella and put into a separate agency, in partnership with museums. Coming from a museum education background herself, Frankel took pains to affirm the value of libraries and librarians and expressed optimism that libraries and museums would work together for mutual benefits. She promised improvements in how LSTA funds would be dispersed to the states ("a simplified plan"), but made no mention of federal support for LIS research.

Further, according to St. Lifer (1998), who interviewed Frankel, some librarians were concerned that the consolidation would link libraries with the culture community and organizations that were supported by private donations rather than by tax dollars. St. Lifer noted that even the location of the new IMLS was worrisome—in the same building as the National Endowment for the Arts (NEA) and the National Endowment for the Humanities (NEH), both of which were "not exactly on the most solid funding footing with Congress" (p. 42). Frankel responded that she did not see this as a problem, as "the Institute of Museum Service has never been embroiled in the kinds of controversies" that NEA and NEH have been (p. 42). Oder (2001) also remarked on the culture clash between libraries and museums that was partly due to the fact that they have different governance structures, they compete for funding, and they use different technology bases. Both St. Lifer and Oder noted that the two types of institutions do share a common educational mission, and that there were numerous successful collaborations between libraries and museums, some of which were supported by federal grants.

In 2002, at the beginning of his term as IMLS Director, Robert Martin expressed concern about the number and quality of proposals being submitted for NLG; LIS researchers and librarians need to be better trained in grant writing. The main shortcomings were lack of detail and "lack of articulation between the budget and the goals" (IMLS Director, 2002). Martin also was concerned that many librarians do not know what IMLS does. Even if they receive LSTA funding, they do not realize that the funds originate with IMLS (Kenney, 2002). They have even less grasp of NLG opportunities. Rowan (2006) recently wrote an overview of IMLS, in an attempt to address Martin's desire to make more professionals aware of it.

In 2003, Martin's job was to get the act that created the IMLS in 1996 reauthorized, which he did successfully. In his hearing before a Congressional committee, Martin emphasized IMLS' role in fostering leadership, creativity, and innovation. In response to questions, he emphasized the impact of LSTA as well as IMLS's partnerships with NEH and NSF to foster digital library development. He made no mention of funding LIS research except for two cases. One was for research in Colorado and Pennsylvania that demonstrated that well-supported school libraries strongly affect student achievement. The other was a Florida State University study that found that the combination of funding from LSTA, the E-rate, and Gates Foundation had resulted in "significant experimentation and innovative information services development by public libraries" (Equipping, 2002, pp. 21, 46). The final bill included a provision for consolidating the separate library and museum boards into a single national Museum and Library Services Board whose responsibility is to "advise the Director on general policies with respect to the duties, powers, and authority of the Institute relating to museum and library services, including financial assistance awarded under this title" (Museum and Library Services Act, 2003).

The act also required IMLS "to conduct analyses of the need for museum and library services and the effectiveness of funded projects in meeting those needs" (Museum and Library Services Act, report to accompany, 2003). One result of this mandate was a 2004 survey of technology and digitization in the United States—what exists and how well it is funded. The study found that federal support for technology and digitization was shrinking in public, academic, and state libraries. IMLS promised to use the data to shape programs (Institute of Museum and Library Services, 2006).

## B. Funding Priorities

One way to get a snapshot of the IMLS priorities and how they change from year to year is to look at the guidelines and application form (issued annually by IMLS; current ones are at www.imls.gov) that is issued a couple of months before the grant applications are due. Over the years, the guidelines have gotten much more detailed and explicit, in response to requests from applicants. The changes are often subtle, but still worthy of notice.

1998     "Projects of national significance to enhance the quality of library services nationwide . . . . Support collaboration."

1999     "Education of learners in the 21st century . . . Help people develop life-long learning skills."

2000     "Support changing nature of learning in the 21st century . . . Promote collaboration between libraries and museums."

2001     "Must address key concept of leadership . . . may include fresh models for collaboration, innovative educational approaches, or unique combinations of collections." "Stress the development and dissemination of projects that have the potential for adaptation within many settings." "Address the specific needs faced by small and mid-sized libraries." "Strengthen community life, provide educational services, build collections, and emphasize access for all."

2002    "Special emphasis on projects that help museums and libraries take a leadership role in the education of lifelong learners in the 21st century." (It was called a special emphasis, but this language was essentially the same as prior years.)

2003    Same as 2002, with this addition: "The vision for the 21st Century Learner Initiative is that museums and libraries are recognized as places that will encourage and support free-choice, lifelong learning."

2004    Same concepts, but a new catchphrase: "a nation of learners." "Address issues such as improving literacy; furthering school reform; preserving knowledge, artistic, and cultural heritage; teaching science and technology; sustaining the natural environment; enhancing global understanding; and stimulating creativity."

2005    First mention of "archives" along with museums and libraries. Another new term is "globalization" and the need for insights that cross cultural, geographic, and economic boundaries. Another new concept: "civic engagement"—"libraries foster community involvement and provide important spaces, both virtual and physical, for dialog and debate."

2006    "Spotlight on the many ways that libraries support youth development." Proposals are wanted that "invest in our nation's future by engaging young people."

In addition to these statements from the guidelines, Ray (2004) underscored that digitization projects (described elsewhere in this volume) were always a very high priority for IMLS because IMLS is the only federal funding agency with statutory authority to fund digitization—meaning that, even though other federal agencies may support digitization projects, Congress had indicated in the authorizing legislation that IMLS should make increasing public access to online content a top priority. Ray (2001, p. 93) explained, "With Internet access rapidly becoming ubiquitous, digital content is beginning to supersede connectivity as the hot-button issue."

Ray also indicated (personal communication, July 13, 2007) that IMLS would like to see more proposals for research on the LIS profession and Early Career Development grants.

## C. National Leadership Grants

Since the beginning of IMLS, the director has reported every year in *Bowker Annual* the amounts dispersed the previous year to the states under LSTA, amounts given to other small programs targeting special populations (Native Americans and Native Hawaiians), and details of the grants awarded under the NLG program. The NLGs have been the second component of IMLS funding after the LSTA—although a far smaller one. From the beginning they were not intended for basic research, but rather for applied research that would support innovative model programs to enhance the quality of library services nationwide.

Over 500 NLGs were awarded between 1998 and 2006. Table 1 shows the breakdown year by year of the grant categories and the number awarded in each. The numbers are not perfectly precise, since the two sources of ostensibly the same data—*Bowker Annual* and a database on the IMLS web site—reveal a few discrepancies in number of grants in each category and dollar amounts.

The Education and Training grants were primarily for recruitment and training of librarians, including funding for masters and doctoral students. In 2002, First Lady Laura Bush announced a new grant program to recruit and educate the next generation of librarians. The first year the program was called simply "Recruiting and Educating Librarians for the 21st Century," but beginning in FY2006, the program was renamed the Laura Bush 21st Century Librarian program (shortened here to LB21 in the tables and text). As it had from its inception, it continued support for research on the demographics and needs of the profession and it offered Early Career Development grants for new LIS faculty on a variety of topics. This support for research was in addition to its primary function of supporting masters, doctoral, pre-professional, and continuing education programs, and the building of institutional capacity of LIS educational programs. Table 1 shows that the original Education and Training grants continued through 2004 (although far fewer were awarded after 2002), but the LB21 grant program greatly expanded the number and variety of institutions involved and supported significant research studies as well. LB21 awarded five Early Career Development grants for junior faculty and nine for other research on the profession. Since 2003, 21 LB21grants have been awarded for developing and strengthening doctoral programs. It is unknown yet how much of those monies will directly fund dissertations, but it can be presumed that strengthening doctoral programs will build capacity and increase research productivity in the future.

The Preservation or Digitization grants were for projects that addressed the challenges of preserving and archiving digital media, and enhanced access

Table 1
National Leadership Grants 1998–2006

| Year | Research and demonstration | Education and training | Recruiting librarians for 21st century | Preservation or digitization | Building digital resources | Library/ museum collaboration | Partnership for nation of learners | Advancing learning communities |
|---|---|---|---|---|---|---|---|---|
| 1998 | 10 | 6 | | 13 | | 12 | | |
| 1999 | 14 | 12 | | 12 | | 12 | | |
| 2000 | 10 | 14 | | 12 | | 14 | | |
| 2001 | 7 | 9 | | 18 | | 15 | | |
| 2002 | 15 | 8 | | 12 | | 11 | | |
| 2003 | 7 | 5 | 27 | 14 | | 10 | | |
| 2004 | 10 | 3 | 27 | 5 | | 19 | | |
| 2005 | 15 | | 39 | | 10 | 7 | 7 | 3 |
| 2006 | 12 | | 35 | | 9 | | 13 | 4 |
| Total | 100 | 57 | 128 | 86 | 19 | 100 | 20 | 7 |
| Grand Total | 510 | | | | | | | |

of library resources useful to the broader community. This program was recast in 2005 as Building Digital Resources and described as supporting "the creation, use, preservation, and presentation of significant digital resources as well as the development of tools to manage digital assets" (Radice, 2006).

The Library and Museum Collaboration grants were for model programs of cooperation between libraries and museums, as well as to support research and other activities to enhance interoperability, integration, and seamless access to digital library and museum resources. In 2005, a new program was introduced called Partnership for a Nation of Learners Community Collaboration Grants which brought public broadcasters into the mix of collaborations.

Also in 2005 another new program called Advancing Learning Communities was introduced. It encouraged collaborations "with other educational and community organizations to support the educational, economic, and social needs of learners of all ages" (Radice, 2006).

As noted earlier, the Research and Demonstration grants supported applied research (the word "applied" perhaps is not the best—but it is a way to distinguish the more formal or pure types of research typically funded by NSF and NLM). Table 1 shows 100 R&D grants. Of the 128 LB21 grants, nine were for research on the profession, bringing the total number of research studies to 109. Many different types of institutions received Research and Demonstration grants and LB21 research study grants. The grant descriptions are sometimes vague as to whether the grantee was affiliated with an academic program or the academic library. Nevertheless, the breakdown by type of institution receiving awards is approximately as follows:

| | |
|---|---|
| 45 | Schools of library and information science |
| 39 | Academic libraries |
| 10 | Public libraries |
| 1 | School library media center |
| 1 | Special library |

The remaining were "other" organizations such as historical societies, research institutes, and state libraries.

Table 2 details year by year the specific amounts IMLS spent each year for LIS research under the NLG. The sources of the data are the IMLS chapters in *Bowker Annual*: Frankel (1999), Sheppard (2000, 2001), Martin (2002, 2003, 2004, 2005), Radice (2006), and Radice and Chute (2007).

Table 2
NLG Research Grants, 1998–2006: Number of Studies and Expenditures

| Year | Total NLG expenditures | Research and demonstration expenditures | Number of research and demonstration awards | LB21 expenditures for research | Number of research studies funded by LB21 | Total number of research studies funded | Total expenditures for LIS research |
|---|---|---|---|---|---|---|---|
| 1998 | $6,487,750 | 1,483,103 | 10 | | | 10 | 1,483,103 |
| 1999 | 10,565,000 | 2,860,268 | 13 | | | 13 | 2,860,268 |
| 2000 | 10,906,289 | 2,400,354 | 10 | | | 10 | 2,400,354 |
| 2001 | 11,116,150 | 1,381,727 | 7 | | | 7 | 1,381,727 |
| 2002 | 12,013,000 | 4,181,959 | 15 | | | 15 | 4,181,959 |
| 2003 | 12,117,000 | 3,328,671 | 7 | 444,091 | 2 | 9 | 3,772,762 |
| 2004 | 11,913,674 | 3,147,096 | 10 | 1,341,388 | 2 | 12 | 4,488,484 |
| 2005 | 10,850,995 | 5,346,684 | 15 | 958,111 | 2 | 17 | 6,304,795 |
| 2006 | 7,065,177 | 3,641,574 | 12 | 888,325 | 3 | 15 | 4,529,899 |

Other grants awarded under the NLG are not in Table 2; one could legitimately question about whether or not those other grants should be included in the total. It is true that some of the continuing education and training, library and museum collaborations, and preservation or digitization projects had an element of research or evaluation that would add to the knowledge base of the field. To be fair, then, we must say that that *at least* the amounts reported in this table were allocated to research. The real amounts are likely to be somewhat higher.

On the other hand, although it appears that the amounts IMLS spent under the NLG program represented a huge increase over what had been available from the USDE Office of Library Programs, much of the money was not spent on research. The education and training, digital and preservation projects, and other projects involving collaboration by museums and libraries were mostly not research, not even applied research. The amount IMLS spent for research has been spread around to many more projects than was true at USDE, but the total amount spent each year on research (as represented in the right-most column in Table 2) is not a great deal more than it was back in the mid-1990s [recall that Dunn (1998) had reported that USDE had $5 million available for research funding in 1997, even though they expended only $3 million on three studies that year].

The *Bowker* chapters also tell how many proposals were submitted to NLG and how many were funded. The percentage funded ranged from a low of 16.4% in 1998 (not surprising, since there was much excitement and optimism at the beginning of the program and an unusually high number of proposals were submitted) to a high of 37.1% in 2001. Table 3 shows how

Table 3
IMLS NLG Proposals Funded, by Year

| Year | Number of applications | Number of grants awarded | Percentage of applications funded |
|------|------------------------|--------------------------|-----------------------------------|
| 1998 | 250 | 41 | 16.4 |
| 1999 | 187 | 50 | 26.7 |
| 2000 | 173 | 50 | 28.9 |
| 2001 | 132 | 49 | 37.1 |
| 2002 | 188 | 46 | 24.4 |
| 2003 | 205 | 42 | 20.4 |
| 2004 | 154 | 37 | 35.5 |
| 2005 | 147 | 28 | 19.0 |
| 2006 | 110 | 25 | 22.7 |

the numbers of applications and percentage funded has fluctuated dramatically over the years. With such sharp fluctuations, it is impossible to predict from one year to the next how likely it is that a proposal will get funded, but it appears that overall about a quarter of the proposals are successful—similar to the success rates at other federal funding agencies.

## D. Future of IMLS Funding

When Robert Martin left IMLS in June 2005, Berry (2005) noted how much the LSTA program had increased under the Bush administration. Berry interviewed Martin and asked him whether federal library aid would be sustainable. Martin hedged and simply said, "There is opportunity to sustain it," as it depends not only on who is in the White House, but on the wishes of Congress. Martin also noted, "When you compare the funding we have to some other federal agencies, it's miniscule. I think the NLG program has the potential for having the kind of impact that the National Science Foundation has had" (para. 11). The data so far, however, do not appear to support Martin's cheerful optimism.

# IV. National Library of Medicine (NLM)

## A. History of Extramural Programs

The NLM 2008 Congressional appropriations justification reviewed the history and focus of the extramural grant programs:

> The NLM has for more than 40 years had a program of grant assistance to improve medical library resources, conduct specialized research and development in informatics and biocommunications, and train health information personnel. The Library's grant programs ... have supported pioneering research and development in bioinformatics, artificial intelligence in medicine, clinical decision support, biomedical ontology, imaging, electronic medical records, regional health data exchange, health applications of advanced communications networks, automated biosurveillance, and emergency management systems. (Department of Health and Human Services, n.d., p. 16)

This $57 million budget request also relayed how NLM grants had "supported the first Internet connections for many health sciences libraries, community hospitals, local public health departments, and community organizations." Currently, the program supports "projects to improve health literacy," including "projects to improve patient access to health information, increase understanding of literacy requirements in consumer health information, and encourage healthy behavior ... " (p. 16).

## B. Potential Opportunities

On a web page for frequently asked questions about NLM grants (http://www.nlm/nih.gov/ep/FAQGeneral.html), is a description of the kinds of projects NLM funds: "All NLM grants focus on use of computers and telecommunication technologies for improving storage, retrieval, access, management and use of biomedical information." In an article in the *ASIST Bulletin* (presumably targeted to the information science community), Bean and Corn (2005, p. 551) declared that "opportunities abound for obtaining research funding in bioinformatics." They described the program focus:

> NLM supports research and development into more effective and efficient ways to organize and analyze vast amounts of data, knowledge, and information in any medium relating to molecular control of life processes. Problem areas of interest relevant to bioinformatics include, but are not limited to, design and management of large-scale databases and other data repositories, representation and discovery techniques for complex molecular and cellular biological knowledge, retrieval and integration of information from heterogeneous databases, pattern-matching algorithms for biological sequences, and the potential role of techniques such as artificial intelligence for uncovering knowledge otherwise concealed by massive and complex data. (pp. 551–552)

Bean and Corn described the various grant programs available in 2005 as well as 30 examples of funded studies. Not one of the 30 grantees mentioned was from the LIS community—they were researchers in bioengineering, biostatistics, biochemistry, bioinformatics, biotechnology, computer science, human genetics, neurobiology, pharmacology, and similar fields.

One of the grant programs seems tailor-made for the LIS community. Information System grants (G08) "are available to health-related institutions to improve the organization and management of health-related information using computers and networks, with emphasis on the use of information technology to bring appropriate information to end users" (Bean and Corn, 2005, p. 555). However, according to Corn (personal communication, September 21, 2007), no one from LIS has applied.

Writing earlier in the *Bulletin of the Medical Library Association* (and therefore presumably targeted to medical librarians and health informatics faculty), Zink *et al.* (1996) described the Extramural Programs (EP) that supported medical libraries, academic medical centers, individual researchers, and industry. They emphasized that NLM grants are awarded on the basis of good ideas. In fact, anyone who asks the question, "What is NIH/NLM funding this year?" displays naïveté as to how NIH works (p. 168). NLM/NIH does not set the agenda; researchers do. Bean and Corn (2005) echoed this sentiment:

> The NLM rarely sets aside extramural funds for specific topical areas, preferring to fund the best new projects available proposed by the community of scientific investigators. In

other words, the NLM approach permits the research community to determine the pool of projects considered for funding rather than setting boundaries through predefined topics of interest ... Applications for groundbreaking research in novel areas are always welcome, and indeed, encouraged. (pp. 551–552)

Even though most of the research funded is not awarded in response to applications solicited by announcement of Requests for Proposals, but rather from unsolicited proposals for innovative research, it is a good idea for potential grantees to pay attention to the occasional RFP because these are issued when NIH needs to distribute a reserve of funds (which is true as well for the other federal agencies). Each year about 3% of the grant pool is spent on special solicitations.

The NLM web site offers a wealth of information about the grant programs and how to apply for funding (http://www.nlm.nih.gov/ep/extramural.html). The programs are not detailed here because, as we shall see, the reality is that very few of these grants have been awarded to LIS researchers or medical librarians. In a nutshell, a proposal must address a biomedical need. While NLM-funded projects could, as a by-product, advance the state of knowledge in LIS, what NLM really cares about is research that benefits the biomedical community. Furthermore, in its FY08 appropriations justification, NLM indicated that it plans to focus its extramural budget on "high-risk, high-payoff projects."

## C. EP Funding for LIS

In spite of how relevant the NLM topics may sound to the LIS research community, NLM EP have provided very little support for research and demonstration in the field of LIS. As we saw earlier from Altman (1991), for many years the proposals at NLM have come from biomedical researchers with a lot of knowledge about computers—some held both medical degrees and doctorates in computer science and thus their proposals were highly competitive in the bioinformatics arena. LIS researchers with lesser credentials were not likely to be competitive. Therefore, according to Corn (personal communication, September 21, 2007), they have seldom tried. Corn indicated that the reason NLM does not give grants to LIS researchers is not because their proposals are poor; they fund very few because NLM receives almost no applications from LIS researchers.

Learning what NIH has funded in the past is facilitated by Computer Retrieval of Information on Scientific Projects (CRISP), a searchable database of federally funded biomedical research projects conducted at universities, hospitals, and other research institutions. As entries in CRISP are indexed with a controlled vocabulary, I scoured the database for funded projects having relevant subject headings:

- Health care facility information system
- Information and communication
- Information dissemination
- Information gathering methods evaluation-standards
- Information retrieval
- Information system analysis
- Information systems
- Libraries, library
- Vocabulary development for information system indexing.

In addition, I searched the names of the full and part-time faculty in the ALISE Directory who claim a teaching or research interest area in health informatics or medical libraries.

After this broad, if not completely exhaustive search, only a handful of grants were found in the period 1990–2007. One was for a senior training program in informatics (F38), several were grants to medical institutions for disseminating information over a network (G08—not a research grant), and several were for improving IT connections (G07—also not research). According to Corn (personal communication, September 21, 2007), NLM no longer thinks it necessary to give monies to medical libraries to improve Internet connectivity.

Most NLM extramural grants are for basic, rigorous, investigator-initiated research (R01). Overall, NLM awards about 25% of the proposals that come in, but the award rate for R01s is only about 10–15%. The CRISP search yielded only three projects that had been submitted by LIS researchers in the R01 competition:

1. Padmini Srinivansan, University of Iowa, School of Library and Information Science. $89,000, 2 years (2000–2002). "The UMLS for Text Retrieval—A Rough Set Approach." This proposal presents a framework that supports the systematic and exploratory investigation of the UMLS metathesaurus. This research is part of an overall goal to contribute to the knowledge base on improving effectiveness of information retrieval in health care.
2. Nancy Roderer, John Hopkins University, Welch Medical Library. $750,000, 3 years (2004–2007). "Evaluating Patient Information Prescriptions." A proposal to extend and evaluate a tactic for meeting patient's information needs by having librarians offer a "prescription" (IRx) for offering information services tailored to individual patients' needs. The research hypothesis is that the program will improve patient satisfaction, provider knowledge, and attitudes regarding patient information needs. The evaluative data will help care organizations decide whether to implement IRx in their own environment.
3. Wanda Pratt, University of Washington, the Information School. $900,000, 3 years (2007–2010). "Managing Health Information in Your Life." The long-term objective is both

to understand patients' information management work and to develop new technology that will
support that work.

It is possible that the CRISP database search missed a grant or two, but
nevertheless, the number over a 17-year period is shockingly small.

Zink *et al.* (1996) said that most successful grants are for studies
involving a team composed of individuals with different disciplinary
backgrounds. It would behoove LIS researchers therefore to become aware of
biomedical researchers and computer scientists at their own or neighboring
institutions who would welcome their information skills and knowledge as
members of a collaborating team.

## D. Support from the National Network of Libraries of Medicine

Another opportunity for support from NLM is from the National Network
of Libraries of Medicine (NN/LM), which provides funds to the eight
institutions that serve as Regional Medical Libraries (RMLs) in the
NN/LM. The RMLs in turn provide funding to Network Member libraries,
in similar fashion to the way IMLS distributes federal monies to the states
under LSTA and each state agency in turn distributes the funds to libraries
within its state. Ruffin *et al.* (2005) described how the process worked, how
the recipients or NN/LM Member libraries used the funding (either under
$10,000 for a single institution or under $40,000 for a multi-type library
collaboration) to improve consumers' access to electronic health information. The most common strategies for accomplishing the improvements
used by the libraries who participated in this round of funding were
community partnerships and collaborations with community-based organizations and public libraries. Many of the projects targeted racial and ethnic
minorities and seniors, and a large proportion of them included training
programs for consumers. Developing web sites and pages, and energetic
marketing and publicity were elements of many as well. Evaluation of the
efforts was critical, and one of the key findings was the importance of
evaluating the interest and enthusiasm of potential partners before
committing to work with them.

In answer to whether this program is going to be continued, Ruffin
(personal communication, October 1, 2007) said that it depends on funding.
The specific projects reported in Ruffin *et al.* (2005), were a special focused
initiative made possible by additional Congressional funding. However, the
RMLs do have as part of their regular outreach and consumer health
programs to fund projects which promote the access and use of electronic
resources.

## V. National Endowment for the Humanities (NEH)

For almost 40 years NEH has supported library and archives collections and public programs to promote reading, especially in the humanities. Established by Congress in 1965, NEH has provided funding for significant reference materials; poetry readings; bilingual reading programs; cataloging and preservation of significant library collections including oral histories, photographs and newspapers; traveling exhibitions; online libraries such as Perseus; Supreme Court resources; and Civil War archives for use in libraries and schools. NEH grants have helped libraries enhance web sites, make electronic databases accessible, and establish standards for integrating digital technology into the study of the humanities. Preservation projects have included disaster recovery training and microfilming of brittle books.

NEH has also worked with other federal agencies to support connecting public libraries to the Internet, in order to make library materials and digitized resources more accessible to the public (NEH, 1998). NEH was a partner with NSF on the Digital Library Initiatives. NEH and the Library of Congress have worked together in recent years to support the National Digital Newspaper Program, a project to digitize and make accessible on the web the microfilms of historically important US newspapers (Testimony of Bruce Cole, 2005). NEH also has its own digital humanities initiative (http://www.neh.gov/grants/digitalhumanities.html).

The primary sources of information about grant opportunities are NEH's web site (http://www.neh.gov) and yearly articles in the *Bowker Annual* (Phelps, 1997, 1998, 1999, 2000, 2001, 2002, 2003, 2004, 2005, 2007). These opportunities include Challenge Grants, a category of funding that helps public libraries plan long-term programming. However, they require significant matching—three or four dollars in new or increased donations for every federal dollar offered.

Some NEH funds (about 22% in 2006) are designated for the Federal–State Partnership program. Each state, US territory, and the District of Columbia has its own state council to fund humanities programs in its own jurisdiction. These grants typically are for reading programs, lectures, conferences, institutes, and traveling exhibitions.

Representing about 11% of the NEH budget, the Division of Research Programs gives fellowships to individual scholars and grants for collaborative research projects that will contribute to the creation of knowledge in the humanities. Phelps (2006, p. 359) described the research support: "Grants provide up to three years of support for collaborative research in the preparation for publication of editions, translations, and other important works in the humanities, and in the conduct of large or complex interpretive studies." Thus the grant program seeks to benefit humanities scholars and the general public, through fostering their understanding and appreciation of the humanities.

Since 1980, Thomas Phelps has been a key staff member at NEH for LIS, serving as program officer for grants to libraries, library associations, systems, consortia, and library schools. Phelps (personal communication, July 19, 2007) said that the NEH research agenda to a certain extent is set by NEH staff and the National Council on the Humanities, the members of which are appointed by the White House. The staff and the Council react to what they see happening in the field. The Council reviews the annual guidelines developed by the staff and they may exert a great deal of influence on them. Other influences come from the reviewers. The greatest influence on the agenda, however, comes from the grassroots—the individuals and research teams who write proposals. In the past 10 years or so, the greatest external or environmental factor influencing the research agenda is technology (in the form of new delivery systems) and digitization.

Recent NEH awards are listed at http://www.neh.gov/news/recentawards. html. None were given to LIS researchers; they were awarded to scholars in core humanities disciplines. However, Phelps (personal communication, July 19, 2007) said that collaborative research grants would be more competitive if the humanities scholars included a librarian or LIS researcher on the team. Phelps said the typical percentage of grants funded is about 25%, similar to other federal agencies, and it is not uncommon for applicants to apply two or three times before getting funded. As a program officer, he offers to work closely with applicants—the main problem is that sometimes the applicants do not listen to the advice offered.

## VI. National Science Foundation (NSF)

Congress created the NSF in 1950 as an independent agency to promote the progress of science by funding basic scientific research and research fundamental to the engineering process, as well as education programs that will ensure the nation's supply of scientists and engineers and future educators. NSF accounts for about one-fourth of federal support to academic institutions for basic research. (http://www.nsf.gov/funding/about/aboutfunding.jsp). About 11,000 out of 44,000 proposals (25%) are funded each year, which is in line with other federal funding agencies (http://www.nsf.gov/funding/aboutfunding.jsp). According to Kasprowski, (2005), "Funds awarded by NSF are typically contractual agreements, not grants, with more loosely defined objectives. This is meant to encourage researchers to pursue their ideas more freely if the payoff is potentially significant" (p. 19).

NSF is presently organized into seven directorates and five offices. A few are relevant to LIS: the Directorate for Computer and Information Science and Engineering (CISE), the Directorate for Education and Human Resources, the Directorate for Social, Behavioral, and Economic Sciences, and the Office of Cyberinfrastructure. The web sites for each of these detail their goals and the general areas they fund. Within CISE (http:// www.nsf.gov/cise/about.jsp) are three divisions—the most relevant is Information and Intelligence Systems (IIS). IIS covers human-centered computing (roles and relationships between people and the information technologies they develop and use as well as the study of the impact of these technologies on individuals, groups, and society at large), information integration and informatics (process and technologies for creating, storing, and interacting with digital content), and robust intelligence (includes natural language processing and other areas of artificial intelligence). Not surprisingly, most of the grants and contracts from this division are awarded to computer scientists, often working in teams with other disciplines, including LIS.

Stretching across all the program areas is an opportunity of special interest to new researchers. Small Grants for Exploratory Research (SGER) are for novel, untested ideas or ventures into emerging and potentially transformative research areas. Proposals may be abbreviated, reviews are expedited, and the award amounts limited to under $200,000 for a period of two years or less. NSF does not recommend submitting a SGER without first talking to a program officer and sending a short written summary of the idea. Nevertheless, inquiries are encouraged and welcomed.

As NSF welcomes proposals in a wide range of areas of innovation, it is hard to determine a "research agenda," much less pinpoint the source of the agenda. As the program officers in other agencies emphasized, it is the best ideas generated by applicants themselves. In the last decade or so, the programs at NSF most closely related to LIS are in the area of digital libraries (covered elsewhere in this volume). Both Griffin (2005) and Lynch (2005) said that substantial government funding of digital libraries research is at an end, at least for the near future. Nevertheless, NSF's latest strategic plan (National Science Foundation, 2006) highlights the importance of information to the scientific endeavor: "Today's science employs revolutionary sensor systems and involves massive, accessible databases, digital libraries, unique visualization environments, and complex computational models" (p. 2).

Messerschmitt (2003) reported that a NSF Blue-Ribbon Advisory Panel recommended a new Advanced Cyberinfrastructure Program (ACP):

> The program offers a chance ... for libraries to contribute to scholarly activity in science and engineering research in new ways. Research libraries house core competencies and expertise highly relevant to ACP and its challenges. However, the natural organization of scientific repositories around disciplinary needs presents challenges to the institutionally based organization predominant in the research library community. (p. 1)

Messerschmitt underscored that a central theme of ACP is preservation, which has been the domain of libraries for millennia. NSF funded a two-day Association of Research Libraries workshop in September 2006 to examine the role of research and academic libraries in partnering with others to provide stewardship of scientific and engineering digital data. It appears that this area may provide the next big opportunities for federal support for LIS. The final report of the workshop, titled *To Stand the Test of Time*, is available at http://www.arl.org/bm ~ doc/digdatarpt.pdf

A search of the NTIS database (US government-sponsored research and reports from federal agencies) on the term "national science foundation" and the classification code "88B (Library and Information Sciences: Information systems)" plus various LIS subject terms, yielded all the studies NSF-funded. From the indexing of these reports, it can be seen that the most popular topics were, in rank order: information retrieval (36 hits), classification (16), information processing (7), user needs (6), relevance ranking (5), ontology (4), archives (3), and vocabulary (3). All other terms had two or fewer hits.

A similar search of the ERIC database yielded hits for studies on a children's digital library; music notation search in digital libraries; automatic identification and organization of index terms for interactive browsing; and a literature review on implications of information technology for scientific journal publishing. All of these NSF-funded projects involved at least one faculty member from an LIS program.

Because NSF is so large and complex, it makes available a wealth of general descriptive information about its programs and the process for submission and review. NSF also offers a grant policy manual, an electronic bulletin and e-mail updates, and regional one-day conferences for orienting new and prospective applicants. More information about how to take advantage of each of these is on the NSF web site. In addition, program officers are ready to help with individual questions. It is important to note that some NSF program solicitations may require or request a letter of intent or a preliminary proposal before applicants send full proposals. This allows the program staff to plan for the number and range of submissions and line up the appropriate type and number of reviewers and panelists, as well as to discourage proposals for which the chance of success is very small.

At a NSF Regional Grants Conference held in 2006 at the University of Maryland, the presenters cautioned that the current environment is difficult for federal agencies because of constrained budgets, a "war time" mentality, need for federal funds for disaster relief, desire for deficit reduction, and various other economic uncertainties. Nevertheless, the NSF presenters declared, the future looks bright because national leaders (presumably in Congress and the White House) understand the importance of investing in research that will strengthen the United States in the long run.

## VII. Evidence of Federal Funding from *JASIST* Authors

Getting a handle on opportunities from federal agencies other than IMLS, NEH, NLM, or NSF is difficult because there are so few scattered throughout many different agencies that are not typically viewed as funding agencies, much less LIS funding agencies. Even pinpointing the amount of funding for LIS is challenging because LIS is so difficult to define. Oard (personal communication, July 19, 2007) suggested letting LIS researchers define themselves—let those who *want to be* LIS researchers (as at least part of their identity) *be* LIS researchers. Thus we can consider LIS researchers to be people who teach and research in LIS programs, who publish in LIS journals, and who present at LIS conferences. This does not completely solve the conundrum because one still has to figure out what are LIS programs, journals, and conferences. Nevertheless, this chapter has focused on faculty in LIS programs, librarians, authors whose articles are indexed in *Library Literature & Information Science* or *Library, Information Science & Technology Abstracts* (*LISTA*), and in particular, who publish in *Journal of the American Society for Information Science & Technology* (*JASIST*), a scholarly research journal whose scope encompasses the entire field of LIS.

An examination of *JASIST* from 1998–2006 (vols. 49–57, 14 issues each year) reveals that 356 articles acknowledged receipt of research support from an outside funder in the form of a grant, contract, or dissertation scholarship. Of the 356, 166 (47%) were funded by an agency or organization in the United States and 190 (53%) were funded by a foreign government agency or other organization outside the United States. Of those funded in the United States 94 (26%) received funding from an organization or agency other than the federal government (universities, research institutes, professional associations, or other). 114 (32%) received their funding from one or more government agencies. There is some overlap between these two groups, because some studies received funding both from non-governmental as well as from government agencies.

A total of about 17 US government agencies provided grants or contracts that supported the research reported in *JASIST* from 1998 to 2006. The agencies and the number of studies funded by each are shown in Table 4.[1]

NSF is clearly the top funder for information research in the United States, with a total of 76 grants acknowledged in *JASIST* between 1998 and 2006. The library-oriented agencies (NLM, IMLS, and LC) funded a total of 18. DoD awarded 11, from various separate units. DARPA and the National Aeronautics and Space Administration (NASA) awarded 10 each. The other agencies awarded only a few each, and a large percentage of those were contracts to produce specific deliverables, not for original or exploratory research. By far the most likely sources of federal funding for research in library and information science, at least as reported in *JASIST*, are NSF, DARPA, NASA, NLM, IMLS, and LC.

Other than support for digital library research, the NSF grants reported in *JASIST* just since 2003 have been on the topics of information retrieval (far and away the most popular area), electronic publishing, scholarly publishing, web site development, web portals, search engines, databases for music and geography, database searching, data mining, cognition, indexing vocabularies, information systems design, information needs, use studies of virtual libraries, children's use of microcomputers, scientific and technical periodicals, computer-assisted instruction, information policy, government information, information dissemination, and electronic mail messages. This backward look of a few years, however, is probably of little use in predicting what NSF will fund in the future.

Overall, between 1998 and 2006, the number of federal grants reported in *JASIST* increased 36%. However, this is not as good news as it sounds.

---

[1]The data in the table are not guaranteed to be 100% accurate. Part of the problem is that *JASIST* authors reported their funding sources at differing levels of specificity. In the case of NIH, for example, sometimes the source is listed as only "NIH" and other times the specific institute is identified. The Department of Defense (DoD) and Department of Energy represent a similar problem. It is hard to be precise about the number of agencies involved, as some agencies are units of others, and some receive funding from each other. Although the Defense Advanced Research Projects Agency (DARPA) is a division of DoD and NLM is part of NIH, they are separated out in the table because of their distinct roles in funding information research. Lastly, the number of studies funded is presumed to be equal to the number of articles in which a funding source is acknowledged. However this number is probably inflated a bit because occasionally an author will report on the same study in more than one article.

Table 4
Funding Sources for Research Reported in *JASIST*, 1998–2006

| Agency name | Number of studies funded |
|---|---|
| Bureau of Labor Statistics | 2 |
| Bureau of the Census | 1 |
| Defense Advanced Research Projects Agency (DARPA) | 10 |
| Department of Defense, (DoD), including one from Army Research Laboratory, two from Defense Intelligence Agency, two from Naval Research Laboratory and four from Office of Naval Research (ONR) | 11 |
| Department of Energy, including two from Sandia National Laboratories | 5 |
| Department of Education, | 2 |
| General Services Administration, Office of Information Technology Integration | 1 |
| Institute for Museums and Library Services (IMLS) | 5 |
| Department of Justice, National Institute of Justice | 2 |
| Library of Congress (LC) | 5 |
| National Aeronautics and Space Administration (NASA) | 10 |
| National Computational Science Alliance | 2 |
| National Institutes of Health, including two from the National Institute of Mental Health, and two from the National Center for Research Resources | 8 |
| National Library of Medicine | 8 |
| National Institute of Standards (NIST) | 1 |
| National Science Foundation (NSF), including 10 for Digital Libraries Initiative and 10 for Digital Library Initiative-2 | 76 |
| National Center for Supercomputer Applications, which is funded by NSF, the state of Illinois, the University of Illinois, and industrial partners | 3 |

The total number of studies that reported getting some form of outside funding increased overall 70%. A large percentage of the growth in outside funding was accounted for by studies by authors with affiliations in foreign institutions, funded by a foreign government or other organization; the foreign studies increased 185% during this period. Overall, the page count of *JASIST* increased 54%, so it is clear that as a percentage of the LIS research being published in *JASIST*, the American government was responsible for a reduced amount.

## VIII. Advice for Getting Federal Grants

An article about federal funding would not seem complete without a recap of the highlights of the bits of advice and tips from the literature and program officers in the federal agencies. For example, Zink *et al.* (1996) offered these suggestions for increasing one's chances of obtaining federal funds:

- Do not wait for the federal agency to provide explicit guidance on what they are funding. Most grants are given to support good ideas coming from the field itself.
- Do not blame the reviewers if they do not understand a proposal. It is the applicants' responsibility to write clearly.
- Research ideas often require "seed money" to collect feasibility data or conduct a pilot study. Researchers can often get small grants from their own or partnering institutions for seed money. Showing evidence of having obtained seed money and having done this preliminary work greatly strengthens a proposal.
- Grant writing is extremely time-consuming and requires a long lead time; negotiate with supervisors for an intensive period devoted to the grant proposal, but also start planning it many months in advance, to allow time for consultation, pilot studies, and data gathering.

Humes (1998) offered an indirect way to increase the number and quality of proposals—which should begin with researchers improving the dissemination of research findings and doing a better job of translating research findings into useful information for practitioners. Then research should be connected to practice by involving more library practitioners in research projects.

Ray (2001) emphasized the importance of reading and following the program guidelines, as well as consulting with program staff throughout the proposal process and having a colleague who knows nothing about the proposal to read it and make suggestions for revision. Ray said that, in addition to meeting all the criteria in the program guidelines, "Successful proposal writers will inspire readers with a sense of excitement and even urgency about the project. They convey the message 'This is important work and it should be done as soon as possible!'" (p. 96).

Theiler (2002) suggested using the Catalog of Federal Domestic Assistance (in print or on the web) and grants.gov to search for grant opportunities. However, she admitted that they could be cumbersome to use; she suggested looking instead at the web sites of the individual agencies—IMLS being the best source of information.

Becker (2003) cautioned that one burden of federal grants is writing interim and final reports. Applicants must plan time for this.

Kasprowski (2005) summed up suggestions made by Joyce Ray (IMLS), and Sangtae Kim (NSF) and several recipients of grants in human information behavior:

- Start applying for grants early in your career to establish a history.
- Pick something you are prepared to study for several years.
- Connect with peers and programs officers—through conference attendance, committee work, and research presentations. Serve on review panels and actually participate in review process.
- Find partners—barter tasks. Make clear you are a researcher, not just a supporter.
- Do not submit the same proposal to more than one agency.
- Propose an innovative but risky idea that will yield a big payoff.
- Use the staff and tutorials at each federal agency; really listen to what they say.
- "Public libraries are good topics for research [in human information behavior] because they are open to researchers and can provide resources like patrons as study participants." (p. 18)

Larsen (2005) called the Federal research agenda "malleable." He suggested that researchers can influence the research agenda not only by the ideas and topics in their proposals but also by serving on peer review panels, or even by serving a year or more in Washington as a visiting member of the NSF or DARPA staff.

Ray (personal communication, July 13, 2007) emphasized the concern at IMLS that they cannot always award all the monies they have because the proposals themselves are not top-notch and the reviewers will not reduce their standards. Those applicants who have grant-writing skills will be far more successful than those who do not, no matter what the value of the project itself is. The skilled grant writer not only tells a compelling story and situates it in a bigger context, but also tells how the project will benefit not just one institution. Applicants without these skills should seek partners to help them.

Clark (personal communication, July 16, 2007) underscored the importance of writing a proposal that conveys passion, caring, and commitment. She said she is amazed that applicants display all these qualities in preliminary telephone conversations and then they write very dry proposals.

Crawley (personal communication, July 13, 2007) emphasized the importance of writing clear research questions and methods. Grant writers who lack the skills to do full statistical planning, should enlist the help of a statistician or take more courses on statistics and surveys. Formal study of other quantitative and qualitative methods is also important; even qualitative methodologies need to be structured and rigorous.

Langile and Mackenzie (2007) added a few more points:

- In order to persuade the reviewers of the value of your project, "spark the interest and imagination ... by using a variety of types of information and formats including statistics, stories, quotes, frameworks, and tables." (p. 25)

- Address ethical issues, obtain approval for human subjects research from your institution, and also describe any ethical dimensions of your proposed research (such as informed consent, confidentiality).

Finally, a good strategy for breaking into the federal grant process is to serve on a review panel, to gain first-hand knowledge of the peer review process, learn about common problems with proposals, discover strategies to write strong proposals, and meet agency program officers who manage the programs related to one's own research. Each agency has directions for offering one's services as a grant reviewer on its web site.

In addition to these tips, every agency has some tutorial guidance tailored for its particular grant programs. For example, a page designed for NLM extramural grants has a list of six created tutorials: (http://nlm.nih.gov/ep/Tutorial.html). The National Network of Libraries of Medicine web site offers guidance, tutorials, tips, and funding opportunities for a wide variety of programs at the NIH/NLM as well as at external agencies and programs (http://nnlm.gov/funding/grants.html). It does not claim to be comprehensive, but it offers a wealth of links to get one started.

## IX. Conclusions

A large number of federal agencies have provided some form of support for LIS, in the form of grants or contracts. Only a few, however, have full funding programs for which the LIS community may compete. Even in these cases, however, with the exception of IMLS, LIS researchers have not had much success.

Why do not more LIS researchers get federal grants? Everywhere, competition for funds is fierce. In some cases, even at IMLS, it is because their research ideas are too esoteric, lacking the grounded, applications component that would appeal particularly to IMLS. Also, many practitioners simply do not have the expertise (they were not required to take any type of statistics or research methods course in their master's program) or awareness of the grant application process. Even academic librarians may not be motivated unless they have faculty status and are pressured to bring in outside grants. Program officers at all the agencies say they never run out of money for R&D for LIS research—they simply do not receive enough good proposals. More and better proposals would be welcomed.

It is important to know your agency and its mission. For NLM, a proposal must address a biomedical need. An NSF proposal must address a need of the science and technology community. NEH grants must serve the humanities. IMLS wants to serve the communities of learners who use libraries and museums.

It is also critical to understand the types of activities each agency funds—whether research and demonstration (applied research or projects that provide models for other organizations), programming to advance literacy or other agency objectives, or basic research, including innovative, cutting-edge ideas. NLM and NSF are particularly looking for high-risk, high-payoff projects.

Occasionally agencies issue a call for proposal on a particular topic or problem area, or are interested in awarding contracts for specific deliverables. Much more often, however, federal agencies are looking to the research community to generate fresh ideas.

The task of setting a research agenda for any given year in each agency is divided among many people, including agency staff, members of Congress and the White House, an advisory board, and reviewers—but mostly by researchers themselves. External factors influencing the priorities and amount of money available are political and economic, and also driven by technological developments.

Trends in topics funded are difficult to ascertain; within the broad mission of each agency, a wide variety of studies may be funded. Prospective applicants are advised to discuss their ideas with program officers before writing a full-blown proposal.

It is not unusual for researchers to try two or three times before being successful. Collaborating on multi-disciplinary, multi-skilled research teams improves the chances. Researchers who are successful in securing grants are more likely to get more grants in the future. There is a lot of advice available for prospective grant writers; the key thing is to take the advice to heart and also to listen—really listen—to the feedback on a failed proposal.

## Acknowledgments

Karen Patterson and Benjamin Brown at the University of Maryland provided research assistance. Interviews with Tom Phelps (NEH), Milton Corn (NLM), Stephanie Clark, Joyce Ray, Mary Chute, and Martha Crawley (all at IMLS) enriched and interpreted the literature review and web sites. Others with whom I exchanged messages and who sent materials included Jeffrey Pomerantz (University of North Carolina), Denise Davis (ALA),

Angela Ruffin (NN/LM), Glen Holt (consultant), and Douglas Oard and
Kenneth Fleischman (both at the University of Maryland).

## References

Altman, E. (1991). Whither LIS research: Ideology, funding, and educational
standards. In *Library and Information Research: Perspectives and Strategies for
Improvement* (C. R. McClure and P. Hernon, eds.), pp. 114–127, Ablex Publishing
Corporation, Norwood, NJ.

Altman, E. (1993). National Science Foundation's support of information research.
In *Encyclopedia of Library and Information Science*, vol. 52, supp. 15, pp. 273–290.
Marcel Dekker, Inc., New York.

Altman, E., and Brown, S. (1991). From retrieval to robotics: The National Science
Foundation's support of information research. *Government Information Quarterly*
8(4), 359–373.

Bamford, H. E., and Brownstein, C. N. (1986). National Science Foundation
support for computer and information science and engineering. *Information
Processing and Management* 22(6). 449–442

Bean, C. A., and Corn, M. (2005). Extramural funding opportunities in
bioinformatics from the National Library of Medicine. *Journal of the American
Society for Information Science and Technology* 56(5), 551–556.

Becker, B. (2003). Grant money on the web: A resource primer. *Searcher* 11(10).
Retrieved on July 11, 2007 from http://www.infotoday.com/searcher/nov03/
becker.shtml

Berry, J. N. (2005). The post-Martin era. *Library Journal* 130(1), 42–44. Retrieved
on July 11, 2007 from Library Literature & Information Science.

Department of Health and Human Services, National Institutes of Health, National
Library of Medicine. (n.d.). *FY 2008 Congressional Justification*. National Library
of Medicine, Bethesda, MD. Retrieved on September 28, 2007 from http://
www.nlm.nih.gov/about/2008CJ.pdf

Dunn, C. (1998). US department of education discretionary library programs, fiscal
year 1997. In *The Bowker Annual: Library and Book Trade Almanac*, 43rd ed.,
pp. 307–327, R. R. Bowker, New Providence, NJ.

Equipping Museums and Libraries for the 21st Century. (2002). Hearing before the
Subcommittee on Select Education of the Committee on Education and the
Workforce, House of Representatives, 107th Congress, second session. Serial No.
107-45. Washington, DC: GPO. Retrieved on April 4, 2007 from http://
www.eric.ed.gov/ERICDocs/data/ericdocs2sql/content_storage_01/0000019b/80/
1b/28/bb.pdf.

Fitzgibbons, S. G. (1984). Funding of research in librarianship. *Library Trends* 32,
537–556.

Frankel, D. (1997). A natural cultural partnership: libraries, museums, and
government. *American Libraries* 28, 35–36. Retrieved on from *Library Literature &
Information Science*, July 11, 2007

Frankel, D. (1998). Institute of Museum and Library Services library programs. In
*The Bowker Annual: Library and Book Trade Almanac*, 43rd ed., pp. 302–306, R. R.
Bowker, New Providence, NJ.

Frankel, D. (1999). Institute of Museum and Library Services library programs. In *The Bowker Annual: Library and Book Trade Almanac*, 44th ed., pp. 340–349, R. R. Bowker, New Providence, NJ.

Griffin, S. M. (2005). Funding for digital libraries research. *D-Lib Magazine* 11(7/8). Retrieved on March 25, 2007 from http://www.dlib.org/dlib/july05/griffin/07griffin.html

Hernon, P., Hunt, C. D., and McClure, C. R. (1990). Research. In *ALA Yearbook of Library and Information Services: A Review Of Library Events 1989*, vol. 15, p. 218, American Library Association, Chicago.

Humes, B. (1998). Building and Supporting Library Research: A National Focus. *Proceedings From an Exploratory Workgroup Meeting, 1998*. Washington, DC, National Institute on Postsecondary Education, Libraries, and Lifelong Learning (ED/OERI). Retrieved on July 11, 2007 from http://www.ed.gov/offices/OERI/PLLI/libresearch.html

IMLS Director Gets His Message Across: Federal Dollars Deliver Service (2002). *American Libraries* 22(2), 15–16. Retrieved on July 11, 2007 from Library, Information Science & Technology Abstracts database.

Institute of Museum and Library Services (2006). *Status of Technology and Digitization in the Nation's Museums and Libraries*. Retrieved on May 26, 2007 from http://www.imls.gov/publications/TechDig05/Technology%2BDigitization.pdf

Kasprowski, R. (2005). Funding opportunities for research in human information behavior. *Bulletin of the American Society for Information Science and Technology* 31(6), 17–20.

Kenney, B. (2002). Libs., education, and the IMLS. *Library Journal* 127(1), 18. Retrieved on July 11, 2007 from Library, Information Science & Technology Abstracts database.

Klassen, R. (1997). US department of education library programs, 1996. In *The Bowker Annual: Library and Book Trade Almanac*, 42nd ed., pp. 302–312, R. R. Bowker, New Providence, NJ.

Langile, L., and Mackenzie, T. (2007). Navigating the road to success: A systematic approach to preparing competitive grant proposals. *Evidence Based Library and Information Practice* 2(1), 23–31.

Larsen, R. L. (2005). Whence leadership?. *D-Lib Magazine* 11(7/8). Retrieved on July 8, 2007 from Library, Information Science & Technology Abstracts database.

Libraries for the Future (1998). *Library Research: 1983–1997; A Report to the National Institute on Postsecondary Education, Libraries, and Lifelong Learning and the National Library of Education, Office of Educational Research and Improvement, US Department of Education (1997)*. Report prepared by Libraries for the Future, New York, NY. Retrieved on March 25, 2007 from http://www.ed.gov/offices/OERI/PLLI/LibraryResearch/iffnew2.pdf

Lynch, C. (2005). Where do we go from here? *D-Lib Magazine* 11(7/8). Retrieved on July 2007 from http://www.dlib.org/dlib/july05/lynch/07lynch.html

Martin, R. S. (2002). Institute of Museum and Library Services library programs. In *The Bowker Annual: Library and Book Trade Almanac*, 47th ed., pp. 343–357, Information Today, Medford, NJ.

Martin, R. S. (2003). Institute of Museum and Library Services library programs. In *The Bowker Annual: Library and Book Trade Almanac*, 48th ed., pp. 348–362, Information Today, Medford, NJ.

Martin, R. S. (2004). Institute of Museum and Library Services library programs. In *The Bowker Annual: Library and Book Trade Almanac*, 49th ed., pp. 321–340, Information Today, Medford, NJ.

Martin, R. S. (2005). Institute of Museum and Library Services library programs. In *The Bowker Annual: Library and Book Trade Almanac*, 50th ed., pp. 353–375, Information Today, Medford, NJ.

Mathews, A. J. (1991). The role of the US Department of Education in library and information science research. In *Library and Information Research: Perspectives and Strategies for Improvement* (C. R. McClure and P. Hernon, eds.), pp. 45–62, Ablex Publishing Corporation, Norwood, NJ.

Messerschmitt, D. G. (2003). *Opportunities for research libraries in the NSF cyberinfrastructure Program*. Association for Research Libraries, Washington, DCARL Bimonthly Report No. 229. Retrieved on April 7, 2007 from http://www.arl.org/resources/pubs/br/br229/br229cyber.shtml

Museum and Library Services Act of 2003 (2003). Washington, DC: Superintendent of Documents, US government Printing Office. Retrieved on April 10, 2007 from http://www.imls.gov/pdf/2003.pdf

Museum and Library Services Act of 2003: Report (to accompany S. 888). (2003). Washington DC: US Government Printing Office.

National Science Foundation (2006). *Investing in America's Future; strategic plan FY 2006–2011*. National Science Foundation, Arlington, VA. Retrieved on March 25, 2007 from http://www.nsf.gov/publications/pub_summ.jsp?ods_key = nsf0648

NEH. (1998). *NEH and America's Libraries*. Washington, DC: National Endowment for the Humanities.

Oder, N. (2001). IMLS addresses lifelong learning. *Library Journal* 126(20), 17–18.

Phelps, T. C. (1997). National endowment for the humanities. In *The Bowker Annual: Library and Book Trade Almanac*, 42nd ed., pp. 293–301, R. R. Bowker, New Providence, NJ.

Phelps, T. C. (1998). National endowment for the humanities. In *The Bowker Annual: Library and Book Trade Almanac*, 43rd ed., pp. 293–301, R. R. Bowker, New Providence, NJ.

Phelps, T. C. (1999). National endowment for the humanities. In *The Bowker Annual: Library and Book Trade Almanac*, 44th ed., pp. 331–339, R. R. Bowker, New Providence, NJ.

Phelps, T. C. (2000). National endowment for the humanities. In *The Bowker Annual: Library and Book Trade Almanac*, 45th ed., pp. 273–279, R. R. Bowker, New Providence, NJ.

Phelps, T. C. (2001). National endowment for the humanities. In *The Bowker Annual: Library and Book Trade Almanac*, 46th ed., pp. 273–285, R. R. Bowker, New Providence, NJ.

Phelps, T. C. (2002). National endowment for the humanities. In *The Bowker Annual: Library and Book Trade Almanac*, 47th ed., pp. 333–342, Information Today, Inc, Medford, NJ.

Phelps, T. C. (2003). National endowment for the humanities. In *The Bowker Annual: Library and Book Trade Almanac*, 48th ed., pp. 335–347, Information Today, Inc, Medford, NJ.

Phelps, T. C. (2004). National endowment for the humanities. In *The Bowker Annual: Library and Book Trade Almanac*, 49th ed., pp. 307–320, Information Today, Inc, Medford, NJ.

Phelps, T. C. (2005). National endowment for the humanities. In *The Bowker Annual: Library and Book Trade Almanac*, 50th ed., pp. 339–352, Information Today, Inc, Medford, NJ.

Phelps, T. C. (2006). National endowment for the humanities. In *The Bowker Annual: Library and Book Trade Almanac*, 51st ed., pp. 347–360, Information Today, Inc, Medford, NJ.

Phelps, T. C. (2007). National endowment for the humanities. In *The Bowker Annual: Library and Book Trade Almanac*, 52nd ed., pp. 293–305, Information Today, Inc, Medford, NJ.

Radice, A. (2006). Institute of Museum and Library Services library programs. In *The Bowker Annual: Library and Book Trade Almanac*, 51st ed., pp. 361–382, Information Today, Inc, Medford, NJ.

Radice, A. M., and Chute, M. L. (2007). Institute of Museum and Library Services library programs. In *The Bowker Annual: Library and Book Trade Almanac*, 53rd ed., pp. 306–330, Information Today, Inc., Medford, NJ.

Ray, J. (2004). Connecting people and resources: Digital programs at the Institute of Museum and Library Services. *Library Hi-Tech* 22(3), 249–253. Retrieved on July 11, 2007 from Library, Information Science & Technology Abstracts database.

Ray, J. M. (2001). Digitization grants and how to get one: Advice from the Director, Office of Library Services, Institute of Museum and Library Services. *The Bottom Line* 14(2), 93–96. Retrieved on July 11, 2007 from Library Literature and Information Science database.

Rowan, E. (2006). The Institute of Museum and Library Services. *Information Research Watch International*, June, 1–2.

Ruffin, A. B., Cogdill, I., Kutty, L., and Hudson-Ochillo, M. (2005). Access to electronic health information for the public: Analysis of fifty-three funded projects. *Library Trends* 53(3), 434–452.

Sheppard, B. (2000). Institute of Museum and Library Services library programs. In *The Bowker Annual: Library and Book Trade Almanac*, 45th ed., pp. 280–293, R. R. Bowker, New Providence, NJ.

Sheppard, B. (2001). Institute of Museum and Library Services library programs. In *The Bowker Annual: Library and Book Trade Almanac*, 46th ed., pp. 286–298, R. R. Bowker, New Providence, NJ.

St. Lifer, E. (1998). A "promised land" for federal *library* funding? *Library Journal* 123(8), 40–42. Retrieved on July 11, 2007 from Library Literature and Information Science database.

Stone, A. (2006). Presidents' 2006 and 2007 budgets boost library funding. *American Libraries* 37(3), 11. Retrieved on July 11, 2007 from Library Literature & Information Science database.

Testimony of Bruce Cole (2005). Testimony of Bruce Cole, Chairman, National Endowment for the Humanities Before the Appropriations Subcommittee on Interior, Environment, and Related Agencies. US House of Representatives, March 10, 2005. Retrieved on March 25, 2007 from http://www.neh.gov/pdf/chairmansstatementfinal.pdf

Theiler, T. (2002). Government funding—Getting money from Uncle Sam. *Information Outlook* 6(6). Retrieved on March 25, 2007 from http://www.sla.org/content/Shop/Information/infoonline/2002/jun02/policy.cfm

White, H. S. (1994/95). Library research and government funding—A less than ardent romance. *Publishing Research Quarterly* 10(4), 30–38. Retrieved on March 26, 2007 from Library Literature & Information Science database.

Zink, S., Illes, J., and Vannier, M. W. (1996). NLM extramural program: Frequently asked questions. *Bulletin of the Medical Library Association* 84(2), 165–181.

# The Development and Impact of Digital Library Funding in the United States

Jeffrey Pomerantz, Songphan Choemprayong and Lori Eakin
School of Information and Library Science, University of North Carolina at Chapel Hill, Chapel Hill, NC, USA

## Abstract

This chapter traces the history of digital libraries (DLs) in the United States through the funding sources that have supported DL research and development over the past decade and a half. A set of related questions are addressed: How have the mission and goals of funding agencies affected the types of projects that have been funded? What have been the deliverables from funded projects and how have the goals of the funding agencies shaped those deliverables? Funding agencies have exerted strong influence over research and development in DLs, and different funding agencies have funded different types of projects, with varying sets of concerns for driving the various fields that feed into DLs. This chapter will address the impact that DL funding has had on the development of research in the field of Library and Information Science, as well as on the practice of librarianship.

## I. Introduction

Digital libraries (DLs) have emerged as one of the most vibrant areas within library and information science (LIS). DLs exist at the intersection of many, if not all topics within the field of LIS, and introduce much from computer science (CS) and other fields into the mix as well. As a result, trends in these fields have influenced research and development on DL-related topics. Furthermore, the fields and subdisciplines that feed into DLs are themselves active areas of research and development, funded by a range of agencies. Some of these agencies fund DL and DL-related projects specifically, while some have agendas in which DLs simply play a role alongside other types of projects. This chapter traces the history and development of DLs through the funding sources that have supported them, and investigates the goals of

INFLUENCE OF FUNDING ON ADVANCES IN LIBRARIANSHIP
ADVANCES IN LIBRARIANSHIP, VOL. 31
© 2008 by Emerald Group Publishing Limited
ISSN: 0065-2830
DOI: 10.1016/S0065-2830(08)31002-2

the funding agencies and the impact that these goals have had on both the current shape of DLs and on the profession of librarianship in general. This history and development is extracted from the literature on DLs, from the earliest DLs and DL-like projects to the present day. A few informal interviews were conducted with researchers involved in DL projects early in their history, but these were not a primary source for this chapter, serving instead to point the authors to bodies of literature to review.

DLs, like physical libraries, are expensive to build and expensive to maintain. Since their inception, DLs have commanded large sums of money, and have benefited from major funding initiatives from many organizations. Funding for DLs, however, differs in at least one important respect from funding for physical libraries. A physical library necessarily reflects the mission of its host institution, be that a city, a school, a university, a corporation, or any other organization. In order to justify its existence, therefore, a physical library must demonstrate that it assists its host institution in fulfilling its objectives, whether those objectives are educational, political, financial, or anything else. DLs, on the other hand, are often grant-funded research and development projects, testbeds in which new technologies and new processes are tried out, often with a longer-term timeline for payoff in fulfilling institutional objectives. The goals of a physical library are shaped to a great extent by the goals of its host institution, which is generally also the library's primary funding agency. The goals of a DL are also shaped by the goals of its funding sources; however, these sources are not necessarily tied to the institution that hosts the DL. For example, the Canadian Council on Social Development (Scott, 2003) notes that grants, as generally unrestricted and unaudited forms of support, tend to allow a much greater level of process and content freedom to their recipients than do other forms of funding. The goals of DL projects, often being grant-funded, may be different than the goals of the DL's host institution. As a result, DLs must balance the goals of its host library (and of the profession of librarianship in general) with the goals of its funding agencies. This difference between DLs and physical libraries is of course a difference of degree and not of kind, since even traditional libraries receive funding from various sources.

As a DL moves from being a testbed to a viable operational entity, it often loses some of the freedom from institutional restrictions that it originally was granted during its start-up phase. In most cases, a DL that originates within an institutional environment must find a way to integrate its operations with the mission of its host institution as time goes on. This is likely to impact its financial structure, sometimes placing additional pressures on its funding requirements. Indeed, in a study of the DL programs in Digital Library Federation (DLF) member libraries, Greenstein and Thorin (2002) found that "core funding"—funding provided by the institution, not from external sources—was essential to libraries in funding their DL programs as they matured. Further, as Letts *et al.* (1997) point out, because grants tend to support the start-up stage of projects, they often fail to provide incentives for these projects to focus upon organizational goals such as the long-term ability for the initiative to support routine overhead costs and organizational capacity, which are essential factors in long-term sustainability. Those factors are often considered more carefully in projects' later stages, either due to requirements from longer-term governmental funding initiatives or restrictions placed upon the program by its host institution as it begins to receive more core funding.

Given that DL research and development is more heavily funded through grants than most other work in libraries, then, it has had the potential to radically reshape the field of LIS and the profession of librarianship via the relative freedom to implement innovative new technologies and experiment with new services. But has it actually done so? As this chapter explores the history of funding for DLs, the question of just what that funding has paid for over the years will be addressed, and the impact of DLs and DL-related technologies will be explored. In fact this impact extends beyond what can be explored here, since DL funding has led to far more than the development of DLs: database and publishing ventures, software development, even Google has been supported by DL funding sources. It is also difficult, if not impossible, to establish a direct cause-and-effect relationship between historical events. DL funding has had an impact on a great many areas within LIS and librarianship, but it is unreasonable to suggest that this funding is the sole influence. This chapter will therefore attempt to disentangle the influence that DL funding has had on LIS and librarianship, as opposed to other influences, but this influence will be interpreted liberally.

One of the greatest challenges in writing any paper about DLs is simply defining the term "digital library." Definitions of DLs abound in the LIS and CS literature, and reviewing these definitions requires an entire paper unto itself (as, e.g., Borgman, 1999). Instead, two representative and widely cited examples are presented here. Arms (2000) defines a DL as a "managed collection of information, with associated services" (p. 2). Borgman (1999) defines DLs as "a set of electronic resources and associated technical capabilities" that are "constructed, collected and organized, by (and for) a community of users" (p. 234). Most definitions of DLs include the elements that Arms and Borgman introduce: a DL is a collection of electronic materials; that collection is managed and organized; it is created and managed by one or more user communities; and technical and user services are provided that add value to the materials. Duguid and Atkins (1997) extend this definition by suggesting that a DL is "an environment to bring together collections, services, and people in support of the full life cycle of creation, dissemination, use, and preservation of data, information, and knowledge" (Introduction Section), thus introducing the social function of DLs.

These definitions are useful for most purposes, but are too broad for the purposes of this chapter, given the need to identify funding sources that support DL work specifically, and exclude funding that supports other types of managed digital collections, such as digital archives, institutional repositories, electronic publishing initiatives, and others. Consequently, a purely pragmatic definition will be employed here: a funding source will be said to support DL work if the Call for Proposals, Program Solicitation, or other documentation states that it supports DL work. Additionally, a funded project will be said to be a DL if the published literature on that project states that it is a DL. This definition would be insupportable in the context of formal DL research, as it opens the door to all manner of semantic imprecision; however, semantic imprecision needs to be allowed here. As will be discussed below, the term DL was not always in widespread use, and projects that evolved into DLs were called by other names first. This pragmatic definition of DLs also allows different agencies the latitude to define DLs differently, which, again, might be insupportable in other contexts. This latitude is, however, precisely what is needed here: given that different agencies may define DLs differently, and fund DL projects accordingly, what impact have these different approaches had on the development of DLs and on librarianship?

A significant limitation of this chapter is that it focuses exclusively on DL initiatives and funding streams based in the United States. There are extensive and important DL initiatives around the world (e.g., the European Digital Library Project, www.edlproject.eu; the Digital Library of China, www.d-library.com.cn; multiple digital collections from the National Library of Australia, www.nla.gov.au/digicoll/), and there are many collaborative efforts between institutions in the U.S. and other nations (e.g., the Digital Library Federation, www.diglib.org). This chapter will not address these initiatives, though the authors suggest that a chapter or a book on DL initiatives worldwide would be a fascinating read and well worth someone's time to write.

## II. Prior to the Digital Libraries Initiative

The first large-scale funding effort for DL projects was the National Science Foundation's Digital Libraries Initiative (DLI), which will be discussed in detail below. However, the idea of the DL did not emerge, Athena-like, mature and armored, from the head of the National Science Foundation. Rather, there were many streams of research and development that presaged DLs and directly fed into DL research and development. For example, in his vision of libraries of the future, Licklider (1965) predicted that by the year 2000 computers would be able to provide automated library services that could be simultaneously accessed by numerous users. Even earlier, Vannevar Bush (1945) described his now-famous "memex" as "a sort of mechanized private file and library," foreshadowing personal DLs of 60 years hence (Beagrie, 2005). By the late 1970s, technology development was beginning to have a profound impact on libraries. Observing this trend and projecting its future, F. W. Lancaster published his now classic *Toward Paperless Information Systems*, in which he described the "library in a box," a system which he predicted would shake the foundations of traditional, physical libraries and lead to an ever-increasing number of computerized libraries (Lancaster, 1978). Lancaster recognized the significant cultural and technical difficulties involved in achieving such technological change to libraries, but he also pointed out that it was more than a pipe dream: in the late 1970s the CIA was already engaged in a project to build a prototype system that would allow widespread storage, indexing, and searching of large bodies of documents (Sapp, 2002).

Such early thought experiments and prototype projects encouraged libraries to act as early adopters of many computer technologies designed to manage a range of functions (Borgman, 1997; Kilgour, 1970). For example, as early as the mid- to late 1960s, libraries adopted innovations such as databases of published and gray literature (Neufeld and Cornog, 1986), machine-readable cataloging records (McCallum, 2002; Spicher, 1996), and databases for sharing these records (Borgman, 1997). These early uses of technology began the shift toward what Buckland (1992) refers to as the "electronic library" and Rusbridge (1998) the "hybrid library": libraries that utilize technology both to manage their administrative operations and to deliver materials to patrons. Publishers too were experimenting with computer and network technology for delivering materials as early as the 1960s (Peek and Pomerantz, 1998). Most of these, however, were experiments with alternative forms of delivery for scholarly journals and other forms of scholarly communication. As such, these projects were not framed as being library-related, except insofar as the published content might be delivered to libraries and library users. While it is clear in hindsight that these projects were precursors of DLs, they were described at the time as publishing or database ventures.

During the 1980s, a number of research studies to explore the possibilities for electronic libraries were conducted by and in physical libraries, and funded by traditionally library-oriented agencies. In 1986, The University of Texas at Austin received a grant from the Council on Library Resources (CLR) to conduct a study on users' interest in digitized images (Libraries for the Future, 1998). Also supported by CLR, in 1988 the University of Hawai'i at Mānoa conducted a study of users of full-text databases (Libraries for the Future, 1998). In 1989, two projects supported by the U.S. Department of Education were launched by Ohio State University and The University of Houston to develop a prototype system for "intelligent information retrieval" and an "intelligent reference information system" (Libraries for the Future, 1998). In 1988, the Online Computer Library Center (OCLC)—always an active funder of studies on the creation and use of electronic information in libraries—conducted a self-funded project called Bibliographic Control and Document Architecture in Hypermedia Databases, to identify potential designs "for electronic documents that enable algorithmic derivation and generation of a variety of bibliographic representations" (Hjerppe, 1989, p. 6). Today, all of these projects might be framed as DL services.

Perhaps the first DL both funded and developed by a library was the American Memory Project, launched in 1990 by the Library of Congress (LC) (Lamolinara, 1995a; Bellinger, 2002). This project will be discussed in more detail below. Another early library DL project was Project Open Book, launched in 1991 by the Yale University Library and supported by the Commission on Preservation and Access (which later merged with CLR to become CLIR, the Council on Library and Information Resources) (Conway, 1996; Conway and Weaver, 1994). Both of these projects focused on digitization of materials and preservation issues, however, rather than on collection building or the technical aspects of DL development.

Identifying the first funded project that might reasonably be called a DL (in or out of a library) is quite difficult. One of the earliest examples is the University of California, Irvine's *Thesaurus Linguae Graecae* (TLG), a project which originally began in 1972 with funding from the Andrew W. Mellon Foundation as a CD-ROM database collection, and which has since developed into a widely used web-based DL of classical texts (www.tlg. uci.edu). Like the TLG, many early DL projects were originally distributed on physical media: American Memory, for example, was originally distributed on laser disc. In part bound by the limitations of physical media, many early DL-like projects were efforts undertaken by a single institution, with no connection to other related projects, thus differentiating them from later, networked DLs. Further, before the term "digital library" came into widespread use, the TLG and other projects were often simply called "databases."

Perhaps the first project that was described in writing as a DL (rather than as a database or a form of publishing) was the Envision project (Fox *et al.*, 1993; Heath *et al.*, 1995). Envision was a project to develop a digital collection of computer science materials, specifically bibliographic records and full text from several publications produced by the Association for Computing Machinery (ACM). Envision was referred to as a DL, however, only in the published literature written about the project; in the grant proposal, Envision was described as a "hypermedia database" (NSF, 1993). When the Envision project was launched in September 1991, the term "digital library" was not yet in widespread use.

The first use of the term "digital library" in print appears to have been Kahn and Cerf's (1988) report to the Corporation for National Research Initiatives, in which they describe an architecture for a DL system as a "new kind of national information infrastructure" (p. 3), on par with other critical national infrastructure such as the highway and telephone systems. In July 1992 the NSF held a Workshop on Electronic Libraries, while in December 1992 a second NSF workshop was called Workshop on Digital Libraries (Fox, 1993): at the NSF and among the workshop attendees, at least, a terminology shift had taken place in the intervening 6 months. Griffin (1998) notes that the reason for the adoption of the term "digital libraries" rather than any alternative term was that "'electronic' refers primarily to the nature of the technologies which operate on information and 'virtual' implies a synthetic environment which resembles the original, physical environment ... 'Digital' refers to a representation of information on electronic (and other) media." The term "electronic library" is still used, though nowadays this term more often refers to portals to a wide range of electronic publications, often provided by government agencies, as in the case of the Florida Electronic Library (www.flelibrary.org) and the Michigan eLibrary (www.mel.org).

Surprisingly, during all of the time that research was being conducted by libraries on functionality for electronic libraries, and library-like functionality was being developed outside of libraries, little attention was being paid to these trends by the mainstream communities of library science researchers and librarian practitioners. Neither of two reports that articulate research agendas in LIS in the 1980s (Cuadra Associates, 1982; Matthews, 1989) mention DLs among their research priorities. Even after the DLI had been underway for several years, DLs were largely ignored in the context of agenda-setting for the profession of librarianship. The report from Libraries for the Future (1998) acknowledged that the DLI "will doubtless shape the future of information research and access," but nevertheless somewhat myopically excluded the DLI from its analysis of funding trends in library research, in part because "most of the work is being done by researchers in computer science and information science, with comparatively little input from traditional library researchers." (p. 13) As predicted in the Libraries for the Future report, the DLI, and DLs in general, did indeed shape the future of information research and access, with far-reaching impact for library research and the profession of librarianship. One cannot fully understand the impact of the DLI without considering the overall environment in which it was created.

Programmatically, the DLI was a subcomponent of the High-Performance Computing and Communications (HPCC) Initiative, set up under the auspices of the High-Performance Computing Act of 1991 (HPCA), an act passed in large part to ensure that the United States maintained its global economic and military superiority, a concern to the nation in the late 1980s. Americans had emerged from the Cold War worried about the United States' ability to adapt and survive in a global economy no longer driven largely by military expenditures (Savage, 1994). Increasing competition from abroad fueled these concerns, and the 1987 stock market crash and recession, followed by a renewed recession in the United States in 1990 and 1991, led Americans to the startling recognition that the country's foreign competitors were potentially in a better economic position than the U.S., largely due to their technology policies. Specifically, the economies of both Germany and Japan, recognized as our prime technological competitors, continued to thrive in the early 1990s while that of the U.S. stagnated (Mitchell, 1997). When then-senator Al Gore introduced his "National High-Performance Computer Technology Act" (a.k.a. the "Gore Bill") in 1989, his statement that "the nation which most completely assimilates high-performance computing into its economy will very likely emerge as the dominant intellectual, economic, and technological force in the next century" reflected much current economic and political thinking (National High-Performance Computer Technology Act, 1989). Indeed, the military had long recognized the potential benefits of computing technologies for defense purposes: in a 1981 report the Department of Defense (DoD) had noted that "the military power of the United States is inextricably tied to the programmable digital computer" (Yudken and Simons, 1988). In fact, military (especially DoD) funding of computer science research rose dramatically between 1977 and 1985, well overtaking the funding provided by the NSF, and sparked intense debate regarding the appropriate role for military spending in both basic and applied computer science research (Thompson, 1986; Yudken and Simons, 1988; Winograd, 1991). A compromise bill that allowed both economic and military goals to be achieved and that re-balanced and clarified the relationships between the top federal funding agencies was clearly a winning combination. As a result, the amended Gore Bill was passed in 1991 as the High-Performance Computing Act of 1991. This bill led to the implementation of the National High-Performance Computing and Communications initiative (NHPCC), which identified DLs as one of four fundamental applications that have "broad and direct impact on the Nation's competitiveness and the well-being of its citizens, and that can benefit by the application of HPCC technology and resources" (FCCSET, 1994, Section 6).

In short, the political climate in the U.S. in the early 1990s was favorable to a large-scale, multi-agency project that would utilize the National Research and Education Network (NREN) and would lead to new research in high-performance computing. In addition, computing and networking had already been widely adopted by research and educational institutions across the U.S., and had achieved speeds that made it conceivable for the bill to call for transmission rates nationwide of "one gigabit per second or greater" within five years (Zakon, 2003). In this environment of computing and networking power, and political support for harnessing this power, the recommendation to develop DLs could gain traction, as perhaps never before or since in the history of the United States.

# III. The NSF's Digital Libraries Initiatives

## A. Digital Libraries Initiative

Thus, while the idea of DLs did not originate with the NSF and in fact predated the DLI, the DLI nevertheless marked a turning point in the history of DLs by focusing attention on DLs as a legitimate area for research and development. Specifically, three NSF-sponsored workshops held in 1991 and 1992 had a strong influence on the DLI, and consequently on DLs as they exist today: the October 1991 Invitational Workshop on Future Directions in Text Analysis, Retrieval and Understanding, held preceding that year's ACM Special Interest Group on Information Retrieval (SIGIR) conference (Lesk et al., 1991); the July 1992 Workshop on Electronic Libraries; and the December 1992 Workshop on Digital Libraries (Fox, 1993). These workshops were themselves the culmination of discussions between program directors at a range of federal agencies, including the National Science Foundation (NSF), the Defense Advanced Research Projects Agency (DARPA), and the National Aeronautics and Space Administration (NASA). These three agencies were to go on to fund the DLI, along with a host of other agencies that could benefit from the development of and access to shared online collections of materials.

These workshops were also the culmination of discussions between researchers in fields that were to feed into DLs, and between researchers and program directors. It was no accident, for example, that the 1991 workshop was held alongside that year's SIGIR conference: the workshop participants were prominent researchers in the field of information retrieval (IR) and related areas. Lesk *et al.* (1991) list a wide range of research areas related and complementary to the DL work that they propose; many of these were (and still are) central to DLs, including such areas as indexing and classification, interface design, hypertext, natural language processing, and knowledge representation, to name only a few. There were many funded projects in all of these research areas in 1991 and before, a few of which have been discussed above. Funding for IR and related areas itself grew out of a federal focus in the late 1980s on funding research on networking and infrastructure. Griffin (2005) notes that this focus was due to concerns that the U.S. was lagging behind other nations (specifically Germany and Japan) in the area of large scale computational science, and the concomitant desire to rapidly develop the United States' capabilities in this area. As often occurs with technological developments, however, the infrastructure development made possible by this federal support brought about unintended consequences: specifically, the popularization of computing and networking technology. The development of the World Wide Web then led to the development of tools designed to ease non-experts' use of the Web, including search engines and better interfaces. Mass use of online resources led to the need for better ways to organize and retrieve the data now widely available, and the need to make more high-quality data available. In their recommendations, Lesk, Fox, and McGill articulated what must have been the *zeitgeist* of the 1991 workshop: that diverse threads of IR-related research already underway could be applied to the development of an online library that would not only enable electronic access to materials, but could also benefit the education and research communities.

A number of recommendations came out of the 1991 and 1992 NSF workshops, both for the NSF specifically and for the community of researchers and funding agencies generally. The overarching recommendation from these workshops was for the NSF to launch "an initiative to build a basic science, engineering, and technology library on-line, available over the Internet/NREN, and for research regarding building and exploiting it" (Lesk *et al.*, 1991, p. 12). Lesk, Fox, and McGill also stated that existing infrastructure and technology must be used wherever possible in building this "library on-line." The NREN was singled out as "the most important resource" to bring to bear on this library. The NSF, as the agency that coordinated the NREN and the HPCC, was singled out as the logical federal agency to launch this initiative.

While influential, the recommendations from the 1991 and 1992 NSF workshops were not the sole influence on the creation of the DLI. From a broader perspective, the DLI was the result of a happy confluence of a congenial political environment, a positive economic climate, and the then-state of the art of computing and networking technology. Without all of these elements in place, the various federal agencies involved in the DLI might have been unlikely to engage in such a large-scale and financially intensive initiative, especially during a period in which a federal budget deficit and economic recession were growing concerns to the nation's citizens. The fortunate convergence of these factors, however, set the stage for future DL research and practice.

It is worth pointing out that the "precursor" DL projects (those that were not yet being called DLs: e.g., the American Memory Project, the Envision project, etc.) were all projects to develop collections of digital materials. The DLI therefore has the distinction of being the first funded research project on DLs, a project specifically to develop new technologies and to explore issues involved in building and maintaining DLs. Indeed, the DLI and DLI-2 remain to this day among the few basic research projects on DLs.

Six grants were awarded under the DLI: to Carnegie Mellon University, the University of California at Berkeley, the University of California at Santa Barbara, the University of Illinois at Urbana-Champaign, the University of Michigan-Ann Arbor, and Stanford University. The total amount awarded under the DLI was $26.8 billion; the average amount of these awards was $4.5 million. Five of these grants were to schools of Computer Science; only one was to a school of Library and Information Science (the University of Michigan). The University of California at Berkeley and the University of Illinois at Urbana-Champaign, however, both have LIS programs (and had when the DLI grants were awarded), and researchers from these programs collaborated with the principal investigators on the grants to these institutions. While the DLI's goals were not directly derived from the High-Performance Computing Act of 1991, the projects funded under the DLI did address some of those agencies' responsibilities. The six funded projects developed DLs containing a range of formats of materials, including the full text of periodical publications, images, maps, audio and video recordings, and large data sets. The University of Michigan, for example, was one of the institutions involved in The University Licensing Project (TULIP) project, Elsevier Science's project "to jointly test systems for networked delivery to, and use of journals at, the user's desktop" (Borghuis *et al.*, 1996), and the University of Michigan's DLI proposal was an extension of their efforts in that project. The University of California at Santa Barbara proposed to develop a DL of spatially indexed information, including collections of maps and images. Carnegie-Mellon University, in addition to other work, proposed to study the economics of charging for online content. The University of Illinois at Urbana-Champaign proposed to conduct sociological and economic analysis of DL use. Thus the DLI projects covered a very broad range, the work on which was, as Lesk *et al.* (1991) had suggested, divided between "the creation of the library and the research on its exploitation" (p. 20)—in other words, between collection development and basic research.

As often happens with technology, an event that could not have been predicted dramatically changed the course of the DLI projects. In November 1993, the National Center for Supercomputing Applications (NCSA) released Mosaic version 1.0. Mosaic was the first graphical browser application for the World Wide Web and, unlike previous hypertext applications, enabled the integration of both text and images into hypertext documents. This integration of text and images was the tipping point for the popularization of the internet, and within months, Mosaic had achieved a user base of millions worldwide (NCSA, 2007). The DLI program announcement was released in the autumn of 1993 (Griffin, 1998), and the start date for projects was September 1994. Project proposals were therefore written during that intervening year: in other words, precisely at the time that Mosaic was first released and was gaining a user base. It would have been nearly impossible during that year for anyone to predict just how much Mosaic would change the internet and users' interaction with it, and as a result, the DLI project proposals did not address the Web. With the advent of the graphical Web, however, the Web became the obvious platform for the dissemination of the materials in these DLs, thus employing the Hypertext Transfer Protocol (HTTP) as the protocol and the browser the interface for this dissemination.

## B. Limitations of the DLI

The DLI was perhaps as important for focusing attention on DLs as an area for research and development as it was for its support of the individual projects it funded. As the first major funding program for DL-related projects, however, there was much that it did not and could not do. The DLI received a good deal of criticism, often from the very researchers who were funded by it, who were naturally in a position to see its limitations. Criticism of the DLI focused largely on four points: its primarily CS-driven agenda, a lack of connection to libraries and other cultural institutions, too little attention to user needs, and too little attention to evaluation.

As mentioned above, five out of six grants under the DLI were provided to CS programs; only one went to an LIS program. According to Saracevic and Dalbello (2003), only two projects focused on specific domains or topics, while the remaining four focused on the development of domain-independent technologies (p. 8), echoing the divide between collection building and basic research. To be fair, however, the connection between theory and practice was in fact a component of the DLI agenda from the beginning: the DLI's call for proposals required that funded projects "will digitize a significantly large and important information collection, or use an existing collection, to serve as an experimental platform to demonstrate scale-up potential and as an experimental testbed for the research proposed" (NSF, 1993). In other words, the NSF required that projects create and disseminate useful collections, both as project deliverables and as environments for basic research. Nevertheless, this supposed disconnect between theory and practice in the DLI added fuel to the criticism that the DLI agenda was largely "set by the computer science community" when in fact there were "other constituencies whose voices need to be heard" (Levy, 2000, Paragraph 19).

Griffin (1998) identified some of these other constituencies, such as "libraries, museums, art departments, schools of music, archeology, history and other humanities departments" (Conclusion section, Paragraph 3), thereby suggesting that research and development for DLs needed to expand to encompass cultural institutions of all types. Although some DL-like projects in cultural institutions predated the DLI (e.g., the American Memory Project and the *TLG*), these were piecemeal efforts, largely disconnected from each other and from the DLI projects (Saracevic and Dalbello, 2003); the DLI projects themselves focused primarily on technology development rather than collection building and management. Although all of the DLI projects built their own testbed collections, the published literature contains little discussion of the scope of these collections.

Others also recognized this disconnect between DL research and practice (Hirtle, 1999), and identified important research areas within that gap. Schatz and Chen (1996), for example, argued for increased attention to user needs, suggesting that "large-scale testbed" collections are necessary "as the only method for determining which information system features are actually useful in practice" (pp. 47–48). Griffin (1998) echoed this sentiment, bemoaning the "unnatural separation between the producers and consumers of digital libraries" (Conclusion section, Paragraph 3) and arguing for increased collaboration between researchers and users.

Evaluation was also an area of concern for DLI. Evaluation is always a challenge, and it was especially so for the DLI projects, since they were interdisciplinary and aimed to fulfill the goals of multiple agencies. Bishop (1995) articulated four levels of evaluation for the DLI projects: adequacy of the collection, functionality, interface, and usability; search and retrieval performance and behavior; effect on the work and processes of users; and public policy implications. She further commented that "the six projects are devoting varying amounts of attention to each of these evaluation levels" (Synchronizing Work Across the Six DLI Projects section, Paragraph 2). Griffin (2005), however, argues that the impact of and new research questions raised by a project are often apparent only in the "latter stages of the research program" (Critique of the DLI Program, Section 4).

Another drawback of the DLI was the short-term nature of the funding it provided. The DLI provided funding for projects for 4 years, which, as anyone who has been involved in the development of a DL knows, is insufficient time to bring a DL project to maturity. Years after the conclusion of the DLI, Griffin (2005) argued that the DLI's "funding models did not work optimally, particularly for the mid-size, longer-term, interdisciplinary research and testbed projects" (Critique of the DLI Program, Paragraph 2). This comment echoes Griffin's comment of years earlier, that "larger-scale projects require several years to complete and require a stable and predictable funding stream to retain essential staff and resources" (DLI Program Constraints section, Paragraph 1). Of course, this problem is not unique to the DLI: stable funding is a challenge for any grant-funded project, and DL projects in particular, since DLs tend to span disciplinary boundaries and "research agencies tend to be limited to support of those research activities and infrastructure building that stay within their defined missions" (DLI Program Constraints section, Paragraph 2).

These criticisms of the DLI had a significant impact on the scope of the DLI Phase 2. DLI-2 was more interdisciplinary, and had a stronger focus on collection development and user needs. Additional public and private agencies were included in DLI-2 in order to provide support from an interdisciplinary perspective. Evaluation was a more central concern for DLI-2, corresponding with an increased focus on evaluation within the NSF as a whole (Directorate for Education and Human Resources, 1998). Not all limitations of the DLI were, or could be, addressed by the DLI-2, however. Furthermore, increasing awareness of DLs led to an explosion in the number of DL-related projects, and researchers and practitioners working on such projects. This created a need for funding sources beyond the NSF, and these funding sources presented themselves, in the form of both public and private agencies.

## C. Digital Libraries Initiative Phase 2

Before discussing the projects funded by sources beyond the NSF, however, the NSF's two other major DL initiatives will be addressed briefly. In 1997, the NSF sponsored the Planning Workshop on Distributed Knowledge Work Environments, which has come to be known as the Santa Fe workshop (Duguid and Atkins, 1997). The Santa Fe workshop, like the workshops in 1991 and 1992, brought together the community of researchers working in DL-related areas (naturally including researchers from the original six DLI projects) to brainstorm about the possible futures for DLs, and to make recommendations to the NSF about the need for a continued funding program focused on DLs. Perhaps unsurprisingly, the consensus from the Santa Fe workshop was that there was a continued need for a Digital Library Initiative. Workshop participants identified three "central issues" in DL research: systems, collections, and users.

By 1998 the HPCCs initiative had evolved into the Federal Computing, Information, and Communications (CIC) programs, with a narrowed focus on developing technologies for scientific applications and education (NSTC, 1999). The DLI-2 was part of the Human Centered Systems (HuCS) Program of the Federal CIC Program. The overarching goal of the HuCS program was to enable "increased accessibility and usability of computing systems and communications networks" (NSTC, 1999, p. 5); the goals of the DLI-2 therefore remained consistent with those of the DLI. Griffin (1998) points out that although the DLI-2 accounted for only about 0.6% of the total budget for the CIC, it was considered to be "a CIC R&D Highlight, testimony both to its achievements and to the mounting importance of the area generally" (DLI and the Federal Context: HPCC section, Paragraph 4).

Twenty-eight projects were funded under DLI-2, including a continuation of four of the six DLI projects (Fox, 1999). The two DLI projects that were not continued by DLI-2 were, however, continued by other funding sources (Fox, 1999). Conversely, some of the projects funded by DLI-2 were underway prior to DLI-2 (Saracevic and Dalbello, 2003), funded under other NSF programs, by other federal agencies, or by the projects' host institutions. Eight DLI-2 projects had a specifically undergraduate emphasis, investigating various ways in which the materials in DLs could be utilized in undergraduate education in a range of disciplines. As early as the 1991 NSF workshop, DLs were seen as presenting a benefit to education; this perspective was clearly at the forefront at the NSF, as recommendations concerning access to educational materials and use of technology from the NSF's review of undergraduate education (Advisory Committee to NSF, 1996) clearly informed the DLI-2 program.

The DLI-2 was funded collaboratively by the original three agencies behind the DLI (NSF, DARPA, and NASA) but also by additional federal agencies, including the National Library of Medicine (NLM), the LC, the National Endowment for the Humanities (NEH), the Federal Bureau of Investigation (FBI), the Institute for Museum and Library Services (IMLS), the National Archives and Records Administration (NARA), and others (NSF, 1998). These agencies contributed large sums to DLI-2, incurring about twice the expenditures of the DLI (Lesk, 1999), but they also played a significant role shaping the projects funded by DLI-2—and the DL projects more generally—in a variety of ways. Brogan (2003) observed that major DL initiatives "cluster around the mission of those government agencies supporting the Digital Library Initiative Phase 2—predominantly in the sciences and cultural heritage" (p. 7). Similarly, Griffin (1998) acknowledges that the DLI-2 addressed "a narrower technology research agenda than DLI" (DLI Programmatic Context section, Paragraph 6). On a more positive note, however, Griffin suggests that the potential range of DLI-2 projects was "expected to involve content in subject areas across the continuum of human interest" (DLI Programmatic Context section, Paragraph 7). Schatz and Chen (1999) likewise suggested that DLI-2 "presages the even bigger efforts recommended in the PITAC report" (Research initiatives section, Paragraph 5), referring to the 1999 President's Information Technology Advisory Committee report, which recommended a substantial increase in federal support for information technology research (PITAC, 1999). DLI-2 funded projects within the three central issues in DL research identified during the Santa Fe workshop—systems, collections, and users—and "across the information lifecycle," but de-emphasized projects to digitize collections. It is of course impossible to separate the practical issues of DL collection development from the basic research on these collections and the technologies underlying and serving them; each relies on the other. The fact that DLI-2 de-emphasized digitization therefore created a need for other funding sources that could step in and fund the many cultural institutions that desired to digitize their unique and valuable collections.

## D. National Science Digital Library

Even before the DLI-2 program ended in 2004, the NSF had already launched another DL program: the National Science, Mathematics, Engineering, and Technology Education Digital Library (NSDL) (NSF, 2000). The idea of such a DL predates the DLI-2, however, having been proposed while the DLI was still underway (Wattenberg, 1998; Zia, 2000). The scope of the NSDL is, quite obviously, materials that may contribute to education in science, mathematics, engineering, and technology (STEM) education (alternatively referred to as STET or SMETE).

The NSDL is a program of the NSF's Directorate for Education and Human Resources (EHR), Division of Undergraduate Education (DUE), while the DLI and DLI-2 were programs of the Information & Intelligent Systems (IIS) Division of the NSF's Computer and Information Science and Engineering (CISE) Directorate. This change in directorates is telling. From as early as the 1991 and 1992 NSF workshops, a central element of the conception of a DL was that it should benefit education, in particular undergraduate education. It was appropriate for the first major DL initiative that the projects funded under the DLI focused largely on developing the infrastructure to make DLs possible, and less on collections and their uses. With work on infrastructure well underway, some projects funded under the DLI-2 were able to focus more on developing collections, and services that could be provided to add value to those collections. As mentioned above, several DLI-2 projects focused on undergraduate education. By moving its DL initiative into the EHR, the NSF emphasized their increased focus on undergraduate education as a central element of DLs. The EHR oversees the NSDL program, but sister directorates to the EHR, including the Directorate for Mathematical & Physical Sciences, the Directorate for Geosciences, and the Directorate for Biological Sciences, provide "significant co-funding" (NSDL, n.d., Funding section).

This focus on education is demonstrated in other ways as well. When it was established in 2000, the NSDL program solicited proposals in four "tracks": Core Integration System, Collections, Services, and Targeted Research (NSF, 2000). The Core Integration track was the extension of the infrastructure-related work begun in the DLI and DLI-2; the purpose of the Core Integration track was to coordinate between all of the NSDL projects, develop standards and requirements, and develop and maintain the "central portal" to the NSDL (Core Integration System Track section). The Collections track supported projects to develop DL collections that would be accessible through the NSDL's "central portal," such that the NSDL became a collection of collections. The Services track supported projects "to develop services to increase the impact, reach, efficiency, and value of the digital library in its fully operational form" (Services Track section); what constituted a service was conceived broadly, to allow room for innovative uses of the materials within the NSDL. The Targeted Research track supported short-term projects that could be applied to the other three tracks, such as user studies, or development of new applications or interfaces. By 2002, the Core Integration effort had become established as an ongoing component of the NSDL project, conducted by a stable group of institutions (NSF, 2002);

this perhaps is an indication of how critical a central "command and control" group is for a large distributed collection of collections. In 2004, the Collections Track was replaced with the Pathways track: instead of supporting projects to develop new collections, the Pathways track supported projects to "assume a stewardship role for the educational content and/or the services" under the NSDL, and to "aggregate the efforts of existing resource providers" (NSF, 2004a, Pathways Track section). With the shift from Collections to Pathways, the NSDL began to emphasize sustainability of existing projects by organizations or consortia, "beyond the period of NSF funding" (Program Description section). Sustainability is, however, an ongoing effort, as demonstrated by a survey conducted by the NSDL's Sustainability Standing Committee (Giersch, 2003).

The NSDL program has supported the development of many DL collections of materials useful for education in the various STEM fields. Some of these DLs were developed from the start with NSDL funding, and some existed prior to the NSDL program (e.g., the Digital Library for Earth System Education, DLESE, www.dlese.org). The many projects funded under the Services track span a wide range of types of services, and address the full lifecycle of educational materials from creation to dissemination to review to reuse (for a complete list of projects funded by the NSDL, see nsdl.org/about/ ?pager = projects). What unifies these projects, however, is that their overarching purpose is to increase the reach and usefulness of the materials in the NSDL. For example, the Instructional Architect (ia.usu.edu) enables instructors to create lesson plans and learning objects from materials across the NSDL's many collections, and package and share these educational materials (Recker, 2006).

## IV. Proliferation of Funding Streams

The criticisms of the DLI discussed above, and the increased interest in DLs that the DLI helped to create, led the NSF to modify the program goals for the DLI-2 and again for the NSDL in favor of projects to deliver operational DLs and services to add value to DLs. In addition, in the 1990s other agencies began to provide large sums to fund DL-related projects. Lynch (2005) characterizes the period from about 1994–2004 as "the first time that digital library research could really get substantial programmatic funding from the major research funding agencies in the United States" (Paragraph 5). He also notes that many of these same agencies funded precursors to DLs, but that this programmatic funding served to legitimize DLs as a field of research.

As might be expected, the direction of the DLI projects were initially shaped by the missions and requirements of the agencies funding the DLI: the NSF, NASA, DARPA, the U.S. Environmental Protection Agency (EPA), and others. With the DLI in place, other agencies rapidly began to see the potential for DLs to support their own goals, causing "divergent evolution" among DLs, such that DLs emerged that reflected the varying concerns and purposes of their founding institutions, original funders, managing organizations, and user bases. This divergent evolution is certainly at least partly responsible for the "competing visions" of the nature of DLs referred to by Borgman (1999), and the lack of clarity as to precisely what a DL is, which persists to this day (Lagoze *et al.*, 2005). Additionally, as Griffin (1998) points out, "digital libraries projects can extend in scope well beyond agency missions, and demand support beyond a single agency's means" (DLI Program Constraints section). Therefore, many DL-related projects have been funded by multiple agencies, though like the DLI, this support is often coordinated by a single agency. This section presents some of the most prominent agencies that have funded (and continue to fund) DLs and DL-related projects, the motivations of these agencies for doing so, and some of the outcomes of this support. The next section presents the impact that this longer-term "evolution" of DLs and the widespread interest in them has engendered.

Larsen and Wactlar (2003) point out that significant DL initiatives have been funded by large scale federal agencies (e.g., NARA, NASA, NSF, DARPA, the National Institutes of Health (NIH), and NEH); smaller yet still significant federal and state agency programs (e.g., the LC's National Digital Library Program, and the University of California's California Digital Library); private foundations such as the Andrew W. Mellon Foundation and the Alfred P. Sloan Foundation; and private industrial research projects, such as IBM's and Sun's efforts. Although the number of funding agencies focusing on DL projects may only be in the dozens, as Schonfeld (2003) points out, there may be hundreds of projects that have created significant DLs. For example, while the W. K. Kellogg Foundation does not explicitly fund DLs or even technology in libraries in particular, it has supported several DL-related initiatives through its Youth and Education and Learning Opportunities program areas (W. K. Kellogg Foundation, 2007). Kellogg has funded projects and studies on service-oriented and operational aspects of DLs (e.g., Lamolinara, 1995b; Library of Congress, n.d.c; University of Michigan, 1996, n.d.). Additionally, Kellogg supported one of the earliest DL policy projects through Harvard University (Greenstein and Thorin, 2002) and LIS education and curriculum regarding DLs (e.g., Durrance, n.d; Fox, 1996). These projects will not be discussed further here, however, as Smith's chapter in this volume addresses the impact of grant funding on education for LIS. It is simply not possible to discuss all of the potentially relevant projects and funding agencies that have shaped the development of DLs. Consequently, only those agencies and projects that have had the most direct and profound impact on library science and the profession of librarianship are discussed here.

## A. Library of Congress

Libraries have traditionally been early adopters of technology for promoting dissemination of and access to information resources, and the technology of DLs was no exception. One of the first large-scale DLs developed outside of the DLI project umbrella, and, as mentioned above, perhaps the first developed by a library was the LC's American Memory Project. American Memory actually predates the DLI, having been launched in 1990, though at that time it was distributed on physical media (CD-ROM and videodisc) rather than via the internet (Lamolinara, 1995a). As soon as the World Wide Web entered the public eye, the LC, like the DLI projects, began to disseminate materials via the web and the web browser.

In 1994, the LC began the National Digital Library Project (NDLP) to expand their digitization efforts, with the goal of digitizing five million items by the year 2000, a goal which was met and exceeded (Library of Congress, n.d.b). The LC's digitization efforts were a two-phase effort: phase one was the American Memory Project, in which "unique historical collections [and] extensive bodies of primary-source materials of the Library were digitized" (Davis, 1998, p. 198). A component of this project was to develop a model for sharing electronic materials between libraries. Phase two continued the digitization of materials in the LC's collections, and also began to digitize materials from other libraries.

From the beginning, given the sheer scope of digitizing the LC's collections, the LC's digitization and digital library efforts required a "concerted effort and partnerships among many entities" (Davis, 1998, p. 199). These efforts were funded by a collection of agencies in addition to Congress. The NDLP was initially established with $13 million in private sector donations, followed by a $15 million appropriation from Congress and an additional $48 million from the private sector (Library of Congress, 2004).

The American Memory Project still exists (memory.loc.gov), making it one of the oldest extant DLs; it is also one of the largest collections of any DL. From early days, LC has developed creative organizational structures to support the American Memory Project, partly out of the need to find novel ways to manage a DL program of much larger scope and complexity than had been attempted by any other entity before it. In 1996, for example, LC partnered with Ameritech to offer a three-year competition in which individual projects could receive funding to build digital collections that would then be available on the American Memory website. A total of 23 awards were made during this period, supporting the efforts of 32 organizations (Library of Congress, n.d.a). This creativity has paid off in the novelty of design and the variety of collections: Time Magazine named American Memory one of the 10 best Websites of 1996, calling it a "treasure trove of memorabilia converted into easily downloadable recordings, images and text" (Bellafante and Corliss, 1996). The site also placed among the six finalists in the Education category of the National Information Infrastructure Awards Program in 1996. It has continued to rack up awards and citations for creativity of design and usefulness of content since its inception over a decade ago. American Memory has also been a leader on the research front, having conducted perhaps the first user evaluation by any DL project (Library of Congress, 1993).

The LC continues to fund digital library-related initiatives under the NDLP. In 2000, the LC launched the National Digital Information Infrastructure and Preservation Program (NDIIPP), a grant program funding research into digital preservation as part of an effort "to implement a national digital preservation strategy" (NSF, 2004b). NDIIPP was originally funded by an appropriation from Congress of nearly $100 million, "with $75 million contingent on a dollar-for-dollar match from non-federal sources." (Lefurgy, 2005) The funding was provided for the LC "to lead a national planning effort for the long-term preservation of digital content" (Friedlander, 2002, Paragraph 1). NDIIPP has tackled the problem of digital preservation on many fronts, including the creation of preservation networks of multiple institutions and types of institutions (Smith, 2006), and the interoperability and transfer of digital archives between institutions (Shirky, 2005). NDIIPP has also worked on developing standards, including the *Audit Checklist for the Certification of a Trusted Digital Repository*, which outlines the requirements for an institution to consider itself a "Trusted Digital Repository" (Kaczmarek *et al.*, 2006). A Study Group sponsored by NDIIP and the U.S. Copyright Office is, as of this writing, investigating Section 108 of the U.S. Copyright Act, with the goal of providing "balanced, solid recommendations for revising Section 108 to meet the way libraries work in the Digital Age" (Harris, 2006, p. 36). Thus, via NDIIPP, the LC has been marshaling the efforts of many different organizations and agencies from business, government, and academia. Currently, there are over 36 individual partners working on 12 primary projects, along with 10 additional grant recipients working on specific aspects of digital preservation research. In addition, over 150 government representatives from all 50 states have participated in workshops associated with this project.

However, the future of NDIIPP's activities may hang on the balance of political and economic agendas. After the 15 February 2007 passage of P.L. 110-5, as part of an across-the-board series of funding cuts, Congress rescinded $47 million of NDIIPP's approved funding (LibraryJournal.com, 2007), thereby also threatening "an additional $37 million in matching, non-federal funds that partners would contribute as in-kind donations." (Barksdale and Berman, 2007)

However, the LC continues to provide leadership in the design of DLs. The LC maintains a number of Research Centers online, including the American Folklife Center (www.loc.gov/folklife/), the Geography & Map Reading Room (www.loc.gov/rr/geogmap/), and the Recorded Sound Reference Center (www.loc.gov/rr/record/). These Research Centers maintain extensive online collections in addition to their considerably more extensive physical collections; the LC does not even present these collections as DLs, but in any other hands they would clearly be so. Unlike many DLs, some of these Research Centers have also developed resources for their online collections more commonly associated with traditional physical libraries, such as bibliographies, guides, and finding aids. In short, from the very earliest days of DLs, the LC has been on the cutting edge of the development of DL collections and of services within DL environments.

## B. Institute for Museum and Library Services

The Institute for Museum and Library Services (IMLS) is the only federal agency with Congressionally granted statutory authority to fund digitization projects (Ray, 2004). As Ray points out, while other federal agencies also fund digitization projects, the IMLS was created specifically to "make increased online public access to library and museum content an agency priority" (p. 249). This mission has inevitably led the IMLS to focus much of its energies and granting on DLs and DL-related projects.

The National Leadership Grant program is one of the IMLS' largest granting programs, and has supported many digitization projects in both libraries and museums since the creation of the IMLS in 1996. Indeed, the creation of a federal agency whose mission includes funding digitization projects was timely for both libraries and museums, and significantly contributed to the "widespread acceptance" that Fox (1999) points out "of the broadening of the digital libraries field; not only libraries but also museums and archives are within scope" (Assessment and Conclusion section, Paragraph 3). Some portion of most libraries' collections, and often most or all of the collections held by museums and archives are unique. Part of the purpose of these institutions is to make these collections available to users, but access to these collections has traditionally been limited to users who could physically visit the library, museum, or archive. With the advent of the World Wide Web, it quickly became clear that access to unique collections could be greatly expanded by digitization. Libraries, museums, and archives tend, however, to be chronically under-funded, and it is often difficult to justify new projects in a tight budget cycle. Thus the very existence of the IMLS' National Leadership Grant program was a boon to these cultural institutions, and, the present authors suggest, single-handedly greatly expanded the amount of cultural heritage materials available online.

The IMLS has launched many efforts to support cultural institutions in making cultural heritage materials available online. Among the earliest efforts were two studies, conducted in 2001 and 2004, of the status of new technology adoption and digitization in museums and libraries (IMLS, 2002, 2006). These studies investigated the goals, plans, policies, practices, hindrances, and funding of digitization activities conducted in museums and libraries, as well as the roles played by IMLS. Institutions surveyed included museums, both public and academic libraries, and State Library Administrative Agencies (SLAAs); archives were included in the second study. The studies also compare digitization activities between small, medium, and large institutions based on annual budgets. The results from the studies provide insights about trends and developments in digitization activities, and the needs of cultural institutions—data which are very useful for IMLS in shaping their programs.

The *Framework of Guidance for Building Good Digital Collections* (NISO Framework Advisory Group, 2004) articulates many principles concerning digital collections, digital objects, metadata, and projects as a whole. As of this writing, a third edition of this document is in progress, supported by the IMLS. The *Framework* document was developed "to encourage institutions to plan their digitization practices strategically in order to develop collections that will be accessible and useful for the long-term, and that can integrate with other digital collections to support a growing network of broadly accessible digital information resources" (p. iv). This document is indicative of the IMLS' efforts to encourage libraries and museums to think strategically about the future of cultural heritage institutions, and, as stated in the IMLS' mission, to "connect people to information and ideas" (www.imls.gov/about/about.shtm).

Since 2004, the IMLS has also sponsored the WebWise Conference, which was one of the first and has become one of the most important conferences to address issues faced by cultural institutions in making resources available digitally. Every year, many cultural institutions present their most recent research and innovations at WebWise, as examples for other institutions, and every year's conference has a theme that reflects current thinking and concerns for libraries and museums in making digital materials available online.

In short, the IMLS has provided leadership to cultural institutions in the arena of digitization and the development of useful and sustainable collections of cultural heritage materials online. The IMLS occupies an important niche in the environment of DL funding, in that it brings museums and archives under the DL umbrella, and focuses specifically on DLs as vehicles for the dissemination and sustainability of cultural heritage materials.

## C. Andrew W. Mellon Foundation

Although the Andrew W. Mellon Foundation (hereafter referred to as Mellon, www.mellon.org) has not historically had an explicit interest in libraries *per se*, libraries have nonetheless often been in a position to fulfill some of the social functions that *are* of interest to Mellon. Mellon's mission is "to aid and promote such religious, charitable, scientific, literary, and educational purposes as may be in furtherance of the public welfare or tend to promote the well-doing or well-being of mankind" (Mellon, 2006). Beginning in the late 1970s, Mellon began to fund individual digitization projects and projects to develop CD-ROM databases of individual collections of materials. For example, the foundation provided some of the start-up funding to enable the University of California at Santa Barbara to develop the *TLG* (Mellon, 1978). It also supported the work of the Association of Research Libraries (ARL) in Washington to build a database of materials in microform and funded numerous electronic catalog projects that paved the way both for future digitization projects and for the sharing of collections via the Internet. These library- and DL-related projects were funded under the Higher Education and Scholarship program, historically the largest single program area for Mellon's giving. Almost every year since 1987, approximately 50–70% of all of Mellon's grants have been within this area, with total annual appropriations in this area ranging from almost $32.5 million to over $132 million. After 1990, Mellon's DL-related funding skyrocketed until, by 2005, spending on DL-related activities represented over 70% of Mellon's total giving.

Indeed, over the years, enough grants under Higher Education and Scholarship have been oriented toward libraries that in 2004 Mellon created the Scholarly Communication program area, to support the "creation, dissemination, accessibility, and preservation of high-quality scholarly resources" (http://www.mellon.org/grant_programs/programs/scholarly communications). Much of Mellon's grant-making in this area has supported digital initiatives such as JSTOR (www.jstor.org), its offshoot ARTstor (www.artstor.org), and Mellon's new "incubation" institution, Ithaka Harbors, Inc., which was launched "to accelerate the productive uses of information technologies for the benefit of higher education worldwide" (Ithaka Harbors, 2007).

JSTOR, arguably the flagship of journal archiving, was initially the brainchild of Mellon's then-president William Bowen, who envisioned the project as a means for saving library space by enabling back issues of journals to be digitized, indexed, and made available on the Internet, thereby allowing libraries to drop their physical holdings of those issues (Bowen, 1995; Schonfeld, 2003). The original space-saving impetus rapidly shifted, however, to a recognition of the potential reduction in communications costs and increased access that users of electronic forms of communication would enjoy. Although Mellon realized that it was not interested in permanently assuming the role of either a production shop or publishing management enterprise, it did recognize that the type of back issue archiving it was proposing could provide a great deal of value to scholars, students, and research institutions. It simultaneously realized that the archiving mission it desired was unlikely to be offered via the private market in any manner that would help to allay the rapidly increasing scholarly communications costs with which libraries already were burdened, and that the capital costs involved in a for-profit version of a JSTOR-like entity would require a huge capital outlay that would make the archiving mission of JSTOR take back seat to more profit-driven motives (Schonfeld, 2003). As a result, Mellon engaged in the management of the initial prototype development, and when the viability of JSTOR was verified, aided in the creation and funding of an offshoot non-profit entity that subsequently took over the management of JSTOR production activities.

## D. Host Institutions

This section has thus far focused on agencies that fund DL programs, but DLs are increasingly being funded by libraries themselves, and by libraries' host institutions. Often, however, these programs are begun with and/or supplemented by funding from sources external to the library. In a study of the DL programs in DLF member libraries, Greenstein and Thorin (2002) found that "core funding" (funding provided by the institution, not from external sources) was essential to libraries in funding their DL programs.

As Greenstein and Thorin (2002) suggest, an institution may allocate funds to DL programs in a variety of ways, and these funds may come from a variety of sources both within and without the library's budget. Interestingly, "as digital library programs mature, reallocated library funding becomes more important" (p. 9). The implication of this last point is that numerous DL programs in libraries are launched using funding from external agencies, but sustained using funding from the library's budget. The present authors suggest that this is as it should be, and corresponds to other library services and programs once their value has been established: virtual reference services, for example, are often launched using grant funds but later integrated into the library's "core funding" (McGlamery and Coffman, 2000).

Many DL projects in libraries have been launched with funds awarded through the IMLS' Library Services and Technology Act (LSTA) program (Byrd *et al.*, 2001). One of the goals of the LSTA is to "develop library services that provide all users access to information through local, state, regional, national, and international electronic networks" (Institute of Museum and Library Services, n.d.), which clearly includes digitization and DL projects. Within the authors' own state, the North Carolina Exploring Cultural Heritage Online (NC ECHO, www.ncecho.org) program is a collection of digital library "special collections of North Carolina's libraries, archives, museums, historic sites, and other cultural institutions." NC ECHO is not only funded via the LSTA, but it awards grants of its own "that support collaborative digitization projects among the state's libraries and partner cultural institutions" (North Carolina ECHO, 2007).

Byrd *et al.* (2001) note that the Library of Virginia received funding from both the LSTA and Mellon for a specific sub-project within its larger Digital Library Program. This is a common approach to project funding for libraries: to seek funding for specific sub-projects under a larger umbrella. This is made necessary by two facts that should, by this point in this chapter, be clear: first, DL projects are usually longer-term efforts than any single grant or award would allow, and second, DL projects are often broader in scope than any single agency would be interested in supporting through a single funding program. Two DLs that have existed for over a decade thanks to this patchwork approach to funding are Documenting the American South (DocSouth, docsouth.unc.edu) and the Perseus Digital Library (www.perseus.tufts.edu). Since its launch in 1996, DocSouth has received support from "the National Endowment for the Humanities, the Institute of Museum and Library Services, the LC/Ameritech National Digital Library Competition, the State Library of North Carolina, and private foundations" (Norberg *et al.*, 2005, p. 286). Perseus has been similarly successful over the years in finding support from a range of sources, both private and public (Crane, 1998, 2000).

DocSouth is, as of this writing, over 11 years old, and Perseus is nearly 22 (though early Perseus prototypes in the mid-1980s were, like the American Memory Project, distributed on CD-ROM rather than online; Crane, 1998). These are mature DL projects by any metric, and as Greenstein and Thorin (2002) suggest, as they have matured they have been sustained in part by funding from their host instititutions' libraries. Indeed, the recent adoption of DocSouth by the University of North Carolina Library System's newly created Carolina Digital Library and Archives (CDLA, cdla.unc.edu) officially brings that DL within the fold of the wider institution. French (2003) describes a DL supported even more integrally by its host institutions: the California Digital Library (CDL, www.cdlib.org) is a joint undertaking of the ten campuses of the University of California system, and these ten universities all share the costs of maintaining the CDL. These DLs are all supported in part by "core funding": their host institutions allocate some funding to these DLs as a recurring budget item, like any other resource provided by the institution. Even these mature DLs are not supported entirely by core funding, however, and it is not currently clear that, given the total costs of a DL project, it would even be possible for a library or consortium of libraries to entirely support a DL project.

One project that has gambled on the ability of a consortium of institutions to support a DL, however, is the Internet Public Library (IPL, www.ipl.org). The IPL originated as a project in a graduate seminar in the School of Information and Library Studies at the University of Michigan in the Winter 1995 semester. In the winter of 1995, the graphical web was a mere year and a half old, and so still novel for many. The goal of this seminar was to address issues involved in integrating the web with libraries (Internet Public Library, 2007). What resulted was the IPL as we know it, and has led to new ideas about the nature of libraries in a networked environment. Two characteristics of the IPL make it unique as a DL. First is that the IPL is a "link farm": the collections within the IPL are not digitized versions of material held by physical libraries, nor born-digital materials created by the IPL, but rather are collections of links to resources hosted by others. Importantly, however, these resources are vetted as quality materials, and annotated by librarians and library school students. Second is that the IPL incorporates a human-mediated question answering service, similar to the online reference services that are offered by many physical libraries' reference desks (Pomerantz et al., 2004). Indeed, the IPL's question answering service predates many libraries' online reference services. To the authors' knowledge, the only other DL that has integrated a reference question answering service is the AskNSDL

(nsdl.org/asknsdl/) service, which as of this writing is apparently defunct. Integrating a question answering service into a DL raises a number of issues, which are explored by Pomerantz (2003), including the extent to which the answers themselves should be included in the DL's collection. The IPL also presents an interesting case study in funding. From its founding through 2006, the IPL was funded by the University of Michigan and a series of grants from a range of funders. In January 2007, the IPL moved to Drexel University and, in addition to continued and new grant funding, is now supported by a group of library schools referred to as the IPL Consortium (Lazorko, 2003). This is a creative twist on Greenstein and Thorin's (2002) notion of "core funding": the IPL relies in part on funding from institutions for which it can play a role in fulfilling the institutional mission. By providing services to library schools such as opportunities for students to participate in providing reference service and the management of a DL, the IPL is positioning itself as a resource for the entire community of library educators.

It is interesting to note that DL work within libraries and within the field of library science generally has often been criticized for ignoring the extensive research on DLs being conducted outside of libraries and the field of library science. As mentioned above, the report from Libraries for the Future (1998) largely ignored the DLI, except, paradoxically, to acknowledge that it was expected to "shape the future of information research and access" (p. 13). Borgman (1999) notes that the DLI is also barely mentioned in *Books, bricks and bytes: Libraries in the twenty-first century* (Graubard and LeClerc, 1998), a collection of articles exploring the place of DLs in libraries and librarianship. As in many professional fields, there has traditionally been a split between research and practice in the field of library science/ librarianship. For libraries working on DL projects to ignore the DL research from other fields, however—perhaps specifically because it comes from other fields—is to unnecessarily hamstring library-based DL projects.

## V. Impact of DL Funding

Sociologist Anthony Giddens has noted that "whenever we analyse large swathes of history, we are liable to find ourselves with an aggregate of 'causal influences' rather than conclusive generalizations about why things 'had to happen' as they did." He stresses further that this is because "there are no patterns of universal causation in the social sciences—that is to say, conditions in which circumstance X will, and must, always be followed by circumstance Y" (Giddens, 1991, p. 206). Not only must ideas about social influence rest upon interpretive assessments, they are reflexive: as Borgman and colleagues have noted, "each encounter influences the next" (Borgman *et al.*, 1996). In the final report to the NSF on the 1996 UCLA-based workshop "Social Aspects of Digital Libraries," for example, Borgman *et al.* claim that the participants at this workshop coined the term "social informatics" (Introduction section, Section 3). Within only a few months of that workshop, the term "social informatics" began to be widely used by the NSF and in the published journal literature (Bishop and Leigh, 1996; Kling *et al.*, 1998), as well as in the name of a new academic research organization (Indiana University's Rob Kling Center for Social Informatics). Given this set of historical facts, it is not possible to identify one single causal influence for the now-widespread adoption of the term or the idea of "social informatics."

This reflexivity of influence is particularly apropos when reviewing the historical impact that funding agencies have had on DL research and development; in particular, one is struck by the reciprocal influence of research and practice on funding agencies' decisions. Teasing out the impact of funding streams on DL research and development forces one to face a huge number of interrelations that occurred over time. As only one example, the funding for DLI led to new knowledge and ideas about DLs, which influenced the agencies funding the DLI, leading to the recognition that new types of research and development were required to continue the momentum that the DLI initiated. Although it is impossible to find a strict cause-and-effect relationship by which funding agencies set in motion a few well-oiled gears that then determined the future path of DLs according to the agencies' pre-set agendas, it is nevertheless possible to identify themes and trends throughout the many and varied interactions that have led to the current state of DL research and development. The identification of themes and trends offers interesting insights into the relationship between funding and DL development.

For example, a brief review of citations and acknowledgments (Giles and Councill, 2004) indicates that DLI and DLI-2 have had tremendous impact on DL research. A search of the CiteSeer Scientific Literature Digital Library (citeseer.ist.psu.edu) identifies 64 unique documents published between 1995 and 2004 that explicitly cite or acknowledge DLI or DLI-2, and a further 515 citations to this set of 64 documents. It is reasonable to assume that there are, and will continue to be, additional "generations" of citations. The same is no doubt also true for publications from DL projects funded by other organizations (though publications from NSF-funded projects are especially easy to track, as the NSF provides specific language for authors to include in acknowledgments; NSF, 2007b, Chapter VI, Section E.4.a.).

Thus DL projects continue to influence the DL research community, through an expanding ripple effect in the published literature.

This influence is not confined to the published literature, of course, but extends to the field of LIS and the profession of librarianship in a host of ways. It is nearly impossible to capture the totality of the impact that DLs, and the funding streams that have made them possible, have had. Developments in DLs have had an impact on research and education in fields as diverse as computer science and classics, even on areas of software development as widely dispersed as Optical Character Recognition (OCR) and Geographic Information Systems (GIS) (Ogle and Wilensky, 1996). In particular, at the time of DLI and DLI-2, the NSF did not recommend as strongly as they do today that all funded research projects include an evaluation component (Frechtling, 2002). Griffin (2005), however, claims that the return on investment of the DLI program was high by any measure, suggesting potentially large economic impact in addition to the intellectual. Moreover, every DL project has had its own impact on librarianship and the library research communities, and on society in general. This section has summarized the impact of the DL projects and funders discussed above, in several areas.

## A. Impact on DL-related Research Areas

Given that the DLI emerged from the umbrella of the High-Performance Computing Act of 1991, it is only natural that high-performance computing has, from the beginning, been intimately tied to the development of DLs. That connection continues to this day, though with a semantic shift: instead of "high-performance computing," the term more commonly used nowadays is "cyberinfrastructure." Griffin (2005) notes that the term cyberinfrastructure was coined in the late 1990s, "referring, initially, to the assemblage of high performance computing and networking resources generally available to researchers and educators" (Digital Libraries and Cyberinfrastructure section). The NSF convened a Blue Ribbon Panel to evaluate the NSF's then-current investments in cyberinfrastructure, and to "recommend new areas of emphasis" for the NSF to support cyberinfrastructure (Atkins et al., 2003, p. 5). The report from this panel, which has come to be known as the Atkins Report, has since set the tone for the NSF's funding of cyberinfrastructure research and development. Further, DLs remain central to fulfilling the potential of cyberinfrastructure: one of the goals for the NSF is to "support state-of-the-art innovation in data management and distribution systems, including digital libraries and educational environments that are expected to contribute to many of the scientific breakthroughs of the 21st century" (NSF, 2007a).

Many other organizations as well have articulated ways in which libraries, both digital and physical, may take advantage of the NSF's cyberinfrastructure efforts. The Computing Research Association (2005), for example, discusses how STEM education may take advantage of the "unprecedented access to educational resources, mentors, experts, and online educational activities and virtual environments" (p. 4) that work in cyberinfrastructure will make available, and DLs are included among the virtual environments discussed. Focusing on the humanities and social sciences, the American Council of Learned Societies launched a commission "to articulate the requirements and potential contributions of the humanities and social sciences in developing a cyberinfrastructure for information, teaching, and research" (American Council of Learned Societies, 2006, p. 1). The report from this commission argues for libraries to develop and maintain collections of digital objects generated by humanities and social science scholarship that may in turn inform scholarship. Finally, the ARL convened a forum to address the impact that cyberinfrastructure will have on the "ARL's three strategic directions: scholarly communication, information policies and other public policies, and the roles of libraries in transformations of research and education" (Goldenberg-Hart, 2004, p. 1). The rough consensus emerging from this forum was that while the roles of libraries and experts in libraries may change, the library as an institution must play a central role in managing resources in the e-Sciences. In short, libraries are universally included in the landscape of social institutions that will be affected by cyberinfrastructure but are at the same time necessary for cyberinfrastructure to fulfill its full potential as a tool for change.

As the tools and technologies that cyberinfrastructure enables have become more readily available to researchers in all fields, interdisciplinary and international collaborations that make use of those technologies have proliferated, giving rise to what is often referred to as e-Science (Hey and Trefethen, 2003). The resulting explosion of data being generated by e-Science researchers and the data collection instruments they employ has generated a "data deluge," made possible in part by the improved technical capabilities from high performance computing research. For example, since 2000, an award has been made at the International Conference on High-Performance Computing, Networking, Storage, and Analysis (supercomputing.org) for the High-Performance Bandwidth Challenge, a competition for cutting-edge network applications; the goal of this competition is to support the sorts of scientific endeavors that can only be accomplished with very large data sets and very high data transmission speeds. Moreover, DLs have come full-circle in their role in high-performance computing initiatives: having arisen out of such initiatives, DLs are now being employed to address some of the new issues arising out of them. Borgman *et al.* (2007), for example, propose the use of DLs as mechanisms for organizing and managing the deluge of data being produced by scientific fields, and outline a set of functional and technical requirements for such DLs.

Although the idea of the semantic web emerged prior to the term cyberinfrastructure (Berners-Lee and Fischetti, 2000), the two are closely intertwined. Proponents of the semantic web suggest that it "may be viewed as an infrastructure for supporting the objectives outlined" by the Atkins report (Miller, 2003). Sure and Studer (2005) suggest that semantic web-related technologies enable the development of common naming schemes for digital objects and the repositories in which they are stored, and suggest that such technologies are important in DLs for such purposes as interface design, user profiling, and personalization. Perhaps even more important, however, is the possibility for semantic web-related technologies to aid in interoperability between DLs and to improve end-user searching. The JeromeDL (Kruk, 2005), for example, is a case study of a DL that employs semantic web-related technologies for browsing and searching.

Central to the organizational functionality of DLs is the use of metadata. Just as a physical library could not exist without classification schemes, neither could a DL exist without metadata schemes. Several metadata initiatives are ongoing, all of which are potentially relevant to DLs, but are also broader in scope than DLs alone. The Dublin Core Metadata Initiative (DCMI, dublincore.org), for example, has developed a set of 15 broad and generic metadata elements called "Unqualified, or Simple, Dublin Core" (as opposed to the wider set of elements and refinements called "Qualified Dublin Core") that may be used to describe any resource. The DCMI element set is widely used in DLs, but it is also widely used in other domains, where a number of communities of interest have developed community-specific extensions to the DCMI. The education community, for example, has developed an extensive set of elements to describe educational resources (dublincore.org/groups/education/), as part of the work funded under the NSDL (Sutton, 2004; Greenberg, 2005; Liddy *et al.*, 2001). Other communities have developed their own extensions to the DCMI as well (see: dublincore.org/projects/).

Metadata is only one of many fields that have benefited from DL funding sources. From the very origin of DLs, the field of IR has been one of the most closely tied to DLs. Ironically, however, Smith (2000) found that DLs have implemented only a very narrow range of search features. Nevertheless, a great deal of IR-related work has been funded by DL funding programs, in particular the NSF's initiatives. Much of this IR work has been on improving traditional text retrieval (e.g., Shneiderman *et al.*, 1998), but much of it also is concerned with retrieval of other media, including images (e.g., Tang *et al.*, 2004), audio (e.g, Downie, 2003), and video (e.g., Christel and Huang, 2003; Yang *et al.*, 2004).

One of the best-known and most significant impacts of the IR aspect of DL research and development is the invention of the search engine Google (www.google.com). Hart (2004) relates that Google's founders Larry Page and Sergey Brin were graduate students working on Stanford University's DLI project when they developed a prototype search engine that they called BackRub, due to its functionality of counting incoming links (i.e., backlinks) to web pages (Battelle, 2005). BackRub was later renamed Google, and Google Inc. was incorporated in 1998 (Google, 2007). Since 1998 Google has been one of the great success stories of the technology industry, having become nothing short of a cultural phenomenon.

Google has also had a profound effect on libraries. Of course, web search engines existed prior to the advent of Google (WebCrawler having been the first, released in April 1994; InfoSpace Inc., 2007), and many alternatives for searchers continue to exist. Due to its popularity and ease of use, however, Google has significantly contributed to changes in people's expectations for searching, providing strong implications for *library* search tools. Indeed, some libraries have begun to rethink library automation and the way that services are provided based at least in part on Google's influence (Bibliographic Services Task Force, 2005), and some libraries have integrated tools provided by Google into the services provided online by the library (Pomerantz, 2006). Google has even had an impact on library education, as there have been at least two courses in library schools devoted to Google: one at the University of Washington (Flash, 2004) and one at the University of California at Los Angeles (polaris.gseis.ucla.edu/jrichardson/Courses/19.htm).

## B. Scholarly Publishing

Dissatisfaction with print as a medium for disseminating scholarly publications was evident as early as the mid-1940s (Bush, 1945). In 1962, the Chemical Abstracts Service published Chemical Titles, the first-ever journal in electronic format, and by the mid-1970s there were several projects underway experimenting with the dissemination of scholarly works in networked environments (Peek and Pomerantz, 1998). These projects were not originally framed as DLs, but they had a significant impact on the later development of DLs: for example, as mentioned above, the University of Michigan's DLI project extended their efforts as part of Elsevier Science's TULIP project (Borghuis *et al.*, 1996), and the Envision project (Fox *et al.*, 1993) evolved into the Association for Computing Machinery's DL (portal.acm.org/dl.cfm). Awareness of DLs, combined with dissatisfaction with traditional scholarly publishing, access to the web, and the availability of tools to easily create web content, had—and continues to have—a profound impact on the scholarly community. This impact has manifested itself in at least two ways: the creation of new venues for publication and scholarly communication generally, and the creation of new vehicles for disseminating already-published works.

Two of the most prominent DL-related publication venues are *D-Lib Magazine* (www.dlib.org) and the Joint Conference on Digital Libraries (JCDL, www.jcdl.org). D-Lib was established in 1995 by a grant from DARPA, as a venue for publications from DLI projects (Griffin, 2005), and since 2006 has been funded by the NSF and produced by the Corporation for National Research Initiatives (CNRI) (Corporation for National Research Initiatives, 2007). The JCDL is the result of a merger between two conferences (hence the "joint"): the ACM Conference on Digital Libraries and the Institute of Electrical and Electronics Engineers (IEEE) Forum on Research and Technology Advances in Digital Libraries, both first held in 1996. The ACM and IEEE merged these conferences to form the JCDL in 2001. Since their inception, both D-Lib and JCDL have become established as among the most important publishing venues for DL-related work. Even though D-Lib is not a peer-reviewed publication (submissions are vetted by the editor), it is one of the most influential publications in the DL arena, including as it does research articles, news on current DL-related events and projects, and featured DL collections. An indicator of its influence is that D-Lib is the journal most widely read in DL courses (Pomerantz *et al.*, 2006). JCDL is similarly influential, as it is one of the few conferences where attendees come from the range of institutions with an interest in DLs: LIS and CS programs, academia, corporate research centers, and libraries alike.

One of the reasons that D-Lib is as influential as it is may be that it is freely available online, which Lawrence (2001) has shown increases citations to articles. While the term "Open Access" was not yet in widespread use when D-Lib was established in 1995, D-Lib nevertheless represents what Harnad *et al.* (2004) call the "gold road" of Open Access (OA) publishing: "following" the gold road is to publish an article in a journal that is freely available to readers on the web, while following the "green road" is to publish an article in a subscription-based journal but to self-archive it online.

In short, the purpose of OA publishing is "to make possible an unprecedented public good" by making scientific literature freely available online to the reader (Budapest Open Access Initiative, 2002). While the OA movement can be traced to the mid-1960s (Suber, 2007), it crystallized with the Budapest Open Access Initiative in 2002. Since that time, a number of scholarly publishers have revised their copyright agreements to explicitly allow authors to self-archive preprints and/or postprints—see, for example, the SHERPA RoMEO Project (Securing a Hybrid Environment for Research Preservation and Access, Rights MEtadata for Open archiving), which provides a list of publishers and details of their copyright agreements (www.sherpa.ac.uk/romeo.php). Additionally, some federal funding agencies have developed policies to encourage funded investigators to make their publications available in OA venues: the NIH, for example, "requests and strongly encourages" authors to deposit postprints of publications in PubMed Central (http://www.pubmedcentral.nih.gov) (NIH, n.d.).

Other paths to the OA green road also exist, as authors can put their own work online on their personal websites, or in an OA archive. Many OA archives exist: perhaps the first was the open-access FTP preprints archive for the journal *Behavioral and Brain Sciences*, introduced in February 1991. This was followed closely by the Mathematical Physics Preprint Archive (mp_arc, www.ma.utexas.edu/mp_arc/Z), launched in July 1991, and by perhaps the best-known OA archive, arXiv.org, which includes preprints in the fields of Physics, Mathematics, Computer Science, and Quantitative Biology, which was launched in August 1991 (Suber, 2007). The field of Library and Information Science has two OA archives: dLIST (dlist.sir.arizona.edu) and E-LIS (eprints.rclis.org). In addition to discipline-specific archives, archives exist that contain only specific types of publications, such as the Networked Digital Library of Theses and Dissertations (NDLTD, www.ndltd.org), as well as those that are specific to institutions, such as DSpace at MIT (dspace.mit.edu). Institution-specific OA archives overlap considerably with institutional repositories, which Crow (2002) defines as "digital collections capturing and preserving the intellectual output of a single or multi-university community" (p. 4), although an institutional repository does not necessarily have to be OA. Further, the distinction between OA archives, institutional repositories, and DLs is fuzzy at best.

DL-related projects have also impacted scholarly communication by creating new vehicles for disseminating published works. JSTOR, discussed above, was developed by Mellon to provide libraries with online access to journal backfiles. JSTOR'S goal was to decrease the storage costs and increase the convenience of accessing these materials (Schonfeld, 2003). JSTOR is not unique; other journal backfile repositories currently exist, though as of this writing JSTOR is the only project of its kind that is financially self-supporting. Further, subscription databases existed and libraries subscribed to them for decades prior to the founding of JSTOR. What is particularly interesting about JSTOR, however, is that it embodies the shift away from the "hard-copy" approach to archiving and access traditionally employed by libraries and other institutions. JSTOR has emphasized the importance of archiving in the electronic environment by creating a business model that financially links access and archiving: with the exception of two-year colleges, all university libraries that subscribe to JSTOR pay a fee that includes both access and archiving costs. According to Schonfeld, in the hard-copy era, only the wealthiest libraries could afford the expense of archiving. In the current electronic era, however, all universities participating in JSTOR partake of reduced archiving costs, and gain access to journals that many would otherwise not have been able to afford.

In July 2007 the American Association for the Advancement of Science (AAAS) announced that it would end its participation in JSTOR as of the end of 2007, and that therefore content from Science Magazine would no longer be contributed to JSTOR (AAAS, 2007). The AAAS stated that this decision was made so that the AAAS could "assume the full responsibility for maintaining a complete electronic archive of its flagship publication" (Paragraph 5). In January 2008 the AAAS reversed that decision and rejoined JSTOR. Details of the new agreement between JSTOR and the AAAS are confidential, but changes from the previous agreement are "related to price and to linking of articles within JSTOR to other articles" (Guterman, 2008). On the one hand, the AAAS' renegotiation indicates that publishers, even those that assume the responsibility of archiving their own content, see the value in third-party journal backfile repositories. On the other hand, this incident demonstrates that cooperation with publishers is central to the viability of third-party repositories, and that such repositories are highly vulnerable to pressure from publishers. How relationships between publishers and repositories develop over the next few years, and the influence of OA publishing on these relationships, may have significant impact on the future of scholarly publishing, and on libraries' access to scholarly publications.

## C. Impact on Libraries

OA archives, third-party collections, and other new venues for disseminating published work have had a profound impact on libraries. The existence of materials that are accessible via the library but not part of the library's collection has the potential to change the purpose of the library catalog from a tool for bibliographic control to a more general portal to the internet (Thomas, 2000). Further, the availability of materials via the library that are not under the library's control changes the very definition of a library collection (Lee, 2000). Libraries have thus had to re-evaluate their role in an increasingly networked environment. Since the advent of the subscription literature database, and increasingly since the advent of the DL, libraries have been moving from a model of ownership of materials to a model of access to materials.

While libraries have been increasingly providing access to online collections created and maintained by others, they have simultaneously been creating their own online collections. As discussed above, libraries are increasingly launching their own DL programs, using grant funding and moving toward "core funding" (Greenstein and Thorin, 2002). As libraries create DLs (and other digital content) Troll (2001) suggests that they "become publishers" (The Changing Environment section). Indeed, Wilkin (2005) presents the case that acting as publishers, even to the point of replacing university presses, is central to libraries' mission of "connecting users with information ... [and] as disseminators of information" (Libraries as Publishers section). While many libraries may be unwilling to replace their institution's university press, increasingly academic libraries are partnering with university presses to make scholarly work available. One of the largest-scale library-press collaborations as of this writing is The Ohio State University Press' Open Access Initiative (www.ohiostatepress.org/books/openaccess.htm).

As disseminators of information, libraries have always explored the many vehicles for this dissemination, and as libraries increasingly provide materials online, this means exploring the software options for dissemination of these materials. As far as the current authors can determine, Greenstone (or rather, at the time, New Zealand Digital Library Software) was the first application developed specifically for the purpose of creating DLs, the first project having been launched in 1995 (Witten and Bainbridge, 2007, p. 148). As the 1990s progressed, the idea of developing tools to assist librarians and other collection developers to build their own DLs and DL-like collections, such as archives and collections of commercial content, became increasingly popular. Following Greenstone, a number of applications for building DLs or DL-like collections have emerged: Flexible Extensible Digital Object and Repository Architecture (Fedora, www.fedora.info), DSpace (www.dspace.org), EPrints (www.eprints.org), and CONTENTdm (www.contentdm.com), to name a few of the more commonly-used applications. Each of these is intended to serve a different (though similar) function: Fedora is intended for building general-purpose repositories (Staples *et al.*, 2003), DSpace is designed to manage research materials and scholarly publications (Smith *et al.*, 2003), CONTENTdm is designed for collections of images (Bunker and Zick, 1999), and so on. It is therefore important to point out that these DL-like applications are not competing for "market share" as it were, but rather each fulfill a different niche in the DL ecology. There is, unfortunately, only one article that the authors are aware of that presents a comparison of these applications (Goh *et al.*, 2006); the authors suggest that more such work would be useful for librarians and other DL builders who are deciding on an appropriate platform.

Developing DLs is expensive, in terms of both money and staff time. In order to partially alleviate these expenses, libraries have begun participating in collaborative initiatives to digitize materials in their collections. Often these initiatives are coordinated by third parties, such as Google Book Search (books.google.com) and the Open Content Alliance (OCA, www.opencontentalliance.org). Both the Google Book Search project and the OCA have partnered with many libraries, and as of this writing are in the process of digitizing materials from these libraries' collections. These initiatives are not "traditional" DLs: the OCA refers to itself as an archive, and Google Book Search does not make the full text of all materials available to users (though Google does make full text available to the library that owns the digitized material). While these initiatives cannot realistically be called DLs, they fulfill a role within DL programs in libraries, as libraries move to digitize significant parts of their collections.

DLs have had an impact on libraries as institutions, and the functions that libraries perform. Consequently, DLs have also had an impact on the profession of librarianship, and the functions that librarians perform, both within and without the library. If libraries are disseminators of information, it is in large part because librarians are present to assist users and to help put that information in context. Griffin (1998) suggests that one of the most valuable aspects of DLs "is their ability to preserve and extend discourse—to provide richer contexts for people to interact with information. The real value of digital libraries may prove to be in their ability to alter the way individuals, groups, organizations, etc., behave, communicate, and conduct their affairs" (Introduction section, Paragraph 6). This aspect of DLs places librarianship squarely in the forefront, as the profession whose function it is to preserve discourse and to assist those who are extending discourse—but this also signals significant changes to how these functions will be performed.

## D. Impact on the Profession of Librarianship

Libraries were one of the earliest adopters of computer and network technology, in the service of dissemination of and access to information resources: the MARC standard, for example, was developed by the LC in 1965; and the Linked System Project was conceived in the late 1970s to enable the exchange of bibliographic data between library networks (Fenly and Wiggins, 1988). As tools for the dissemination of and access to information, DLs were likewise quickly adopted by libraries as well. Integrating DLs into more "traditional" library functions has always been a challenge, but many forms of integration have emerged to fill that "ecological niche." Two major themes emerge from this integration: DL-related initiatives that span multiple libraries, and changes to the profession of librarianship itself.

The DLF was founded in 1995 with the goal of implementing "a distributed, open digital library ... accessible across the global Internet," to be composed of digitized and born-digital materials from member and other libraries (Digital Library Federation, 1995). In order to bring this goal to fruition, the DLF has naturally had to become involved in management, funding, standards, evaluation, and a range of other areas of DL research and development. The DLF has emerged as one of the few agenda-setting initiatives in the DL arena, and it has accomplished this due to the strength and diversity of its membership, which includes colleges and research universities at which DL projects are taking place, national and state libraries in the U.S. and abroad (e.g., the LC, the British Library, the CDL), and many of the major institutional players in the library arena (e.g., OCLC, the Coalition for Networked Information). By providing support for new research and development projects, hosting forums at which DL researchers and practitioners can disseminate findings and discuss their work, publishing reports on specific DL-related issues, and demonstrating leadership generally, the DLF has established itself as one of the most influential institutional leaders in the DL arena.

Other multi-institution initiatives have addressed more specific issues faced not only by DLs, but by collections of digital content of all types. Projects such as LOCKSS (Lots of Copies Keep Stuff Safe, www.lockss.org), Building Resources for Integrated Cultural Knowledge Services Project (BRICKS, www.brickscommunity.org), and the Open Archives Initiative (OAI, www.openarchives.org) provide policies and technical solutions to assist institutions to manage various aspects of the lifecycle of digital content, from collection to dissemination and exchange to preservation. Librarians have inevitably participated closely in projects such as these.

Participation in such projects signals a change in the skills that librarians require—and indeed, are expected to possess even to be hired in the first place. Since the advent of DLs, several authors have articulated sets of skills that librarians need to possess in order to develop and manage DL collections and services (Tennant, 1998, 1999; Croneis and Henderson, 2002; Choi and Rasmussen, 2006). These skills break down into three categories: technological skills, management and interpersonal skills, and library-related skills. Technological skills include knowledge of specific applications, standards, and systems. Management skills include project management ability, leadership ability, flexibility, and grant-writing skills, among others. Library-related skills include knowledge of both technical services and user services: knowledge of indexing, cataloging, and metadata; archiving and preservation practices and standards; and how to conduct reference and other user services. In short, the skills that librarians need to possess in order to develop and manage DL collections and services are arguably the same as the skills that librarians need to possess in order to conduct any form of library work in the modern age, though a far greater emphasis is placed on technological skills than ever before.

These technological skills are, however, utilized in the service of the same functions that librarianship has always performed. While the rise of e-Science and the "data deluge" discussed above is causing many fields to attend to the unfamiliar issue of managing large data sets, librarians are perfectly familiar with managing large volumes of information. A few fields have addressed this issue by establishing their own data repositories, complete with standardized formats and tools to manipulate the data. In more fields, however, data is stored locally by individual researchers, and not widely shared, thus impeding the ability of researchers to build on each others' work. In some ways, this state of affairs is to be expected: researchers' skills are in collecting and analyzing data, not necessarily in organizing that same data. It is, in fact, the skills of librarians that are needed in these cases. Partially in response to the increase in the number of scholarly fields that are generating large data sets, therefore, many academic libraries have begun offering "data services," which includes the management of data sets on behalf of researchers, and reference-like public services to assist users to use this data (Read, 2007; Cook et al., 2001). A new category of librarianship has thus emerged in academic libraries to fulfill these functions: the data librarian. While the profession of data librarian is just beginning to emerge and its scope to be defined, it is a good example of the changes to the profession of librarianship currently underway that have been brought about in part by DL-related technologies. The ARL has taken a leadership role in defining the scope of data librarianship—or, as the ARL refers to it, "data stewardship" (ARL, 2006).

In their report to the NSF, the ARL recommends that the NSF should support a number of stewardship initiatives, including funding research and development, and educational efforts.

Data librarianship is only one area in which new roles are being identified that libraries and librarians will assume in the future. As these new roles evolve and become more clearly articulated, librarians will need to be trained to fill those new roles. DL funding has had a significant impact on the development of the profession of librarianship, and consequently on library education.

## E. Library 2.0

The authors do not claim that all of the impacts discussed so far in this section are direct results of work on DLs; rather, all that is claimed is that DLs and DL-related technologies had some influence on these projects. In this section, the authors will go even further out on a limb and will discuss the idea of "Library 2.0." Library 2.0 is not a DL, nor has it emerged from "traditional" DL funding streams, but the authors suggest that it shares some characteristics with DLs, and that the emergence of the idea of Library 2.0 was influenced by DLs and ideas about the future of libraries that have emerged from DL initiatives.

Habib (2006), in one of the most thorough discussions of Library 2.0 to date, points out that there is no agreed-upon definition of the term, but proposes the following: "Library 2.0 describes a subset of library services designed to meet user needs caused by the direct and peripheral effects of Web 2.0" (p. 9). Habib then suggests that Web 2.0 can be understood as a set of "key concepts and methods" (p. 11) that are united in the goal of enabling users to contribute content, functionality, and services to existing web-based resources. While the idea of Web 2.0 was only formulated in 2005 (O'Reilly, 2005), the idea of online resources benefiting from user contributions considerably predates that, from Kranich's (2004) description of the information commons to Marchionini's (1999) description of the "sharium" as a DL environment.

Habib (2006) suggests several ways in which Web 2.0-related ideas may affect libraries, including "application of these concepts and methods to library services. An example of this would be to allow user tagging in the OPAC" (p. 22). Indeed, this application is currently being pursued, both formally and informally. Spiteri (2006) discusses ways in which folksonomies (metadata created collaboratively by users) can be used to supplement the controlled vocabularies used in libraries' online public access catalogs (OPACs). She suggests that combining controlled and uncontrolled vocabularies may aid users in searching the OPAC, and that providing features to allow customization in OPACs may enable users to personalize their usage experience. Less formally, a number of services have emerged on the web in the past few years that emulate or extend traditional library services. LibraryThing (www.librarything.com) is a prime example of this: LibraryThing is a web-based service that assists users to catalog their books, and enables social networking-like functionality around the books in users' catalogs. In short, LibraryThing extends and, perhaps more importantly, makes available to the individual user the functionality of the OPAC, by providing a simple cataloging interface and a shared uncontrolled vocabulary.

Habib (2006) also suggests that libraries may make more direct use of Web 2.0-related technologies to provide services (p. 22). LibraryThing has recently launched a service to make this possible: LibraryThing for Libraries is a service to enhance OPAC records with content from LibraryThing (www.librarything.com/forlibraries/). Like LibraryThing, many Web 2.0 services harness the efforts of individuals in the service of the community. In this vein, Beagrie (2005) discusses personal DLs, though he prefers instead the term "digital collection." Beagrie defines digital collections as containing "material from the individual's private life, work, and education, as well as from external communities and content sources" (Defining Personal Digital Collections section). Personal digital collections, according to Beagrie, may be solely for personal use, or may be shared with defined communities of which the collector is a part. And just as services are provided in physical libraries to add value to the collections, so too Beagrie discusses the sorts of services that may be provided to add value to personal digital collections. One of the types of services that Beagrie (2005) examines is the management of personal data on remote servers, analogous to data librarianship, only at a personal rather than an organizational level. Beagrie also discusses web-based services like blogging applications and image sharing services (e.g., Flickr, www.flickr.com) as enabling the creation, organization, and sharing of personal content.

None of these applications and services are DLs or even services that are commonly provided by DLs. However, they have grown, at least in part, out of an idea of DLs as community spaces, just as physical libraries have (Pomerantz and Marchionini, 2007). Furthermore, applications for libraries that utilize Web 2.0 concepts and methods are at the vanguard of new types of services that have the potential to have an impact on DLs, just as they have had an impact on physical libraries. If Library 2.0 means enabling users' contributions to library content, functionality, and services, then Library 2.0 and "Digital Library 2.0" may be so inextricably linked as to be indistinguishable.

# VI. Conclusion

DLs have emerged in the past decade as one of the most active areas of library research and practice. In part, this is due to the large sums of money that have been and continue to be spent by many funding agencies on DLs and DL-related projects: in this, as in many areas, innovation and progress tend to follow the money. In part, however, this vibrancy is due to the fact that DLs exist at the intersection of most or arguably all of the areas in modern librarianship. As such, DLs have focused attention—and funding—on libraries and librarianship as few areas of research and development ever have. With the popularization of the internet and the proliferation of full-text resources online, there has been much ink spilled on the topic of the "death of the book" and its corollary, the death of the library (see, e.g., Nunberg, 1996). The authors suggest, however, that the vibrancy of DLs and DL-related funding programs are strong evidence that rumors of the death of the library have been greatly exaggerated. Agencies such as Mellon that have little or no stake in libraries per se, but rather fund educational, scientific, and other social programs, have provided funding to libraries for DL projects. Technical fields such as CS have discovered areas of overlap in research and development with LIS, and many fields in both the sciences and the humanities have discovered a need for the skills possessed by librarians. The image of the profession of librarianship is undergoing a change (Jesella, 2007), and the authors suggest that the spread of DLs is at least partly responsible for the rise in the public's interest in the profession of librarianship.

It seems clear that DLs will continue to exist in some form, despite significant concerns about their sustainability and long-term preservation of digital objects. There is much about the future of DLs, however, that is unclear, including how DLs will be integrated into libraries and other cultural heritage institutions. Levy and Marshall (1995) suggest that "the better word for these evolving institutions is 'libraries,' not 'digital libraries'" (p. 83), and suggest that DLs will both transform and become integrated into libraries. Time will tell if DLs will indeed become integrated into larger institutions, or if they will remain as separate entities. This has implications for the future of DL funding: will agencies that currently fund DL projects under programs that are not specifically library-related continue to do so if DLs become more tightly integrated into libraries?

It is also unclear how DLs will be integrated into organizations and institutions other than libraries. The IMLS in particular has provided leadership in developing DLs in museums, archives, and other cultural heritage institutions, and consequently in strengthening ties between libraries and these types of institutions. Further, as more and more fields of study are affected by the "data deluge" brought on by access to powerful data collection instruments and inexpensive computing, these fields will discover the need for DLs and the skills possessed by (digital) librarians. Will the skills of digital librarianship diffuse out from libraries to become common knowledge in cultural heritage institutions and scientific fields—and in the public domain generally—as knowledge about searching electronic sources has with the popularization of search engines? Or will it instead be librarians that diffuse out from libraries, to become "embedded" in other fields and institutions, as is starting to happen in the health professions (Davidoff and Florance, 2000)?

DLs are at least partly responsible for the increase in recent years in grant funding to libraries and library-related projects. DLs have therefore been a boon to libraries, but this is a mixed blessing: the future of external funding for libraries is at least partly tied to the future of funding for DLs. While the sustainability of DLs is a significant concern, libraries have always excelled at maintaining ongoing funding (even if this funding has been chronically inadequate). Thus there is a natural affinity between libraries and DLs where funding is concerned: libraries are established as an institution that receives a steady stream of funding, while DLs focus attention on the library and are a point of interest for funders. DLs have already transformed, and will continue to transform libraries, and it is clear that this influence goes in both directions. As Levy and Marshall (1995) suggest, it may indeed be that the term DL needs to fade away, so that DLs may become more fully integrated into libraries and other institutions. This may even be the best possible future for DLs: no single area remains a popular target for funding forever. Should this prove to be the future of DLs, however, it must be within the larger context of an environment in which the collection, management, and dissemination of digital materials is valued. Funding agencies must learn to see the value in DL-like projects across fields; political structures must support infrastructure and basic research to make such projects possible; and librarians and other knowledge workers must provide education and support to designers and users of DLs. DLs may lose their name, but they seem likely to survive by becoming integrated into the infrastructure of cultural and scientific institutions universally.

## References

Advisory Committee to the National Science Foundation Directorate for Education and Human Resources (1996, October 3). *Shaping the Future: New Expectations for Undergraduate Education in Science, Mathematics, Engineering, and Technology (NSF File No. NSF 96–139)*. National Science Foundation, Arlington, VA. Retrieved from http://www.nsf.gov/pubs/stis1996/nsf96139/nsf96139.txt

American Association for the Advancement of Science (2007). *Science Announcement about JSTOR Partnership*, July 19. Retrieved from http://www.sciencemag.org/marketing/jstor_partnership.dtl

American Council of Learned Societies (2006). *Our Cultural Commonwealth: The Final Report of the American Council of Learned Societies Commission on Cyberinfrastructure for the Humanities & Social Sciences*. American Council of Learned Societies, Commission on Cyberinfrastructure for the Humanities and Social Sciences, New York. Retrieved from http://www.acls.org/cyberinfrastructure/

Andrew W. Mellon Foundation (1978). *Report of the Andrew Mellon Foundation 1977*. Andrew W. Mellon Foundation, New York. Retrieved from http://www.mellon.org/news_publications/annual-reports-essays/annual-reports/

Andrew W. Mellon Foundation (2006). *Report of the Andrew Mellon Foundation 2005*. Andrew W. Mellon Foundation, New York. Retrieved from http://www.mellon.org/news_publications/annual-reports-essays/annual-reports/

Arms, W. Y. (2000). *Digital Libraries*. MIT Press, Cambridge, MA.

Association of Research Libraries. (2006). *To Stand the Test of Time: Long-Term Stewardship of Digital Data Sets in Science and Engineering*. (A Report to the National Science Foundation from the ARL Workshop on New Collaborative Relationships: The Role of Academic Libraries in the Digital Data Universe, September 26–27, 2006). Association of Research Libraries: Arlington, VA. Retrieved from http://www.arl.org/bm ~ doc/digdatarpt.pdf

Atkins, D. E., Droegemeier, K. K., Feldman, S. I., Garcia-Molina, H., Klein, M. L., Messerschmitt, D. G., Messina, P., Ostriker, J. P., and Wright, M. H. (2003). *Revolutionizing Science and Engineering through Cyberinfrastructure: Report of the National Science Foundation Blue-Ribbon Advisory Panel on Cyberinfrastructure*. National Science Foundation, Arlington, VA. Retrieved from http://www.communitytechnology.org/nsf_ci_report/

Barksdale, J., and Berman, F. (2007). Preserving our digital heritage. *San Diego Union-Tribune*, May 17. Retrieved from http://www.signonsandiego.com/uniontrib/20070517/news_lz1e17berman.html

Battelle, J. (2005). The birth of Google. *Wired* 13(8). Retrieved from http://www.wired.com/wired/archive/13.08/battelle.html

Beagrie, N. (2005). Plenty of room at the bottom? Personal digital libraries and collections. *D-Lib Magazine* 11(6). Retrieved from http://dx.doi.org/10.1045/june2005-beagrie

Bellafante, G., and Corliss, R. (1996, December 23). The best of 1996 and the worst. *Time* 148(28). Retrieved from http://search.ebscohost.com/login.aspx?direct = true&db = aph&AN = 9612193823&site = ehost-live

Bellinger, M. (2002). *Four Generations of the Digital Library*. Presented at Metropolitan New York Library Council's Digitization Symposium. New York. Retrieved from http://digitalarchive.oclc.org/da/ViewObjectMain.jsp?fileid = 0000016179:000000676854&reqid = 58

Berners-Lee, T., and Fischetti, M. (2000). *Weaving the Web: The Original Design and Ultimate Destiny of the World Wide Web*. Harper, San Francisco.

Bibliographic Services Task Force (2005, December). *Rethinking How We Provide Bibliographic Services for the University of California*. University of California Libraries, CA. Retrieved from http://libraries.universityofcalifornia.edu/sopag/BSTF/Final.pdf

Bishop, A. P. (1995). Working towards an understanding of digital Library use: A report on the user research efforts of the NSF/ARPA/NASA DLI projects. *D-Lib Magazine* 1(4). http://dx.doi.org/cnri.dlib/october95-bishop

Bishop, A. P., and Leigh, S. (1996). Social informatics of digital library use and infrastructure. In *Annual review of information science and technology* (M. E. Williams, ed.), vol. 31, pp. 301–401.

Borghuis, M., Brinckman, H., Fischer, A., Hunter, K., Van der Loo, E., Mors, R. T., Mostert, P., and Jaco, Z. (1996). *TULIP Final Report*. Elsevier Science, New York. Retrieved from http://www.elsevier.com/wps/find/librariansinfo.librarians/tulipfr

Borgman, C. L. (1997). From acting locally to thinking globally: A brief history of library automation. *Library Quarterly* 67(3), 215–249.

Borgman, C. L. (1999). What are digital libraries? Competing visions. *Information Processing and Management* 35(3), 227–243.

Borgman, C. L., Bates, M. J., Cloonan, M. V., et al. (1996). *Social Aspects of Digital Libraries* (A final report to the National Science Foundation of the UCLA-NSF Social Aspects of Digital Libraries Workshop. University of California, Los Angeles: Los Angeles. February 15–17, 1996). Retrieved from http://is.gseis.ucla.edu/research/dl/UCLA_DL_Report.html

Borgman, C. L., Wallis, J. C., Mayernik, M. S., and Pepe, A. (2007). Drowning in data: Digital library architecture to support scientific use of embedded sensor networks. In *Proceedings of the 7th ACM/IEEE-CS Joint Conference on Digital Libraries* (R. Larson, E. Rasmussen, S. Sugimoto and E. Toms, eds.), pp. 269–277, Association for Computing Machinery, New York. Retrieved from http://doi.acm.org/10.1145/1255175.1255228

Bowen, W. G. (1995). The Foundation's Journal Storage Project (JSTOR). In: Andrew W. Mellon Foundation. *Report of the Andrew Mellon Foundation 1994*. Andrew W. Mellon Foundation, New York. Retrieved from www.mellon.org/news_publications/annual-reports-essays/annual-reports/

Brogan, M. L. (2003). *A Survey of Digital Library Aggregation Services*. Digital Library Federation, Washington, DC. Retrieved from http://www.diglib.org/pubs/dlf101/

Buckland, M. (1992). *Redesigning Library Services: A Manifesto*. American Library Association, Chicago.

Budapest Open Access Initiative (2002). *Budapest Open Access Initiative*. Retrieved from http://www.soros.org/openaccess/read.shtml

Bunker, G., and Zick, G. (1999). Collaboration as a key to digital library development: High performance image management at the University of Washington. *D-Lib Magazine* 5(3). Retrieved from http://dx.doi.org/10.1045/march99-bunker

Bush, V. (1945). As we may think. *The Atlantic Monthly* 176(1), 101–108. Retrieved from http://www.theatlantic.com/doc/194507/bush

Byrd, S., Courson, G., Roderick, E., and Taylor, J. M. (2001). Cost/benefit analysis for digital library projects: The Virginia Historical Inventory Project (VHI). *Bottom Line* 14(2), 65–75.

Choi, Y., and Rasmussen, E. (2006). What is needed to educate future digital librarians: A study of current practice and staffing patterns in academic and research libraries. *D-Lib Magazine* 12(9). Retrieved from http://dx.doi.org/10.1045/september2006-choi

Christel, M., and Huang, C. (2003). Enhanced access to digital video through visually rich interfaces. *Proceedings of the IEEE International Conference on Multimedia and Expo (ICME)*. Baltimore, MD, July 6–9.

Computing Research Association (2005). *Cyberinfrastructure for Education and Learning for the Future: A Vision and Research Agenda*. Computing Research Association, Washington, DC. Retrieved from http://www.cra.org/reports/cyberinfrastructure.pdf

Conway, P. (1996). Yale University Library's project open book: Preliminary research findings. *D-Lib Magazine* 2(2). Retrieved from http://www.dlib.org/dlib/february96/yale/02conway.html

Conway, P. and Weaver, S. (1994, June). *The setup phase of Project Open Book* (A report to the Commission on Preservation and Access). Yale University Libraries, New Haven, CT. Retrieved from http://www.clir.org/PUBS/reports/conway/conway.html

Cook, M. N., Hernandez, J. J., and Nicholson, S. (2001). *Numeric Data Products and Services (SPEC Kit 263)*. Association of Research Libraries, Office of Leadership and Management Services, Washington, DC. Retrieved from http://www.arl.org/bm ~ doc/spec263web.pdf

Corporation for National Research Initiatives (2007). *About D-Lib Magazine*. Retrieved from http://www.dlib.org/about.html

Crane, G. (1998). The Perseus Project and beyond: How building a digital library challenges the humanities and technology. *D-Lib Magazine* 4(1). Retrieved from http://dx.doi.org/cnri.dlib/january98-crane

Crane, G. (2000). Designing documents to enhance the performance of digital libraries: Time, space, people and a digital library on London. *D-Lib Magazine* 6(7/8). Retrieved from http://dx.doi.org/10.1045/july2000-crane

Croneis, K. S., and Henderson, P. (2002). Electronic and digital librarian positions: A content analysis of announcements from 1990 through 2000. *Journal of Academic Librarianship* 28(4), 232–237.

Crow, R. (2002). *The Case for Institutional Repositories: A SPARC Position Paper*. The Scholarly Publishing & Academic Resources Coalition, Washington, DC. Retrieved from http://www.arl.org/sparc/IR/ir.html

Cuadra Associates (1982). *A Library and Information Science Research Agenda for the 1980s: Final Report*. Santo Monica, CA.

Davidoff, F., and Florance, V. (2000). The informationist: A new health profession? *Annals of Internal Medicine* 132(12), 996–998.

Davis, H. L. (1998). Economic considerations for digital libraries: A Library of Congress perspective. *Journal of Library Administration* 26(1/2), 195–202.

Digital Library Federation (1995). *America's Heritage: Mission and Goals for a Digital Library Federation*. Retrieved from http://www.diglib.org/about/dlfcharter.htm

Directorate for Education and Human Resources (1998). *User-Friendly Handbook for Project Evaluation: Science, Mathematics, Engineering and Technology Education (NSF File No. nsf93152)*. National Science Foundation, Arlington, VA. Retrieved from http://www.nsf.gov/pubsys/ods/getpub.cfm?nsf93152

Downie, J. S. (2003). Establishing Music Information Retrieval (MIR) and Music Digital Library (MDL) evaluation frameworks: Preliminary foundations and infrastructures. In the *MIR/MDL evaluation project white paper collection*, 3rd ed., pp. 3–6. Retrieved from http://www.music-ir.org/evaluation/wp2/wp1_downie_establishing.pdf

Duguid, P., and Atkins, D. E. (1997, March 9–11). *Report of the Santa Fe Planning Workshop on Distributed Knowledge Work Environments: Digital libraries (NSF File No. NSF-IRI-9712586)*. Retrieved from http://www.si.umich.edu/SantaFe/

Durrance, J. C. (n.d.). *Community Networking Initiative Report*. Retrieved from http://www.si.umich.edu/cristaled/opportunities/flinttext.html

Federal Coordinating Council for Science, Engineering, and Technology (FCCSET), Office of Science and Technology Policy (1994). *High Performance Computing and Communications: Toward a National Information Infrastructure*. Office of Science and Technology Policy, Committee on Physical, Mathematical, and Engineering Sciences, Washington, DC. Retrieved from http://www.nitrd.gov/pubs/bluebooks/1994/

Fenly, J. G., and Wiggins, B. (1988). *The Linked Systems Project: A Networking Tool for Libraries*. Online Computer Library Center (OCLC), Dublin, OH.

Flash, C. (2004, February 2). Google for a Grade: UW Class to Study Popular Search Engine. *The Seattle Times*, p. C1. Retrieved from http://archives.seattletimes.nwsource.com/cgi-bin/texis.cgi/web/vortex/display?slug = google02 &date = 20040202

Fox, E. (1996). *Drexel University Workshop 5/96: Information Retrieval 2000— Workplace Needs and Curricular Implications*. Drexel University, Philadelphia, PA. Retrieved from http://ei.cs.vt.edu/ ~ fox/Drexel96/index.html

Fox, E. (1999, October/November). The Digital Libraries Initiative: Update and discussion. *Bulletin of the American Society for Information Science* 26(1), 7–11. October/November. Retrieved from http://www.asis.org/Bulletin/Oct-99/fox.html

Fox, E. A. (ed.) (1993). *Source Book on Digital Libraries, Version 1*. Virginia Tech, Blacksburg, VA. Retrieved from http://fox.cs.vt.edu/DigitalLibrary/DLSB.pdf

Fox, E. A., Hix, D., Nowell, L. T., Brueni, D. J., Wake, W. C., Heath, L. S., and Rao, D. (1993). Users, user interfaces, and objects: Envision, a digital library. *Journal of the American Society for Information Science* 44(8), 480–491.

Frechtling, J. (2002). *The 2002 User-Friendly Handbook for Project Evaluation (No. NSF02057)*. National Science Foundation, Directorate for Education and Human Resources, Arlington, VA. Retrieved from http://www.nsf.gov/pubsys/ods/getpub.cfm?nsf02057

French, B. (2003). The economics and management of digital resources in a multi-campus, multi-library university: The shared digital collection. *Collection Management* 28(1/2), 45–54.

Friedlander, A. (2002). The National Digital Information Infrastructure Preservation program: Expectations, realities, choices and progress to date. *D-Lib Magazine* 8(4). Retrieved from http://dx.doi.org/10.1045/april2002-friedlander

Giddens, A. (1991). Structuration theory: Past, present and future. In *Gidden's Theory of Structuration: A Critical Appreciation* (C. G. A. Bryant and D. Jary, eds.), Routledge, London, UK.

Giersch, S. (2003). *2003 Sustainability Standing Committee Survey Results*. Retrieved from http://sustain.comm.nsdl.org/doc_tracker/docs_download.php?group_id = $group_id&id = 82

Giles, C. L., and Councill, I. G. (2004). Who gets acknowledged: Measuring scientific contributions through automatic acknowledgment indexing. *Proceeding of the National Academy of Sciences of the United States of America*

1010(51), 17599–17604. Retrieved from http://www.pnas.org/cgi/doi/10.1073/pnas.0407743101

Goh, D. H.-L., Chua, A., Khoo, D. A., Khoo, E. B.-H., Mak, E. B.-T., and Ng, M. W.-M. (2006). A checklist for evaluating open source digital library software. *Online Information Review* 30(4), 360–379. Retrieved from http://dx.doi.org/10.1108/14684520610686283

Goldenberg-Hart, D. (2004). Libraries and changing research practices: A report of the ARL/CNI Forum on e-research and cyberinfrastructure. *ARL Bimonthly Report* (237), 1–5. Retrieved from http://www.arl.org/bm ~ doc/arlbr237.pdf

Google. (2007). Corporate information: Google milestones. Retrieved from http://www.google.com/corporate/history.html

Graubard, S. R., and LeClerc, P. (1998). *Books, Bricks, and Bytes: Libraries in the Twenty-first Century*. Transaction, New Brunswick, NJ.

Greenberg, J. (2005). Understanding metadata and metadata schemes. *Cataloging & Classification Quarterly* 40(3/4), 17–36.

Greenstein, D., and Thorin, S. E. (2002). *The Digital Library: A Biography (CLIR Rep. No. 109)*. Council on Library and Information Resources, Washington, DC. Retrieved from http://www.clir.org/PUBS/reports/pub109/pub109.pdf

Griffin, S. M. (1998, July/August). NSF/DARPA/NASA Digital Libraries Initiative: A program manager's perspective. *D-Lib Magazine* 4(7). July/August. Retrieved from http://dx.doi.org/cnri.dlib/july98-griffin

Griffin, S. M. (2005). Funding for digital libraries research: Past and present. *D-Lib Magazine* 11(7/8). Retrieved from http://dx.doi.org/10.1045/July2005-griffin

Guterman L. (2008). *The Journal 'Science' Rejoins JSTOR*, January 3. The Chronicle of Higher Education. Retrieved from http://chronicle.com/news/article/3696/the-journal-science-has-rejoined-jstor

Habib, M. C. (2006). *Toward Academic Library 2.0: Development and Application of a Library 2.0 Methodology*. Unpublished Master's thesis, University of North Carolina at Chapel Hill, Chapel Hill, NC. Retrieved from http://hdl.handle.net/1901/356

Harnad, S., Brody, T., Vallieres, F., Carr, L., Hitchcock, S., Gingras, Y., Oppenheim, C., Stamerjohanns, H., and Hilf, E. R. (2004). The access/impact problem and the green and gold roads to open access. *Serials Review* 30(4), 310–314. Retrieved from http://dx.doi.org/10.1016/j.serrev.2004.09.013

Harris, L. E. (2006). The section 108 study group. *Information Outlook* 10(2), 36.

Hart, D. (2004). *On the Origins of Google*. National Science Foundation, Arlington, VA. Retrieved from http://www.nsf.gov/discoveries/disc_summ.jsp?cntn_id = 100660

Heath, L. S., Hix, D., Nowell, L. T., Wake, W. C., Averboch, G. A., Labow, E., Guyer, S. A., Brueni, D. J., France, R. K., Dalal, K., and Fox, E. A. (1995). Envision: A user-centered database of computer science literature. *Communications of the ACM* 38(4), 52–53.

Hey, A. J. G., and Trefethen, A. E. (2003). The data deluge: An e-Science perspective. In *Grid Computing: Making the Global Infrastructure a Reality* (F. Berman, G. C. Fox and A. J. G. Hey, eds.), pp. 809–824, Wiley, New York.

High-Performance Computing Act of 1991 (HPCA), Pub. L. No. 102-194, §102(a) (1991).

Hirtle, P. B. (ed.) (1999). Editorial: A new generation of digital library research. *D-Lib Magazine* 5(7/8). Retrieved from http://dx.doi.org/10.1045/july99-editorial

Hjerppe, R. (1989). Bibliographic control and document architecture in hypermedia databases. *Annual Review of OCLC Research*, July 1988–June 1989, 6–8.

InfoSpace Inc (2007). *About WebCrawler*. Retrieved from http://www.webcrawler.com/webcrawler/ws/about/_iceUrlFlag = 11?_IceUrl = true

Institute of Museum and Library Services (2002). *Status of Technology and Digitization in the Nation's Museums and Libraries 2002 Report*. Retrieved from http://www.imls.gov/publications/TechDig02/

Institute of Museum and Library Services (2006). *Status of Technology and Digitization in the Nation's Museums and Libraries*. Retrieved from http://www.imls.gov/publications/TechDig05/

Institute of Museum and Library Services (n.d.). *State Programs: Grants to State Library Administrative Agencies*. Retrieved from http://www.imls.gov/programs/programs.shtm

Internet Public Library (2007). *About the Internet Public Library*. Retrieved from http://www.ipl.org/div/about/

Ithaka Harbors, Inc (2007). *About Ithaka*. Retrieved from http://www.ithaka.org/about-ithaka

Jesella, K. (2007, July 8). A hipper crowd of shushers. *New York Times* [Style section], p. 1. Retrieved from http://www.nytimes.com/2007/07/08/fashion/08librarian.html

Kaczmarek, J., Hswe, P., Eke, J., and Habing, T. G. (2006). Using the audit checklist for the certification of a trusted digital repository as a framework for evaluating repository software applications: A progress report. *D-Lib Magazine* 12(12). Retrieved from http://dx.doi.org/10.1045/december2006-kaczmarek

Kahn, R. E., and Cerf, V. G. (1988). *An Open Architecture for a Digital Library System and a Plan for Its Development (The Digital Library Project: Vol. I. The world of knowbots)*. Corporation for National Research Initiatives, Draft. Reston, VA. Retrieved from http://hdl.handle.net/4263537/2091

Kilgour, F. G. (1970). History of library computerization. *Journal of Library Automation* 3(3), 218–229.

Kling, R., Rosenbaum, H., and Hert, C. (1998). Social informatics in information science: An introduction. *Journal of the American Society for Information Science* 49(12), 1047–1052.

Kranich, N. (2004). *The Information Commons: A Public Policy Report*. The Free Expression Policy Project, New York. Retrieved from http://www.fepproject.org/policyreports/infocommons.preview.html

Kruk, S. R. (2005). *JeromeDL: A Digital Library on the Semantic Web*. National University of Ireland, Digital Enterprise Research Institute, Galway, Ireland. Retrieved from http://library.deri.ie/resource/5b7075c0

Lagoze, C., Krafft, D. B., Payettei, S., and Jesuroga, S. (2005). What is a digital library anymore, anyway? Beyond search and access in the NSDL. *D-Lib Magazine* 11(11). Retrieved from http://dx.doi.org/10.1045/november2005-lagoze

Lamolinara, G. (1995a, September). *How the electronic library evolved*. A Periodic Report from The National Digital Library Program, 1995(2). Retrieved from http://www.loc.gov/ndl/sep-95.html

Lamolinara, G. (1995b). *Kellogg Foundation Grant gives Library Means to Reach out to K-12 Audiences.* A Periodic Report from the National Digital Library Program, 1995(2). Retrieved from http://www.loc.gov/ndl/sep-95.pdf

Lancaster, F. W. (1978). *Toward Paperless Information Systems.* Academic Press, New York.

Larsen, R., and Wactlar, H. (2003). *Knowledge lost in information (NSF File No. PR-94-52).* National Science Foundation, Washington, DC.

Lawrence, S. (2001). Free online availability substantially increases a paper's impact. *Nature* 411(6837), 521. Retrieved from http://dx.doi.org/10.1038/35079151

Lazorko, C. (2003). Deans discuss "Information Schools Movement." *News at SILS.* Retrieved from http://www.ipl.org/div/about/IPLconsortium/consortiumInfo. html

Lee, H.-L. (2000). What is a collection? *Journal of the American Society for Information Science* 51(12), 1106–1113.

LeFurgy, W. (2005). Building preservation partnerships: The Library of Congress National Digital Information Infrastructure and Preservation Program. *Library Trends* 54(1), 163–172.

Lesk, M. (1999). Perspectives on DLI-2—Growing the field. *Bulletin of the American Society for Information Science* 26(1). Retrieved from http://www.asis.org/Bulletin/ Oct-99/lesk.html

Lesk, M., Fox, E., and McGill, M. (1991). A national electronic science, engineering, and technology library. In *Source Book on Digital Libraries, Version 1.0* (E. A. Fox, ed.), pp. 4–24, Virginia Tech, Blacksburg, VA. Retrieved from http://fox.cs.vt. edu/DigitalLibrary/DLSB.pdf

Letts, C. W., Ryan, W., and Grossman, A. (1997). Virtuous capital: What foundations can learn from venture capitalists. *Harvard Business Review* 97(March/ April), 36–44.

Levy, D. M. (2000). Digital libraries and the problem of purpose. *D-Lib Magazine* 6(1). Retrieved from http://dx.doi.org/10.1045/january2000-levy

Levy, D. M., and Marshall, C. C. (1995). Going digital: A look at assumptions underlying digital libraries. *Communications of the ACM* 38(4), 77–84.

Libraries for the Future (1998). *Library Research: 1983–1997.* U.S. Department of Education, New York. Retrieved from http://www.ed.gov/offices/OERI/PLLI/ LibraryResearch/index.html

Library of Congress (1993). *Final Report of the American Memory User Evaluation, 1991–1993.* Retrieved from http://lcweb2.loc.gov/ammem/usereval.html

Library of Congress (2004). The National Digital Library at 10: Library extends its reach worldwide. *Information Bulletin.* Retrieved from http://www.loc.gov/loc/lcib/ 0410/ndl.html

Library of Congress (n.d.a). *About American Memory: Mission and History.* Retrieved from http://memory.loc.gov/ammem/about/index.html

Library of Congress (n.d.b). *The National Digital Library Program, Awards and Collections.* Retrieved from http://memory.loc.gov/ammem/award/collections.html

Library of Congress (n.d.c). *Library of Congress National Digital Library Program.* Retrieved from http://memory.loc.gov/ammem/dli2/html/lcndlp.html

Library Journal (2007). *LC Hit By $47 Million Cut in Digital Preservation Funds.* Retrieved from libraryjournal.com (March 20) and http://www.libraryjournal.com/ article/CA6426077.html

Licklider, J. C. R. (1965). *Libraries of the Future.* MIT Press, Cambridge, MA.

Liddy, E. D., Sutton, S., Paik, W., Allen, E., Harwell, S., Monsour, M., Turner, A., and Liddy, J. (eds.) (2001). Breaking the metadata generation bottleneck: Preliminary findings. In *Proceedings of the 1st ACM/IEEE-CS Joint Conference on Digital Libraries* (p. 464). Association for Computing Machinery, New York. Retrieved from http://doi.acm.org/10.1145/379437.379795

Lynch, C. (2005). Where do we go from here? The next decade for digital libraries. *D-Lib Magazine* 11(7/8). Retrieved from http://dx.doi.org/10.1045/july2005-lynch

Marchionini, G. (1999, September 28–29). *Augmenting Library Services: Toward the Sharium.* Paper presented at the International Symposium on Digital Libraries, Tsukuba, Ibaraki, Japan. Retrieved from http://www.ils.unc.edu/∼march/sharium/ISDL.pdf

Matthews, A. J. (1989). *Rethinking the Library in the Information Age.* Office of Educational Research and Improvement, Library Programs, Information Services, Washington, DC.

McCallum, S. H. (2002). MARC: Keystone for library automation. *IEEE Annals of the History of Computing* 24(2), 34–49.

McGlamery, S., and Coffman, S. (2000). Moving reference to the web. *Reference & User Services Quarterly* 39(4), 380–386.

Miller, E. (2003). *Enabling the Semantic Web for Scientific Research and Collaboration.* Paper presented at the NSF Post Digital Library Futures Workshop, Chatham, MA. Retrieved from http://www.sis.pitt.edu/∼dlwkshop/paper_miller.html

Mitchell, G. (1997). *The Global Context for U.S. Technology Policy.* U.S. Department of Commerce, Office of Technology Competitiveness, Washington, DC. Retrieved from http://www.technology.gov/Reports/globalcontext/nas.pdf

National Center for Supercomputing Applications (NCSA) (2007). *About NCSA Mosaic.* Retrieved from http://www.ncsa.uiuc.edu/Projects/mosaic.html

National High-Performance Computer Technology Act of 1989, S. 1067.IS, 101st Cong., (1989).

National Institutes of Health (n.d.). *NIH public access.* Retrieved from http://publicaccess.nih.gov/

National Science and Technology Council (NSTC). Committee on Technology (1999). *Computing, Information, and Communications: Networked Computing for the 21st Century.* National Science and Technology Council, Arlington, VA. Retrieved from http://www.nitrd.gov/pubs/bluebooks/1999/

National Science Digital Library (n.d.). *Fact Sheet.* Retrieved from http://nsdl.org/about/?pager = factsheet

National Science Foundation (1993). *Research on Digital Libraries (NSF File No. NSF 93-141).* Retrieved from http://www.nsf.gov/pubs/stis1993/nsf93141/nsf93141.txt

National Science Foundation (1998). *Digital Libraries Initiative—Phase 2.* Retrieved from http://www.nsf.gov/pubs/1998/nsf9863/nsf9863.htm

National Science Foundation (2000). *National Science, Mathematics, Engineering, and Technology Education Digital Library (NSDL)—Program Solicitation (Archived).* Retrieved from http://wwwnsf.gov/publications/pub_summ.jsp?ods_key = nsf0044&org = NSF

National Science Foundation (2002). *National Science, Technology, Engineering, and Mathematics Education Digital Library (NSDL) (Archived).* Retrieved from http://www.nsf.gov/publications/pub_summ.jsp?ods_key = nsf02054&org = NSF

National Science Foundation (2004a). *National Science, Technology, Engineering, and Mathematics Education Digital Library (NSDL) (Archived)*. Retrieved from http://www.nsf.gov/publications/pub_summ.jsp?ods_key = nsf04542&org = NSF

National Science Foundation (2004b, June 16). *Digital Preservation Program Launches Research Grants Initiative (NSF Pub. No. PR 04-085)*. Retrieved from http://www.nsf.gov/news/news_summ.jsp?cntn_id = 100399&org = IIS&from = news

National Science Foundation (2007a). *Cyberinfrastructure Vision for 21st Century Discovery (NSF. Pub. No. NSF 07-28)*. National Science Foundation, Washington, DC. Retrieved from http://www.nsf.gov/pubs/2007/nsf0728/index.jsp

National Science Foundation (2007b). *Proposal and Award Policies and Procedures Guide (NSF. Pub. No. NSF 07-140)*. National Science Foundation, Washington, DC. Retrieved from http://www.nsf.gov/pubs/policydocs/papp/index.jsp

Neufeld, M. L., and Cornog, M. (1986). Database history: From dinosaurs to compact discs. *Journal of American Society for Information Science* 37(4), 183–190.

NISO Framework Advisory Group (2004). *A Framework of Guidance for Building Good Digital Collections*, 2nd ed., National Information Standards Organization, Bethesda, MD. Retrieved from http://www.niso.org/framework/Framework2.html

Norberg, L. R., Vassiliadis, K., Ferguson, J., and Smith, N. (2005). Sustainable design for multiple audiences: The usability study and iterative redesign of the documenting the American South Digital Library. *OCLC Systems & Services* 21(4), 285–299.

North Carolina ECHO (2007). *Grant Program*. Retrieved from http://www.ncecho.org/grantinfo.asp

Nunberg, G. (1996). *The Future of the Book*. University of California Press, Berkeley, CA.

Ogle, V., and Wilensky, R. (1996). Testbed development for the Berkeley Digital Library Project. *D-Lib Magazine* 2(7). Retrieved from http://dx.doi.org/cnri.dlib/july96-ogle

O'Reilly, T. (2005). *What is Web 2.0: Design Patterns and Business Models for the Next Generation of Software*. Retrieved from http://www.oreillynet.com/pub/a/oreilly/tim/news/2005/09/30/what-is-web-20.html

Peek, R. P., and Pomerantz, J. P. (1998). Electronic scholarly journal publishing. In *Annual Review of Information Science and Technology* (M. E. Williams, ed.), vol. 33, pp. 321–356.

Pomerantz, J. (2003). Integrating digital reference service into the digital library environment. In *The Digital Reference Research Agenda* (R. D. Lankes, S. Nicholson and A. Goodrum, eds.), pp. 23–47, Association of College and Research Libraries, Chicago.

Pomerantz, J. (2006). Google Scholar and 100 percent availability of information. *Information Technology and Libraries* 25(2), 52–56.

Pomerantz, J., and Marchionini, G. (2007). The digital library as place. *Journal of Documentation* 63(4), 505–533.

Pomerantz, J., Nicholson, S., Belanger, Y., and Lankes, R. D. (2004). The current state of digital reference: Validation of a general digital reference model through a survey of digital reference services. *Information Processing and Management* 40(2), 347–363.

Pomerantz, J., Oh, S., Yang, S., Fox, E. A., and Wildemuth, B. M. (2006). The core: Digital library education in library and information science programs. *D-Lib*

*Magazine* 12(11). Retrieved from http://dx.doi.org/10.1045/november2006-pomerantz

President's Information Technology Advisory Committee (PITAC). (1999, February). *Information Technology Research: Investing in Our Future.* Retrieved from http://www.nitrd.gov/pitac/report/

Ray, J. (2004). Connecting people and resources: Digital programs at the Institute of Museum and Library Services. *Library Hi Tech* 22(3), 249–253.

Read, E. J. (2007). Data services in academic libraries. *Reference & User Services Quarterly* 46(3), 61–75.

Recker, M. (2006). Perspectives on teachers as digital library users: Consumers, contributors, and designers. *D-Lib Magazine* 12(9). http://dx.doi.org/10.1045/september2006-recker

Rusbridge, C. (1998). Towards the hybrid library. *D-Lib Magazine* 4(7). Retrieved from http://dx.doi.org/cnri.dlib/july98-rusbridge

Sapp, G. (2002). *A Brief History of the Future of Libraries: An Annotated Bibliography.* The Scarecrow Press, Lanham, MD.

Saracevic, T., and Dalbello, M. (2003). *Digital Library Research and Digital Library Practice: How Do They Inform Each Other?* Unpublished manuscript. Rutgers University, New Brunswick, NJ.

Savage, J. E. (1994). Why NSF should not change its approach to HPCC/NII research. In *Developing a Computer Science Agenda for High-Performance Computing* (U. Vishkin, ed.), pp. 145–147, Association for Computing Machinery, New York. Retrieved from http://doi.acm.org/10.1145/197912.197995

Schatz, B., and Chen, H. (1996). Building large-scale digital libraries. *IEEE Computer* 29(5), 22–26.

Schatz, B., and Chen, H. (1999). Digital libraries: Technological advances and social impacts. *IEEE Computer* 32(2), 45–50.

Schonfeld, R. C. (2003). *JSTOR: A History.* Princeton University Press, Princeton, NJ.

Scott, K. (2003). *Funding Matters: The Impact of Canada's New Funding Regime on Nonprofit and Voluntary Organizations.* Canadian Council on Social Development, Ottawa, ON.

Shirky, C. (2005). AIHT: Conceptual issues from practical tests. *D-Lib Magazine* 11(12). Retrieved from http://dx.doi.org/10.1045/december2005-shirky

Shneiderman, B., Byrd, D., and Croft, W. B. (1998). Sorting out searching: A user-interface framework for text searches. *Communications of the ACM* 41(4), 95–98.

Smith, A. (2006). Distributed preservation in a national context: NDIIPP at mid-point. *D-Lib Magazine* 12(6). Retrieved from http://dx.doi.org/10.1045/june2006-smith

Smith, A. G. (2000). Search features of digital libraries. *Information Research* 5(3). Retrieved from http://informationr.net/ir/5-3/paper73.html

Smith, M., Barton, M., Bass, M., Branschofsky, M., McClellan, G., Stuve, D., Tansley, R., and Walker, J. H. (2003). DSpace: An open source dynamic digital repository. *D-Lib Magazine* 9(1). Retrieved from http://dx.doi.org/10.1045/january2003-smith

Spicher, K. M. (1996). The development of the MARC format. *Cataloging & Classification Quarterly* 21(3/4), 75.

Spiteri, L. F. (2006). The use of folksonomies in public library catalogues. *Serials Librarian* 51(2), 75–89.

Staples, T., Wayland, R., and Payette, S. (2003). The Fedora Project: An open-source digital object repository management system. *D-Lib Magazine* 9(4). Retrieved from http://dx.doi.org/10.1045/april2003-staples

Suber, P. (2007). *Timeline of the Open Access Movement.* Retrieved from http://www.earlham.edu/ ~ peters/fos/timeline.htm

Sure, Y., and Studer, R. (2005). Semantic web technologies for digital libraries. *Library Management* 26(4/5), 190–195.

Sutton, S. A. (2004). Building an education digital library: GEM and early metadata standards adoption. In *Metadata in Practice* (D. I. Hillmann and E. L. Westbrooks, eds.), pp. 1–16, American Library Association, Chicago.

Tang, J., Avula, S. R., and Acton, S. T. (2004). DIRECT: A decentralized image retrieval system for the National STEM Digital Library. *Information Technology and Libraries* 23(1). Retrieved from http://www.lita.org/ala/lita/litapublications/ital/2301tang.cfm

Tennant, R. (1998). The most important management decision: Hiring staff for the new millennium. *Library Journal* 123(3), 102.

Tennant, R. (1999). Skills for the new millennium. *Library Journal* 124(1), 39.

Thomas, S. E. (2000, November 15–17). *The Catalog as portal to the Internet.* Presented at the Conference on Bibliographic Control in the New Millennium. Retrieved from http://www.loc.gov/catdir/bibcontrol/thomas_paper.html

Thompson, C. (1986). Military direction of academic CS research. *Communications of the ACM* 29(7), 583–585.

Troll, D. A. (2001). How and why are libraries changing. *CLIR Issues*, 21. Retrieved from http://www.clir.org/pubs/issues/issues21.html#changing.

University of Michigan (1996, August 7). *Kellogg Foundation Gives $5 Million to School of Information.* Retrieved from http://www.ns.umich.edu/htdocs/releases/story.php?id = 1238

University of Michigan. School of Information and Library Studies. (n.d.). *Educating Human Resources for the Information and Library Professions of the 21st Century* (A proposal to the W.K. Kellogg Foundation from the Faculty of The School of Information and Library Studies). University of Michigan. School of Information and Library Studies: Ann Arbor, MI. Retrieved from http://www.si.umich.edu/cristaled/Kelloggproposal.html

Wattenberg, F. (1998). A National Digital Library for Science, Mathematics, Engineering, and Technology Education. *D-Lib Magazine* 4(9). Retrieved from http://dx.doi.org/cnri.dlib/october98-wattenberg

Wilkin, J. P. (2005, June). *How the Development of Online Search Tools and the Mass Digitization of Collections Might be Changing the Role of Libraries and Affecting People's Access to Information.* Paper present at SPARC-ACRL Forum, American Libraries Association (ALA) Annual Conference 2005, Chicago, IL. Retrieved from http://www.arl.org/sparc/meetings/ala05/John_Wilkin.html

Winograd, T. (1991). Strategic Computing research and the universities. In *Computerization and Controversy: Value Conflicts and Social Choices* (C. Dunlop and R. Kling, eds.), pp. 704–716, Academic Press Professional, San Diego, CA. (Originally published as working paper No. 7, Silicon Valley Working Group, U.C. Santa Cruz, March, 1987)

Witten, I. H., and Bainbridge, D. (2007). A retrospective look at Greenstone: lessons from the first decade. In *Proceedings of the 7th ACM/IEEE-CS Joint*

*Conference on Digital Libraries* (R. Larson, E. Rasmussen, S. Sugimoto and E. Toms, eds.), pp. 147–156, Association for Computing Machinery, New York. Retrieved from http://doi.acm.org/10.1145/1255175.1255204

W. K. Kellogg Foundation (2007). *Our Mission and Values*. Retrieved from http://www.wkkf.org/default.aspx?tabid = 63&ItemID = 1&NID = 34

Yang, M., Wildemuth, B., and Marchionini, G. (2004, October 10–16). *The Relative Effectiveness of Concept-Based Versus Content-Based Video Retrieval*. Poster session presented at the ACM Multimedia conference, New York. Retrieved from http://doi.acm.org/10.1145/1027527.1027613

Yudken, J. S., and Simons, B. (1988). Federal funding in computer science: A preliminary report. *ACM SIGGRAPH Computer Graphics* 22(2), 99–104. Retrieved from http://doi.acm.org/10.1145/47824.47826

Zakon, R. H. (2003). *Hobbes' Internet Timeline v8.2*. Retrieved from http://www.zakon.org/robert/internet/timeline/

Zia, L. (2000, October). The NSF National Science, Mathematics, Engineering, and Technology Education Digital Library (NSDL) Program: A progress report. *D-Lib Magazine* 6(10). October. Retrieved from http://dx.doi.org/10.1045/october2000-zia

# A Review of Research Related to Management of Corporate Libraries

James M. Matarazzo[a] and Toby Pearlstein[b]
[a]Graduate School of Library and Information Science, Simmons College, Boston, MA, USA
[b]Global Information Services, Bain & Company, Inc., Boston, MA, USA (Retired)

## I. Introduction

The authors began this review of the research available on the topic of managing corporate libraries with the hypothesis that there has been a lack of funding for such research that in turn has limited its production. After reviewing the relevant research literature produced in the last three decades, however, the assumption of inadequate funding causing a lack of research on this topic could not totally be supported. As we sought to identify what funding was available, the literature suggested additional questions: How or if research on the subject of managing corporate libraries was encouraged and funded and by whom? What type of research would be most useful for corporate library managers? Finally, how research results were disseminated and whether the results had been put to use by practitioners? Here the authors are defining the topic of "managing libraries" in the broadest sense and occasionally delve more specifically into the topic of valuing library services. While we address corporate libraries in particular, most of our findings and commentary can be applied to special libraries in general.

In this chapter the authors explore the questions raised above by reviewing the body of literature reporting on research and activities on corporate library management (and in some cases generic library management) since the 1980s. Four major sources of this research were identified. These are the Special Libraries Association (SLA) serving corporate library members in the US, Canada, Europe and increasingly in Asia and the Middle East; and three active research environments covering the United Kingdom, Australia, and New Zealand.

INFLUENCE OF FUNDING ON ADVANCES IN LIBRARIANSHIP
ADVANCES IN LIBRARIANSHIP, VOL. 31
© 2008 by Emerald Group Publishing Limited
ISSN: 0065-2830
DOI: 10.1016/S0065-2830(08)31003-4

Initially some assumptions about who might be impacted by research on corporate library management were made. There appear to be two major constituencies. First, little published research by library school faculties, a significant source of research publications, can be found. This review concludes that this is likely due to a combination of inadequate funding and the discontinuation of SLA's refereed journal that offered a publication channel so critical for the promotion and tenure process.

The second constituency consists of corporate library managers. The literature suggests that they face significant challenges in being able to both undertake and share any research they do on their own and that this has resulted in a chilling effect on the creation of a body of knowledge that could be of use to their peers.

An overview of the research that has been done reveals some additional considerations. As one might expect, research seems primarily to be supported by grants from various professional library associations followed by academic institutions and publishers. Given that SLA is the major professional association for corporate librarians in North America, it was important here to fully review the Association's role in supporting research aimed at these members. When considering SLA's support, we came to believe that funding issues are part of a larger concern. The Association and its members seem to need a better understanding of what types of research will actually benefit corporate library managers so that the research that is funded can have a reasonable expectation of being useful to the audience. We were troubled by the question of whether or not the research generated is providing guidance that is pragmatic enough for the corporate library manager's needs. Finally, the need to reengage with Library School faculty who are positioned to be a driving force for this research is essential.

The main goal of this chapter is to provide a context for understanding why corporate special library managers do not seem to have available to them a body of useful and usable research similar to that available to academic, public, and other types of special libraries. The conclusions and assumptions we put forward here are ripe for further analysis and we hope they will stimulate more discussion on how research can help corporate library managers cope with some of the challenges they face today.

Koufogiannakis and Crumley (2006) point out that most areas of librarianship lack a solid evidence base and most practitioners do not incorporate research into daily practice. Why is this? Genoni *et al.* (2004) suggest that this is due to a lack of funding overall and that what funding is available is made in rather small grants. In our review of SLA's research funding over the past 20 years, for example, we found that interest in research and consequently funding levels have been inconsistent. It is possible that with only small amounts of dollars for research, the researcher's time must be contributed for free or funded through other sources. We have not found much evidence of employers of corporate librarians eager to provide in-kind support for any research project. Our review indicates, though, that under funding is not the whole reason for the disconnect found by Koufogiannakis.

The literature indicates that having the time to conduct research is also critical. Genoni *et al.* (2004) have noted that those in practice do not have the time to conduct research. Relevance of the research is also a concern. Practitioners may well find that the research literature lacks relevance for them. We would argue that while corporate library practitioners do not have the time or the support of their employers to conduct research on their own, they do want research available to them that applies to practical problems in their workplace rather than research that focuses on objective, verifiable data which are presented in scientific and technical terms. The literature reviewed reinforces this assumption.

The SLA (2001) Research Statement also calls for the corporate manager needing practical, relevant research and the more traditional scientific-based researchers to come together to share knowledge. This is quite a challenge. Practitioners seem not to either conduct or use research and if they do, their research is rarely published. Library and Information Science (LIS) faculties conduct research but does this research result in something that can be implemented by the corporate library manager? For instance, Kantor and Saracevic (1995–1997) received funding from SLA to conduct a study on the value of special libraries and information centers. The resulting 60 plus page report, *Valuing Special Libraries and Information Services (1997)*, was intended to guide corporate library managers through the process of demonstrating the value of their libraries. Yet the vast majority of the report was devoted to a discussion of the study's methodology and taxonomy, and a technical review of the conduct of the research. In our opinion, it is doubtful that a practitioner would have taken away something from this report for practical implementation. We see this as symptomatic of the gap between what LIS researchers have received funding to do and what corporate library managers can use. While the SLA Research Statement advocates narrowing this gap, this review indicates that progress has been slow.

## II. Special Libraries Association

With more than 11,000 members representing a variety of disciplines and types of institutions SLA in 2007 is well positioned to drive the development and support of research projects relevant to the management of corporate libraries and information services. The review below of SLA funded research projects indicates that both the Association and its members continue to experience very real challenges in being able to provide or support research directed at answering the critical question of how corporate libraries can contribute most successfully to their parent organizations. While some research on special libraries in general has been produced, the work of several authors examined here suggests it may be lacking in applicability to corporate library managers. The impact of the 2007 launch of a new research funding effort awarded to study and report on the impact of "embedded librarians," a topic that seems very relevant to corporate library managers, remains to be seen.

## A. Research Supported by SLA 1980—1990

Matarazzo (1981) investigated the need for research and its uses in special librarianship. His survey emphasized the role of the SLA and its commitment to research; the seeming lack of LIS faculty in the activities of SLA; the SLA research agenda and its relationship to research needs; the lack of funds for research; the low rewards for practitioners to publish; and a lack of evidence that the little research that does exist was applied to the management of corporate libraries. This review ended with a plea for SLA to join with other associations and organizations to more aggressively drive its research agenda. Much of the agenda, he felt, contained researchable questions which were broad and could benefit more than just special libraries.

From 1980 to 1990, LIS faculty were not involved in SLA by holding office, speaking, or publishing research in SLA's quarterly journal, *Special Libraries*. In fact, from 1980 to 1990, Tees (1989) notes, "It seems clear SLA has not been blessed with a close relationship with library school faculty" (p. 300).

Tees' (1989) study covering the years 1983–1984 to 1987–1988, found 0.5% of faculty had held any office in an SLA geographic chapter and only 4.1% had served on an SLA committee. For the years covered by her study, Tees counted 1148 speaking opportunities at SLA's Annual Conferences. LIS faculty spoke at only 52 of these events. Tees also discovered that few LIS faculty published in what was then SLA's peer reviewed journal, *Special Libraries*.

In1981 SLA's Research Committee had voted to dissolve itself (Tees, 1989). It was not until 5 years later, as a result of a renewed interest in research, that SLA appointed a Special Committee on Research which recommended forming a standing committee as well as hiring an association staff member to support the work of the committee. By 1989, SLA had the Research Committee, a staff member, a research agenda, and funds for research. Of this renewed commitment, Drake (1989) stated, "SLA has made a solid commitment to research" (p. 268) That very same year though, Tees, a past president of SLA, noted that the Association's "commitment to research has been at best, uneven" (p. 302). Matarazzo (1981) also warned "this heightened activity around and the desire for research may pass as quickly as it reappeared" (p. 317).

## B. Research Supported by SLA Since 1990

The authors reviewed SLA's research publications since 1990 guided by the following three questions:

1. What impact on SLA funded research did the growing focus on evidence based research have?
2. Did SLA's renewed commitment to research, as evidenced by increased funding awarded during this period, result in research that was useful to corporate librarians?
3. Who was involved in the research projects funded by SLA (e.g., Library School faculty and/or practitioners)?

## 1. Focus on Funding and Sponsoring Evidence Based Research

Matarazzo (1981) found that SLA's commitment to research seemed cyclical in nature. Celebrating its 10th anniversary as the group charged with "developing the research agenda for action by the Board of Directors," the Association's Research Committee in 1989 called for a revised research agenda. In 1999/2000, the Committee again sought to revise the research agenda by acknowledging that evidence based practice had to become an integral part of the research program if it was to continue to meet the needs of the membership. Before 2000, the Committee had awarded a number of grants to fund research it believed was relevant to the membership. Why the Committee felt that funding research focused on "evidence based practice" is a topic for a different review. The impact this change of focus had on grant applications and research produced is relevant for the purposes of this chapter.

In the new research guidelines accepted by the Board of Directors in 2001, "evidence based practice" in the context of special libraries was defined as follows:

For special librarians, evidence-based practice refers to consciously and consistently making professional-level decisions that are based on the strongest evidence of what would work best for our clients. The areas in which decisions are made in library and information practice are cited in our SLA competencies document: selection and acquisition of information resources; methods of information access; selection and use of information technologies; and management of library and information services. (Putting Our Knowledge to Work, 2001)

Research products resulting from this new agenda were to be directly related to the pragmatic needs of the membership, including corporate library managers.

As Fig. 1 illustrates, putting this evidence based research agenda into practice has been a challenge. From 1994 to 2000, prior to the evidence based research agenda, the Committee received between 7 and 20 grant applications each year for a maximum award of $20,000 during any given year and for no more than two projects and usually only one award each year. From 2001 until 2006 (when SLA ran out of research grant funds) applications dropped dramatically, never equaling that of the previous six years. Between 2004 and 2006, less than five applications were received annually and no awards were made. The body of literature to review since the implementation of the evidence based practice agenda is slim to non-existent (SLA Primary Source Documents, 1993–2007).

In 1991, the Steven I. Goldspiel Memorial Research Fund was established and named in honor of the former President of Disclosure, Inc. In 1995, it

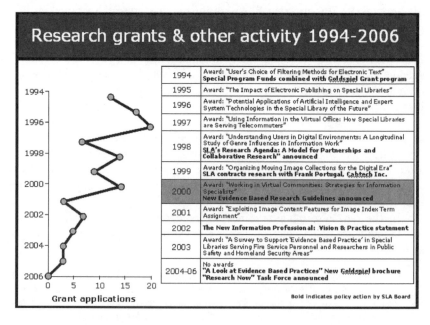

Fig. 1   Research grants and other activity 1994—2006.

was combined with the Association's Special Program Grant Fund to become the major vehicle for providing grants to support research (SLA Primary Source Documents, 1993–2007). Three Goldspiel Grant funded projects since 2000 led to publications covering topics such as organizing digital image collections (Turner *et al.*, 2002), changes in the profession (Barreau, 2003); and applications of evidence-based practice (Smith and Ruan, 2004).

## 2. Disseminating Research

In spite of the decreased amount of funding and published research, SLA continues its efforts to serve the research needs of its members by linking them to research produced elsewhere and by encouraging members to participate in research efforts that will result in information of interest to the professional community. The SLA web site (http://www.sla.org) links Association members to a significant amount of research that has been accomplished either with its support or in which SLA has encouraged its members to participate. These are reviewed below.

*Competencies for Special Librarians of the 21st Century, Library and Information Studies Program Survey, Final Report (Special Libraries Association, 1998).* This survey, done in conjunction with the Medical Library Association (MLA) and the Association for Library and Information Science Education (ALISE), sought to identify curricula in library science programs that "relate to the development of knowledge, understanding, and skills of special librarians and information professionals" (p. 5). The object was to identify needs that could be satisfied through continued education (CE) programs offered by these participating associations. The results from this type of survey could help corporate library managers to better understand the skills and competencies of their potential employees as well as how to continue professional development of their existing employees.

*Information Services Panel Surveys (Phase V Consulting Group Inc., 2000).* This series of surveys aimed to gather statistics relevant to the Association's members, including

> Financial and operating benchmark data, with comparative measures by size, sector, and topical focus;
> Technology environment and trends;
> Internet usage;
> Roles and responsibilities; and
> Usage of products, services, and formats.

The summary of the 2000 Survey contains a variety of statistics and trends useful to corporate library managers, both for strategic planning and in an operational context. For example, 3 years of data on what search engines are being used most frequently are helpful in conducting environmental scans for benchmarking.

Corporate librarians need information for purposes of strategic planning. Although they might not seek such data through formally conducted research, they turn to applied research that presents this type of comparative information. For example, Portugal (2000), created a "workbook" rather than a research product, although it draws on data from interviews with representatives from 125 corporations and organizations. As Portugal notes "this workbook presents four different approaches to the intangible valuation of information resources" (p. ix) by which corporate library managers could measure their organizational contribution. Unfortunately Portugal confirms what other authors reviewed here found; all but two of those interviewed did not conduct valuations of their libraries and information centers. Nonetheless, the four methods he outlines (Return on Investment and Cost Benefit Analysis, Knowledge Value-Added, Intranet Team Forums, and Intellectual Capital Valuations) offer corporate library managers some very pragmatic language to use in thinking about ways to highlight the value of their services in very practical terms.

Coverage of this type of benchmarking data also can be found in the results of a partnership that SLA has formed with Outsell, Inc. Several reports highlighted below have either been prepared in conjunction with SLA or made available to SLA members through special arrangement with Outsell, Inc. These compile survey data that are useful to corporate library managers.

*Information Management Best Practices: 2006 State of the Function* (Outsell, Inc., 2006)

*Information Management Best Practices*: Fortunes Up For Information Management Functions 2005—And With Fortune Comes Accountability (Outsell, Inc., 2005a)

*Information Management Best Practices: Vendor Portfolio Management Rationalizing Content For The Enterprise*: 2004 (Outsell, Inc., 2005b)

*Changing Roles of Content Management Functions*: 2004 (Outsell, Inc., 2004a)

*Trend Alert: The Future of Libraries*: Outsell's InfoAboutInfo Briefing (Outsell, Inc., 2004b)

*Changing Role of the Information Professional*: 2003 Outsell Survey

Compilations of practical information on timely topics are also found recently in a series of 10 Information Portals which the Association has begun to package through links to content at http://www.sla.org (Special Libraries Association Electronic Resources, 2008). Not all the material compiled in these portals has been published in *Information Outlook*, the Association's monthly magazine, nor have all received funding or other support from SLA. Even if not all of the resources assembled (e.g. product reviews, case studies, web sites, monographs, etc.) could be technically defined as evidence based or empirical research, this portal approach is another avenue to meet the pragmatic needs of corporate library managers seeking precedent, creative thinking, and best demonstrated practices to help them answer their management challenges.

The authors found that the mixture of sources covered in any one of these portals appears to be truly international and very timely. Using the LIS Research portal (2008) as an example, articles cited are from a variety of journals, including *Library and Information Science Research, Evidence Based Library and Information Practice, Library Hi-Tech, Journal of Information Science, Journal of the American Society for Information Science and Technology, Health Information and Libraries Journal, Law Library Journal, Journal of the Medical Library Association, Library Review, Library Management*, and *The Library Quarterly*. This suggests that there may be a fair amount of research activity of potential interest to corporate library managers that is not being sponsored or produced by SLA itself and may not be focused on the management of corporate libraries. Given that most corporate library managers would not subscribe to more than one or two of these titles, if any, this compilation by SLA becomes even more valuable.

Another SLA Information Portal, Management/Services—Outsourcing and Offshoring (2008a), offers an equally broad mix of sources. For example, its coverage includes *Fast Company, Library & Information Update, TechWeb, Money, Corporate Library Update, Library Journal, Wall Street Journal, Information Management Journal, MIT Sloan Management Review*, and *CIO.com*. All of the content compiled in this portal could be characterized as offering ideas or concepts possibly useful to corporate library managers facing managerial questions.

For more information on other Information Portals compiled by SLA the reader is referred to http://www.sla.org/content/resources/infoportals/index.cfm.

## 3. Do Corporate Librarians Either Produce or Use This Research?

This review of the literature concludes a partial answer to this question. The literature reinforces the conclusion that corporate library managers continue to need and seek pragmatic research to apply in their day-to-day activities, but that "not much" of this type of research is being produced through their primary professional association.

Dimitroff (1995) attempted to find out if practicing special librarians conducted research and what interest they had in activities related to research.

She reviewed research activity as reflected in the journal literature for special libraries, defined broadly to include law, medical as well as corporate. Of the 279 articles she found for the years 1993–1994, only 53 were reports of research; and academic health librarians wrote over half of these, likely the result of requirements for promotion and tenure. This study found only two research articles written by corporate librarians and six research articles written by LIS Faculty. Dimitroff characterized this small amount of research as "most startling" and observed that it showed no relation between research and what corporate librarians do every day (p. 263). Lack of time and lack of support from their management were the two most frequently cited reasons for not conducting research. Dimitroff further noted that while associations have tried to help with some funding, calls upon individual librarians to conduct and publish research have not been overly successful. It is not surprising, then, that corporate librarians face an enormous challenge to developing a culture of research from such a small base.

Powell *et al.* (2002) found that better than two-thirds of SLA members did not conduct or publish research. In a survey of 1400 members of various professional associations, Powell and his coauthors found that only about one-third of SLA members responded that they had time for research and only 20% of those thought some employer support for research was available. Further, only 13% felt there was external support for research. When asked if they applied research results to practice, only 11% said they did, while 49% said never or seldom. Powell and his coauthor's findings confirm the point made at the beginning of SLA's current Research Statement (2001) that the connection between library and information science research and the day to day problems faced by corporate librarians has not been made in the past.

*Special Libraries* was replaced by *Information Outlook* in 1997. The new publication has color, combines news and several topical columns, and has a few short feature articles in each issue. It is not intended to carry research articles and might not carry the same weight as a referred journal like *Special Libraries* when brought to a university promotion and tenure committee. This does not necessarily diminish the usefulness to corporate library practitioners of articles published there, albeit that usefulness might be at a less granular level than a full research study would offer. So we might conclude that a journal like *Special Libraries* was equally important to practitioners who want to read about research at a deeper level and possibly apply it to practice.

Even when a journal similar to *Special Libraries* is taken into account, though, it is still not clear that corporate library managers are taking advantage of the research found there. Edgar (2004) examined the topic of the impact of a corporate library on its parent organization. He presented the theoretical framework in an article in the journal's print version, and followed with a second article in the electronic version of the same publication where he provided the methodologies that could be used to measure impact. Only two articles have cited Edgar's work in the past three years and neither was written by or for corporate librarians or corporate libraries. If others put Edgar's articles into practice, they have not published their experiences.

That corporate librarians are still struggling with defining what type of research will be most useful to them is evident in two recent efforts by SLA to further define relevant research topics and activities as well as to provide funding for undertaking them: the SLA Research Now Taskforce (2005–2006) and the most recently revised Research Grant Guidelines (August 2007).

The Taskforce set out to accomplish two objectives:

1.  Define subjects for research that will best serve SLA's strategic plan by demonstrating the information professional's value to the organization and
2.  Take one or more of these topics and conduct a research study with results available for the June 2006 conference (Executive Summary Document A06-48 May 2006).

Toward these ends, the Task Force conducted an exploratory research project focused on stakeholders and their perceived value of the information professional and the role of personal networking. The findings of this project suggested the following:

- Timeliness and the ability to locate information are the service attributes that matter most to stakeholders.
- Stakeholders believe the major purpose of the information professional is to provide critical information that helps in making business decisions or solving business problems.
- Conducting research and knowing where to find information are the information services that are most valued.
- Information services save time and money, and allow other staff to be more productive.
- The knowledge and skills for which information professionals are most valued are their expertise in accessing and retrieving reliable information and for their strategic awareness/knowledge of issues of interest to the company/organization.
- Proactive networking by information professionals with other staff helps to further the goals of their organization.
- Stakeholders value librarians who keep knowledgeable of current issues/projects so they are ready to provide information and resources to support their work (Research Now Task Force, Executive Summary 2006).

In its summary report, the Research Now Task Force (2006) expressed some of the same "lessons learned" that have been discussed elsewhere: the difficulties of conducting under-funded research, the challenges of addressing the needs of a broad segment of the special libraries population, and the challenge of getting volunteers to take the time needed to engage with the research. In fact, a review of the Task Force recommendations, offers insights on the relatively recent appearance of Information Portals on the SLA web site as well as the ongoing focus on finding and disseminating relevant research produced beyond the Association sponsorship. The report highlights the following insights:

- Continue to focus research on the value of the information professional to the organization.
- Utilize other related research results conducted by other organizations such as OCLC's (Online Computer Library Center) *Perceptions of Libraries and Information Resources* and Bersin & Associates' research study of the amount of time executives spend searching for information.
- Provide time slots at the annual conference for presenting research results of interest to the entire membership (Research Now Task Force, 2006).

The Task Force even recommended that this might be accomplished by partnering with other library or information professional associations and/or research companies or by providing funding for research by one of three possible means: SLA funded, SLA partnering with other professional associations or non-profit organizations, or SLA negotiating funding support from one or more information related companies.

Within a year of the report of the SLA Research Now Task Force (May 2006), the Association announced new Research Grant guidelines (August 2007) that begin to provide at least some structure of support for research. Two types of grants were offered; one focused on evidenced based practice as outlined in the Research Agenda with awards up to $25,000 and another for projects which directly benefit the operations of SLA and its units by furthering scientific, literary and educational purposes for which the association is organized and operated with awards up to $10,000. Two recipients were chosen in December 2007; "Impulse for Growth! Laying foundations for SLA membership acquisition and growth in Germany for 2008," Michael Fanning ($10,000) and "Models of Embedded Librarianship: A Research Proposal," David Shumaker and Mary Talley ($25,000).

Other funding sources are also attempting to fill some of the gap for research support in this area. There is some overlap between American Library Association (ALA) and SLA in intent, if not practice, especially in the form of ALA's RUSA (Reference and User Service Association) and BRASS (Business Reference and Services Section) groups. For example, in October of 2007 Emerald Group Publishing disseminated an email message throughout ALA which was subsequently also sent to the SLA Business & Finance listserv via a member who belonged both to SLA and BRASS. The "call for grant applications" encouraged readers who had a "business information research idea" and needed financial help to carry it through, to apply for an

Emerald Publishing Group $5000 grant award (Pearlstein, 2007). This effort by a private publisher to encourage research that would be of interest to corporate library managers is one example of other efforts than SLA-sponsorship that are available.

While Drake (1989) made a cogent case for research and its relationship to practice, those in practice do not appear to have been convinced. Perhaps the source of the intermittent quality and lack of pragmatism in SLA's research program to date is in part the responsibility of the membership. Their apparent lack of interest in research and in producing or using research seems clear, at least in North America. In a review of publications in Australia, New Zealand, and the United Kingdom, however, the authors found a somewhat more robust body of research publications.

## III. Australia, New Zealand, and the United Kingdom

Research and publication on corporate libraries in these three countries is frequent and very well executed. While there are more corporate libraries in North America, there appears to be more literature on the subject of corporate libraries in these countries. One reason for this might be that company librarians in Australia, New Zealand, and the United Kingdom (UK) tend to belong to their national library associations which actively encourage research relevant to them and provide adequate resources and interest for this research on par with that for other types of libraries. It is our contention that the opposite seems to be true in North America, with company librarians more likely to be members of smaller organizations (e.g., Special Libraries Association, Medical Library Association, American Association of Law Librarians, etc.) with more narrowly focused interests and correspondingly less interest or resources to fund research.

Not only is research on corporate libraries being actively supported in these countries, it is focusing on those topics that seem directly relevant to corporate library managers. Special librarians in a corporate setting tend to be more pragmatic than their academic or public counterparts when it comes to the type of research findings they need to support them in demonstrating their value to their parent organization. A review of research activities in these countries illustrates this difference.

### A. Measuring "Value" in Australia

Greenshields (1997) reports that in the 1990s the Australian Library and Information Association (ALIA) concluded that the major threat to corporate business libraries was the lack of knowledge about the contributions these libraries made toward corporate goals. As such, ALIA was going to embark on an explanatory study to determine the perceived value of librarians and libraries in Australia's top 100 companies. This research was proposed to add an Australian perspective to studies completed a few years before in the US. The American studies had shown that it was necessary to demonstrate the value of the librarian and the services provided. The Australian study was begun to counter a perceived lack of empirical data on value as measured by the opinions of senior managers at 100 companies. The results would not only be of value to managers of company libraries, but also to library education programs seeking to prepare graduates to work in the corporate sector.

The next year, Walsh (1998) reported most Australian company libraries judged measuring number of requests as a measure of value. Other survey results mirrored a set of earlier research reports conducted in the US. It is interesting to note, however, that 25% of the Australian respondents felt that library resources did not meet the needs of users. A much longer report of the same survey results by Walsh and Greenshields (1998) appeared in *Australian Special Libraries*.

McCallum and Quinn (2004) presented an overview of research reports on the economic value of libraries. While their review addressed the value of both public and special libraries it also discussed reports from the US, Canada and Australia on public libraries and the US and Australia for special libraries. The authors argue that public and special libraries are difficult for financial managers to understand, while users were seen to appreciate the services provided. Since special libraries have to demonstrate value, they found that research that has been completed, shared, and replicated would enable Australian libraries to state objectively their economic value.

That same year, Leavitt (2004) noted in an editorial that one of the hallmarks of a profession is genuine research that underpins both theory and practice. He went on to lament the lack of published research from the many master's and doctoral degree recipients in library and information science. In fact Leavitt speculated that "those who complete these research reports are so burnt out by their projects, they each lack energy or interest to publish the results and share their work with the profession at large (p. 95)".

Missingham (2005) undertook a review of the past decade of research on the value of library services in a variety of settings. She reviewed research in Australia, as well as the US, UK, Canada, and New Zealand and found that demonstrating the value of library and information services had been a theme of library research in these countries for decades. In discussing value, she identified three waves of activity: (1) Efficiency or output oriented studies aimed at proving that libraries are operating efficiently. (2) Studies of financial return to the organization equated the success of the library with the organization's financial success. These studies involved using techniques which allowed the customer to place a monetary value on the service. Missingham found, however, that these studies "did not seem to fully convince managers ... (p. 144). (3) Studies seek to value libraries by establishing their value to managers through data collected on the number of requests, time and money saved, and value added services provided. The reader is referred to Missingham's original review for a more in depth look at these three waves of research activity.

## B. New Zealand

The New Zealand Library and Information Association (LIANZA) has taken a different approach to supporting research on corporate libraries. In 1998, LIANZA engaged Coopers and Lybrand to conduct a study of the library at the New Zealand Dairy Board. At the time, this library had a budget of $300,000 and 3.75 staff members. To accomplish this study, Coopers and Lybrand charged a discounted rate of $21,000 ($19,000 was contributed from the New Zealand Dairy Board and $2,000 from LIANZA). Had it not been discounted, the cost of the study would likely have been closer to $28,000 (LIANZA, 1998). The report states that the study required 146 hours of an analyst's time, 30 hours of supervision and 69 hours of the library manager's time. The end result was a short report which estimates a return on assets of 13% but projected this likely is higher, in the range of 19–20% since some services could not be assigned a value. The report suggested that the New Zealand Dairy Board spend $28,000 annually to continue the study.

In 1997, LIANZA worked with PricewaterhouseCoopers International Limited on a "value added library methodology" (LIANZA, 1999) for the Parliamentary Library. This methodology calculates the return on investment in terms of the value libraries add to information. It measures library usage, services and resources using a top-down and bottom-up approach. The "top-down" approach measures the value of information in the context of what a buyer would pay for it, the time saved by using the library, and the cost of replacing the library and its services, if they did not already exist. This result is compared to the "bottom-up" approach which compares the library to other businesses in order to calculate the return on investment in the library's assets.

This research was completed at a reduced cost of $15,000. The market rate would have been about $32,000 (150 hours of analyst's time, 34 of a supervisor's time and 23–90 hours of library staff time). The report concluded that library services were valued at 2–20 times budget and showed a net benefit for all services provided of 9.8% and 16.4% regardless of how measured.


## C. United Kingdom

Whitehall (1995) provides a review of the literature on measuring value in library and information management in all types of libraries—with a majority in corporate settings—in the UK. This review was completed to provide evidence for libraries to use when they face the harsh reality of the allocation of resources at any organization. It includes a discussion of use, value addition, how to measure the value of information, value of service and many more topics with an extensive bibliography. "The consequence of our focusing on the cost of providing services without being able to demonstrate their value and quality is that we leave the initiative to people whose chief concern is cost control or profit" (p. 10).

Marshall (1993) published an excellent study of libraries in the financial sector in Canada and their contribution to these types of firms. This study was replicated in the UK by the Strathclyde Graduate Business School in the area of retail banking and four other types of organizations and pulled information from all five sectors into one article (Grieves, 1998). The conclusions from all five studies place a high value on information especially as used for better decision making. Differences between the UK studies and the Marshall study were pointed out as were the differences between the other sectors studied. The author warns that these were short-term studies with small samples but nevertheless could give useful insights.

Another study by the staff at the Strathclyde Graduate Business School (Reid et al., 1998) takes an in depth look at the role and value of information in the decision making process and the impact of the corporate library in the UK banking sector. Managers in the banks studied the evaluation and on the whole agreed that information affected how decisions were made. The information they reviewed came not from the company library but from other sources. In those banks with libraries, information was seen to be used in decision making. In fact 79% of the corporate mangers said their libraries "saved them considerable time" (p. 97). The Strathclyde Study warned that libraries need to be proactive about promoting the existence of their services and the kinds of information they can provide. Also of note is the caution that corporate librarians must be familiar with the business of which they are a part. Libraries, they wrote, also need to analyze information for value and relevance to the organization.

Measuring value perceived and received by actual users is challenging. Libraries have non-users too; however research on non-users has been sparse. Brick's (1999) research used a combination of questionnaires and interviews with a small sample of 12 corporate managers which was geographically limited to greater London (p. 15). She found corporate managers were not high users of corporate libraries except in the area of business consulting. Lack of awareness of the library's services was most often given as the reason for non-use. In reviewing older studies, she states that the library level of non-use remains about the same as do the reasons. She reports that 70% of corporate library managers interviewed have not tried to solve the problem of non-use (p. 203).

Foster & Foster (2003) published the 13th survey on *Business Information Resources*. Sixty-two percent of respondents were from financial, legal, property, and consulting firm libraries, making up the largest number of all respondents in the corporate sector. Company library respondents overall stated they were "adding more value and providing more in depth analysis" (p. 22). They appear to be focused on providing a high quality product, improving competitor intelligence and the overall quality of services. These libraries were also adding electronic access to annual reports and journals. In general the survey revealed company libraries were seeking greater recognition of their services, promoting the value of information, developing a knowledge management policy, and wanted a greater role in business development, while also coping with change. The 2003 survey also revealed more work on portals, containing costs and increasing the number of staff to cope with heavy workloads. Respondents were also facing end user training issues to help some employees do more research for themselves.

Broady-Preston and Williams (2004) conducted a series of interviews with a range of small to large law firm libraries to establish how they use information to create value. The respondents all felt that information is perceived to be a valuable asset in law firms. It was, however, difficult to offer any quantitative measure of demonstrating value. The authors assert that "Law is an intensive profession in which there has traditionally been a great reliance on external information" (p. 9). Those interviewed saw information services as adding value to the business, improving service delivery and customer service.

*Library Management* (2007) began a new column, "Theory, Research, and Practice in Library Management." The column will select key management subjects and examine the topic from the viewpoints of theory, research, and practice. The plan is to discuss management issues by moving to an evidence-based model which coincides with a movement to evidence-based library practice. This follows a similar trend toward evidence based research adopted by SLA in 2001; a trend which unfortunately does not seem to have resulted in an increase of pragmatic, sharable, repeatable research projects for the benefit of corporate libraries.

## IV. Conclusion

This chapter on the impact of research funding and support for corporate library management, intends to raise interest on the part of both LIS faculty and corporate library managers to look for ways to address the questions posed at its outset:

- How or if research on the subject of managing corporate libraries was encouraged and funded and by whom? Various attempts to fund such research were made by the SLA, but were not sustained over time. Colleagues in other English speaking countries (Australia, New Zealand, and UK) appear to have more support by national associations to conduct such research.
- What type of research would be most useful for corporate library managers? Research falls into two categories for corporate library managers. Theoretical research about the activities involving corporate libraries is of little interest, except for the emergence of evidence-based research related to decision making. Pragmatic, problem-solving research results or more simply, data gathered for a purpose such as strategic planning and corporate advocacy, are welcomed by practitioners in the corporate library sector.
- How research results are disseminated and whether the results had been put to use by practitioners? SLA previously published research in its peer-reviewed journal, but over time this practice was replaced by maintenance of online portals where links are offered to potentially relevant reports and to articles published in a range of other professional publications. Given limited resources for corporate librarians to purchase publications for internal applications, this referral role shows signs of being helpful to the SLA membership. In other countries, there may be a more active culture of producing and utilizing research than is found in the US among corporate libraries.

There is no question that professional associations, especially those in the US, UK, Australia, and New Zealand have a role to play to engage in research about and for corporate libraries on several levels. For example, associations could conduct the following activities: advocate a research agenda that is practical and of interest to their membership; provide sufficient funding to fully support research so that LIS faculty are attracted to participate; provide channels for distribution of research results that serve the needs of both faculty and practitioners; and investigate further ways to provide guidance to corporate librarians in how they can contribute to a shared knowledge base without compromising their organization's confidentiality or other proprietary requirements.

Leavitt (2004) maintains that one of the hallmarks of maturity in any profession is research and its contributions to theory and practice.

Practitioners do not appear to be convinced, however, of the relationship between research and practice. Perhaps that is the problem corporate library managers are really facing: that the profession has not yet reached maturity.

## References

Barreau, D. C. (2003). *The New Information Professional: Vision and Practice.* Research funded by the Special Libraries Association, Stephen I. Goldspiel Memorial Research Grant, August 7, Final Report. Special Libraries Association, Washington, DC.

Brick, L. (1999). Non-use of business libraries and information services: A study of the library and information managers' perception, experience and reaction to non-use. *Aslib Proceedings* 51, 195–205.

Broady-Preston, J., and Williams, T. (2004). Using information to create business value: City of London legal firms, a case study. *Performance Measurement and Metrics* 5, 5–10.

Dimitroff, A. (1995). Research for special libraries: A quantitative analysis of the literature. *Special Libraries* 86, 256–264.

Drake, M. A. (1989). Research and special libraries. *Special Libraries* 80, 264–268.

Edgar, W. (2004). Corporate library impact, Part I: A theoretical approach. *The Library Quarterly* 74, 122–151.

Foster, A., and Foster, P. (2003). Empowering the end-user: Business information resources survey, 2003. *Business Information Review* 20, 5–24.

Genoni, P., Haddow, G., and Ritchie, A. (2004). Why don't librarians use research? In *Evidence-Based Practice for Information Professionals* (A. Booth and A. Brice, eds.), pp. 49–60. Facet Publishing, London.

Greenshields, S. (1997). The value of corporate libraries. *Australian Special Libraries* 30, 55–56.

Grieves, M. (1998). The impact of information use on decision making: Studies in five sectors-introduction, summary and conclusions. *Library Management* 19, 78–85.

Kantor, P. B., and Saracevic, T. (1995). *Valuing Special Libraries and Information Services.* Special Libraries Association, Washington, DC.

Koufogiannakis, D., and Crumley, E. (2006). Research in librarianship: Issues to consider. *Library Hi Tech* 24, 324–340.

Leavitt, J. (2004). The nature, utility and essential unknowability of research in our disciplines: An editor's view. *Australian Library Journal* 51, 95–97.

LIANZA (1998). *Executive Summary of the N Strategy Methodology.* Library and Information Association of New Zealand, Wellington.

LIANZA (1999). *Parliament library V+LM Trial.* Library and Information Association of New Zealand, Wellington.

*Library Management* (2007). Theory, research and practice in library management: New column. *Library Management* 28, 63–164.

Marshall, J. G. (1993). *The Impact of the Special Library on Corporate Decision Making.* Special Libraries Association, Washington, DC.

Matarazzo, J. M. (1981). Research needs and issues in special librarianship. In *Library and Foundation Science Research: Perspective and Strategies for Improvement* (C. R. McClure and P. Hernon, eds.), Ablex.

McCallum, I., and Quinn, S. (2004). Valuing libraries. *Australian Library Journal* 53, 27–31.

Missingham, R. (2005). Libraries and economic value: A review of recent studies. *Performance Measurement and Metrics* 6, 142–158.

Outsell, Inc. (2004a). *Changing Roles of Content Management Functions, Executive Summary.* http://www.sla.org/pdfs/2006OutsellIMFunctionExecSumm.pdf, March 5, 2008.

Outsell, Inc. (2004b). *Trend Alert: The Future of Libraries: InfoAboutInfo Briefing.* http://www.sla.org/pdfs/2006OutsellIMFunctionExecSumm.pdf, March 5, 2008.

Outsell, Inc. (2005a). *Information Management Best Practices: Fortunes Up for Information Management Functions 2005-and With Fortune Comes Accountability.* http://www.sla.org/content/resources/research/researchlinks/isp99.cfm, March 5, 2008.

Outsell, Inc. (2005b). *Information Management Best Practices: Vendor Portfolio Management Rationalizing Content for the Enterprise.* http://www.sla.org/pdfs/2006OutsellIMFunctionExecSumm.pdf, March 5, 2008.

Outsell, Inc. (2006). *Information Management Best Practices: 2006 State of the Function, Executive Summary.* https://www.sla.org/content/resources/recindreps/imbp2006/index.cfm, March 5, 2008.

Pearlstein, T. (2007). *Personal email correspondence: SLA Business and Finance Division Listserv,* October 10.

Phase V Consulting Group Inc. (2000). *State of the Market 2000, Results from the Information Services Panel Survey.* Readers may link to summary results of this survey at http://www.sla.org/content/resources/research/researchlinks/isp99.cfm, March 5, 2008.

Portugal, F. H. (2000). *Valuating Information Intangibles: Measuring the Bottom Line Contribution of Librarians and Information Professionals.* SLA, Washington, DC.

Powell, R. R., Baker, L. M., and Mika, J. J. (2002). Library and information science practitioners and research. *Library and Information Science Research* 24, 49–72.

Reid, C., Thomson, J., and Wallace-Smith, J. (1998). Impact of information corporate decision making: The UK banking sector. *Library Management* 19, 86–109.

Smith, L. C., & Ruan, L. (2004). *A survey to support 'evidence-based practice' in special libraries serving fire service personnel and researchers in public safety and homeland security areas, funded by 2003 SLA Steven I. Goldspiel Memorial Research Grant,* Special Libraries Association, Alexandria, VA with Additional support funded by the 2004 Campus Research Board Award, University of Illinois at Urbana-Champaign, Champaign, IL.

Special Libraries Association (SLA) (2001). *Putting Our Knowledge to Work: A New SLA Research Statement, 2001.* The Role of Research in Special Librarianship, http://www.sla.org/content/resources/research/rsrchstatement.cfm, March 5, 2008.

Special Libraries Association, association for library and information science education, and medical library association (1998). *Competencies for Special Librarians of the 21st Century, Library and Information Studies Program Survey, Final Report.* Special Libraries Association, Washington, DC.

Special Libraries Association (SLA) – LIS Research Portal. (2008). http://www.sla.org/content/resources/infoportals/research.cfm

Special Libraries Association Management/Services Outsourcing and Offshoring Portal. (2008a). http://www.sla.org/content/resources/infoportals/contract.cfm

Special Libraries Association (1993–2007). Primary Source Documents Collection.
Battaglia, R. D. (1993) to Associate Executive Director, SLA. Original letter re: Steven I. Goldspiel Memorial Research Grant, June 6.
Latham, J. R. (2004). List of Grants awarded from 1991–2004, April 16.
Research Committee, Special Libraries Association (April 29, 1994, May 3, 1995, May 9, 1996, May 1, 1997, April 29, 1998, May 2, 1999, May 8, 2000, May 6, 2001, May 3, 2002, 2002/2003 (undated), 2003/2004 (undated), May 5, 2005, May 4, 2006). Annual Reports to the Board of Directors.
Research Committee, Special Libraries Association (2005). Meeting Minutes, June 6.
Research Committee/Endowment Grants Committee, Special Libraries Association (2006). Coordination meeting minutes, Houston, TX, January 20.
Research Now Task Force, Special Libraries Association (2006). Recommendations, Executive Summary Document A06-48, May 8.
Special Libraries Association (1989). Research Agenda Document A89-72.
Special Libraries Association (2007). Research Grant Guidelines.

Tees, M. H. (1989). Faculty involvement in the Special Libraries Association. *Journal of Education for Library and Information Science* 29, 297–304.
Turner, J. M., Hudon, M., and Devon, Y. (2002). Organizing moving image collections for the digital era: Research results. Research report from the project of the same name funded by the Special Libraries Association under the Steven I. Goldspiel Memorial Grant for 1999. *Information Outlook*, August 2002, 14–25
Walsh, V. (1998). ALIA explores the value of corporate libraries. *InCite* 19, 6–7.
Walsh, V., and Greenshields, S. (1998). The value of libraries and library professionals to Australia's top 100 companies: Draft report of the study conducted by the Australian Library and Information Association. *Australian Library Journal* 31, 59–101.
Whitehall, T. (1995). Value in library and information management: A review. *Library Management* 16, 3–11.

## Further Reading

Special Libraries Association electronic resources. http://www.sla.org, March 2, 2008
*Information Center's Resources Web Site* is a clearing house for all information resources available to SLA members, through SLA's own library, http://www.sla.org/content/resources/inforesour/index.cfm, March 2, 2008.
*Information Portals Web Site* links to articles, Web sites, books and other resources on 40+ topics including corporate and other special library management, http://www.sla.org/content/resources/infoportals/index.cfm, March 2, 2008.

*Recent Industry Reports Web Site* contains reports on information industry issues http://www.sla.org/content/resources/recindreps/index.cfm, March 2, 2008.

*Research Grants Web Site* provides background and additional information on SLA's grants process, http://www.sla.org/content/learn/scholarship/researchgrant/index.cfm, March 2, 2008.

*Research and Surveys Web Site* for assistance with benchmarking and strategic planning http://www.sla.org/content/resources/research/index.cfm, March 2, 2008.

Resources Web Site. Provides access for SLA members to both SLA sponsored and SLA recommended information and research covering management and other topics, http://www.sla.org/content/resources/index.cfm, March 2, 2008.

# Alternative Funding for Public Libraries: Trends, Sources, and the Heated Arguments that Surround It

Denise E. Agosto

College of Information Science and Technology, Drexel University,
Philadelphia, PA, USA

## Abstract

In response to recent public library funding deficiencies, many people both inside and outside
the field of librarianship have suggested that public libraries need to rely less on traditional
government funding and more on alternative funding sources. This chapter reports the results
of a review of the research and professional literature relating to government and alternative
funding for US public libraries and presents a case study of the West Chester (PA) Public
Library, which relies heavily on non-tax funds for its operations. It concludes with an analysis of
the major arguments for and against alternative funding for public libraries and a consideration
of the implications for public librarianship in the United States.

## I. Introduction and Research Questions

In response to recent public library funding shortages, many US public
libraries are turning toward non-tax revenue sources, or "alternative funding,"
to support their programs and services. Although there has been an ongoing
debate in the professional library literature over the merits of alternative
funding for public libraries, little research has been conducted in this area.
This chapter will address three research questions related to alternative
funding for US public libraries:

1. What types of tax-based and non-tax-based funding are available to US public libraries?
2. From what sources do libraries solicit funds, and how do they use them?
3. What are the major arguments for and against alternative funding for public libraries?

INFLUENCE OF FUNDING ON ADVANCES IN LIBRARIANSHIP
ADVANCES IN LIBRARIANSHIP, VOL. 31
© 2008 by Emerald Group Publishing Limited
ISSN: 0065-2830
DOI: 10.1016/S0065-2830(08)31004-6

## II. Methods

This study combined a detailed review of the published literature with an organizational case study (Gorman and Clayton, 2005) of one purposively selected public library. The literature review provided a broad picture of the US tax-based public library funding system and of the various extant forms of alternative funding for public libraries. It focused on literature published in the United States between 1997 and 2007. Items addressing public library funding were gathered for review via systematic searches of *Library Literature & Information Science Full Text* (http://www.hwwilson.com/Databases/liblit. htm), *LISA: Library and Information Science Abstracts* (http://www.csa.com/ factsheets/lisa-set-c.php), the *Web of Science* (http://scientific.thomson.com/ products/wos/), the National Center for Education Statistics web site (http:// nces.ed.gov/), and the Institute for Museum and Library Services (IMLS) web site (http://www.imls.gov/).

While the literature review served to paint a broad picture of the alternative funding scene, it did not provide a clear picture of how public libraries actually use multiple types of alternative funds. An organizational case study was selected in order to provide an in-depth view of alternative funding at one particular institution. The "concept of a case study comes from the practice of law, in which the unit of analysis is a single case before a court ... Often a case study recounts a rare or unusual condition or event, but it may also be a description of a classic situation that can be used as a model or exemplar" (Zach, 2006, p. 4). The West Chester Public Library, located in West Chester, Pennsylvania, was selected for the study due to its heavy reliance on multiple alternative funding sources. Data collection and analysis included content analysis of library newsletters and of the library's web site, combined with an in-depth, semi-structured interview of the library director.

## III. Results: Literature Review

The literature fell into four thematic categories. Three are discussed in the next section: the US public library tax-based funding system, public library funding trends, and sources of available alternative funding. The fourth category is discussed later in the chapter: advantages and disadvantages of alternative funding.

### A. The US Public Library Funding System

The first category corresponds to the first research question ("What types of tax-based and non-tax-based funding are available to US public libraries?")

The items falling into this category described historic and modern tax support for US public libraries. The first tax-supported public library in the United States was begun in Peterborough, New Hampshire, in 1833 (Sessa, 2003, p. 2382). Since then, the traditional source of funding for US public libraries has been federal, state, and local tax funds.

## 1. Federal Funding

At the federal level the Library Service Act, first funded in 1957, originally was intended to fund library services in rural communities in order to bridge service disparities between rural and urban/suburban areas (Sessa, 2003, p. 2390). In 1964, the Library Service Act was expanded and renamed the Library Services and Construction Act. That first year it included $45 million for library services and library construction in all US areas, rural or not.

After more than 30 years of federal library funding focusing largely on construction projects, the Library Services and Technology Act (LSTA) replaced the Library Services and Construction Act in 1996. LSTA is overseen and administered by the IMLS. The mission of IMLS is "to create strong libraries and museums that connect people to information and ideas" (http://www.imls.gov/about/about.shtm), and the agency itself is authorized by the federal Museum and Library Services Act.

Each of the 50 states has a state library agency that distributes federal library funds received from IMLS. When proposed, the fiscal year 2008 funding bill included $253,517,000 for IMLS, a significant increase over the previous year. It included "$167.5 million for the State Programs, $3.638 million for Native Americans and Hawaiians, $12.375 million for national leadership grants, $23.76 million for Laura Bush recruitment and education programs and $2 million for research and analysis" (American Library Association, 2007).

LSTA, which is a part of the federal government's Labor, Health, and Human Services and Education funding bill each year, is one of three programs that IMLS oversees. LSTAs competitive grant-funded projects typically involve information technology and other special services and projects. LSTAs goals are:

- To promote improvements in library services in all types of libraries in order to better serve the people of the United States.
- To facilitate access to resources in all types of libraries for the purpose of cultivating an educated and informed citizenry; and
- To encourage resource sharing among all types of libraries for the purpose of achieving economical and efficient delivery of library services to the public. (http://www.imls.gov/about/about.shtm)

As mentioned above, LSTA replaced the Library Services and Construction Act, which had focused more on funding library construction and on library infrastructure improvements than on library technology and on replicable library programs and research projects. As a result, public funding for construction projects and improvements is now harder to obtain, and many libraries are turning to alternative funds for these projects (Buschman, 2005, p. 5).

## 2. State and Local Funding

In comparison to state and local funding, federal funding is a secondary source of support for public libraries. Funding from state and local governments is usually heavily dependent on local property taxes, meaning that the level of funding varies greatly throughout the United States. Looking at state funding for fiscal year 2004, local operating revenue per capita varies from a high $46.35 per capita in Illinois, to a low $9.42 per capita in West Virginia (excluding Hawaii, for which accurate figures are not available) (National Center for Education Statistics, 2007, p. A-11). Within each state there is also variance in local public library funding. This often translates into funding inequities, with libraries in wealthier communities having larger per capita budgets than libraries in poorer communities (Agosto, 2005).

For example, Table 1 compares per capita fiscal year 2005 funding for the Moorestown Library in Moorestown, NJ, to that of the Camden Free Public Library, located just 11 miles away in Camden, NJ. Moorestown is a much wealthier community, with an annual per capita income (in 1999 dollars) of $42,154, as compared to just $9815 per capita for Camden (United States

Table 1
Per Capita Public Library Funding for the Moorestown (NJ) Library and the Camden (NJ) Free Public Library

| Source (per capita) | Moorestown library | Camden free public library |
| --- | --- | --- |
| Local revenue | $84.39 | $13.02 |
| State revenue | $1.11 | $1.33 |
| Federal revenue | $0.00 | $0.30 |
| Other revenue | $3.35 | $0.02 |
| Total revenue | $88.84 | $14.67 |

*Source*: National Center for Education Statistics, 2005, Library Statistics Program: Compare Public Libraries. Available at: http://nces.ed.gov/surveys/libraries/compare/FocusLibrarySearchResult.asp

Census Bureau, 2007). Library funding in these two communities also varies dramatically. The total per capita library revenue for the Moorestown Library is more than six times that of the Camden Free Public Library, due principally to higher local revenue.

Principal funding from state and local governments can also mean that public library funding can become a political issue. New government officials in charge of state, county, or municipal budgets can decide to cut public library funding in order to reduce local taxes or to solve local budget crises. For instance, in response to a protracted budget impasse, California governor Arnold Schwarzenegger cut two major state library programs by $7 million each in a last-minute attempt to reach a zero deficient budget (California's $14-Million Library Budget, 2007, n.p.). The cuts were a complete surprise to the library community and further reduced state library budgets, which had already been slashed from 88 cents to 39 cents per capita by former governor Gray Davis in 2003. It is possible that a future governor might replace the lost funding, but it is equally possible that a future governor might make even more cuts in response to unforeseeable future political and economic conditions.

## B. Government Funding for Public Libraries: Budget Declines or Budget Stabilization?

The second theme within the literature reviewed was the assessment of government funding trends. For California, there is no doubt that this is a period of severe budget constraints. Many libraries across the state have had to cut operating hours and reduce staff, and collections have suffered as well. But at the national level, budgetary trends are less clear-cut, again due to the fact that most public library funding comes from local government sources and is therefore subject to local politics, local trends, and local crises. Within the literature many authors argued that public libraries are in the middle of a downward funding trend, but there was no clear agreement or irrefutable proof of such a trend.

There have, however, been a number of indicators of funding cuts over the past few years. An American Library Association (ALA) survey in 2005 showed that a slightly more of those libraries surveyed experienced budget increases than budget reductions in the fiscal years 2003, 2004, and 2005 (Davis, 2006). It in not clearly stated within the article, but it is implied that the remainder of the responding libraries (ranging from 58.6% to 64.8%) experienced flat funding. The findings from this survey are summarized in Table 2. (Note that self-reporting and a low response rate greatly reduced the reliability of the findings.)

Table 2

Changes in Operating Revenue for Fiscals Years 2003, 2004, 2005 ($N = 468$)

|  | Fiscal year 2003 (%) | Fiscal year 2004 (%) | Fiscal year 2005 (%) |
|---|---|---|---|
| Increase over prior year | 18.0 | 23.7 | 25.7 |
| Decrease from prior year | 17.2 | 17.7 | 15.7 |
| No increase or decrease reported | 64.8 | 58.6 | 58.6 |

Some librarians, library administrators, and library researchers have suggested that these constraints are part of a new, long-term downward trend in public library funding. Holt (2005) noted a number of public libraries across the country that had suffered budget cuts over the prior 5-year period, but he did not provide supporting statistics.

However, other data point to a minor upward trend in funding beginning in 2006. For example, a 2007 *Library Journal* survey indicated an upsurge in public library funding in 2006 and 2007:

> Libraries seem to be coping [in spite of budget limitations]. Those surveyed this year reported a solid performance last year, from FY05 to FY06, with budget growth of 4.7%. For the next fiscal year, they predict an even better figure, 5.5%, which represents an improvement over a slow-go era a few years ago. (Oder, 2007b, p. 55)

A 2006 *Library Journal* survey of public library book budgets showed a similar reversal in the 1998–2004 downward trend, with a slight increase occurring in 2005 (Hoffert, 2006). Of the 100 libraries surveyed, 43% reported an increase in adult book budgets; 18% reported a decrease; and 39% reported static budgets (p. 39). Again, a limited response rate reduced the reliability of the findings.

While studies such as these can point to possible short-term trends, more important is the consideration of long-term budget trends lasting one or more decades. Long-term data are limited, but overall, it appears that there has been an increase in public library usage over the past few decades, coupled with an aggregate national decrease in public funding since the 1990s:

> Starting in the late 1990s, strains began to appear in library budgets ... Increasingly, library operations felt the pressure. From FY2000 on, both the total income and operating expenditure figures declined in inflation-adjusted terms, causing libraries to lose purchasing power ... During the same period, total circulation went up. (Molyneux, 2006, p. 29)

Perhaps it is necessary to look at even longer periods of time in order to identify a clear upward or downward trend in public funding. Again, data are limited, but looking at the percent of local tax money dedicated to public library support strengthens the idea of a long-term downward trend. Coffman (2004) explained that "The 1950 Public Library Inquiry found that we [public libraries] receive about two cents of the local tax dollar, but NCES [National Center for Education Statistics] data indicates that today we get only a little more than half a cent" (p. 38). However, these statistics indicate only that the percent of total tax dollars dedicated to public funding has decreased. They do not indicate whether or not real spending power, in terms of inflation-adjusted dollars, has changed.

## C. Major Alternative Funding Sources

The third category to emerge from the literature review was the identification of major and minor alternative funding sources. This category corresponds to the second research question ("From what sources do libraries solicit funds, and how do they use them?"). Much of the literature related to alternative funding was published in professional journals, with less attention in the research journals. This literature is largely comprised of opinion pieces, tips for securing funding, and repots of successful projects and programs. Steve Coffman, who works for LSSI, a for-profit company specializing in public library management, has led much of this discussion, a large portion of which has taken the form of a debate over the benefits and appropriateness of alternative funding for public libraries. Coffman has suggested that public libraries' overwhelming dependence on tax funding has made them beholden to economic and political cycles. He argues that:

> It is high time we begin to take a serious look at developing new sources of revenue and we have some great models. Almost every other cultural and educational institution in our communities—including museums, zoos, orchestras, historical societies, nature centers, public universities, public television and radio, and many others—have long ago adopted a plural funding model cultivating a variety of revenue sources that include memberships, contributions, sponsorships [and] business ventures ... These sister institutions no longer depend solely on the largesse of taxpayers, as most libraries do. (Coffman, 2006, p. 27)

The literature review showed that many libraries are indeed taking advantage of these various alternative funding sources. Nonetheless, non-tax funds still account for a relatively small part of most public library budgets:

> The problem is that most public libraries depend almost entirely on local and state tax dollars for operating budgets. Current data from the National Center for Education Statistics (NCES) shows that 91% of the average public library's operating budget comes

from taxes (77% local, 13% state, 1% federal), while all non-tax sources—fines, fees, donations, interest, etc.—account for only 9%. (Coffman, 2004, p. 37)

Examples of popular alternative funding sources described in the literature include community fund drives, grants for special projects, unspecified corporate grants and gifts, in-house product sales, and private endowments. Alternative funds were most commonly used for value-added services and programs, such as advanced genealogy reference services or local author readings, and specialized collections, such as English-language learner collections or local history collections. The literature review revealed four major categories of alternative funding for public libraries in the United States: (1) fees for services, (2) private donations, (3) government grants, and (4) corporate and foundation grants.

## 1. Fees for Services

Most public libraries charge fees for selected services, such as photocopying, placing reserves, or checking out bestsellers, DVDs, and other high-demand items. Other than photocopying charges and fees for materials loans, the most common types of fees are charges for food sales or for commercial items (such as tote bags, books, cards, etc.) sold on library premises (Dempsey, 2004). Craft (1998) has suggested that rather than fundraising, the greatest amounts of money that public libraries can raise is by charging advanced information and community services, in particular "library management in schools and other institutions, or services that cater to community needs such as passports or educational support" (p. 145). However, only a small fraction of public libraries currently engage in these kinds of profit-making services.

While many libraries have set up in-house cafes, coffee bars, or other in-house food and drink outlets since the late 1990s, foods sales typically generate minimal profits, generally earning less than .25% of a library's operating budget (Craft, 1998, p. 141). As a result, most libraries offer food sales more to attract users to the library and for user convenience than to generate revenue.

After food and drink sales, used bookstores operated by public libraries are the most popular type of commercial venture in public libraries. Unlike food sales, library-owned used bookstores usually generate significant profits, particularly if they are staffed by volunteers. In-house bookstores generate an average of $30,000 per year (Craft, 1998, p. 141).

While few users or librarians would object to fees for photocopying or for food, many people do object to fees for other library services, particularly for information services viewed as standard library fare. Common objections include the argument that fees unfairly disadvantage poorer users (e.g. Goldberg, 2004). As Mitch Freedman, ex-president of ALA and a long-time opponent of fees for services, has stated, "As soon as you put fees between the user and the services, in principle, people are denied those services" (Freedman, as quoted in Kniffel, 1997, p. 3).

On the other side of the argument, proponents of fees for services say that if there is a choice between charging a fee for a service and not offering it at all, the public is better served if the service is offered for a fee. Coffman has been an equally vocal proponent of fees for services. He has argued that:

> Wherever we can, we're going to try to provide [services] for free. But if we can't provide them for free, then it's our duty to our patrons to provide them the best information possible at the best price possible. We think it's much better to be able to provide the information and provide the service [for a fee] than it is not to provide it. (Coffman, as quoted in Kniffel, 1997, p. 4)

Another common argument against library fees holds that since public libraries are supported by taxes, the library community has already paid for their services. Library fees therefore amount to double charging (Shoham, 1998). This objection is related to the first objection, as both are based on principles of fairness, and both are tied to the idea of undue financial burden on library users, particularly the poor.

Instead of viewing the fees for services debate solely as a fairness issue, Johannsen (2004) has suggested that the use of fee-based services in public libraries signifies a shift in the general focus of public library services "from an external focus on society to an internal focus on the library itself." That is, an emphasis on the provision of free services indicates an overriding concern for equality of services and for protecting the public from additional tax burdens. Conversely, charging for library services indicates that providing the most advanced services possible is more important than protecting the interests of library users. Johannsen has also suggested that "A similar shift from the user as a citizen with rights to the user as a customer with individual preferences and needs can be observed" (p. 309) when public library fees are implemented.

## 2. Private Donations

For most public libraries, donations from individuals comprise a greater percentage of funding than do any other alternative source. Discussing lessons learned from fundraising for a new library building, the Princeton (NJ) Public Library director and project architect cautioned others to, "Look to individuals, not corporations, to contribute most of the money" (Burger and Garrison, 2006, p. 64) for large capital campaigns.

Private donations as a source of public library support are not a new phenomenon. American public libraries have used private funds since the early 19th century. Just 6 years after the founding of the Peterborough public library, John Jacob Astor made the first significant private donation to a public library, leaving $400,000 of his estate funds in 1839 for the establishment of a public library (Sessa, 2003, p. 2389). Starting his charitable work for libraries almost 50 years later, Andrew Carnegie is probably the best-known of the early public library philanthropists. Between 1886 and 1919, he funded library grants for new buildings in 1418 communities across the United States (Seavey, 2003, pp. 373–374).

There have been objections to private funding for public libraries at least since the time of the Carnegie library funding. In the case of the Carnegie library grants, some communities went so far as to reject Carnegie funding outright. Reasons for rejection varied from disinclination to increase local tax bases, to doubt that Carnegie's motives were purely philanthropic. (See Martin, 1993, for a detailed discussion of the reasons behind the Carnegie rejections.) However, private funds enable public libraries to engage in a wider range of projects and services than they can with just tax funds.

While private funds are often applied to large one-time projects, such as capital fund drives, they are less often applied to daily operations costs, such as staff salaries and overhead. As Nicely (2002) explained, many librarians and library administrators "have come to a realization over the past few years: it is essential to have private funding to augment public resources for major projects" (p. 163). She suggested four ways that private funding can be used as a part of capital projects: "to provide enhancements"; "to establish a fund for maintenance of particular areas"; "to establish funds for particular services or programs"; and "to build endowment" (pp. 164–165).

Although not yet a widespread national trend, in recent years some US public libraries have created library foundations to oversee fundraising. As "a separate non-profit library entity that actively seeks outside funding from individuals, organizations, and corporations" (Boese and Brannon, 2001, p. 219), a library foundation can accept tax-free donations, and it can hire a separate staff whose sole duties involve fundraising and alternative funds administration. And since library foundation employees are not government employees, they can engage in political lobbying on behalf of the library.

These activities are delineated in the mission statement of the Free Library of Philadelphia Foundation:

> The mission of the Free Library of Philadelphia Foundation is to develop resources in order to expand, enhance, and support the services, collections, building programs, and other activities of the Free Library of Philadelphia. Through its Board of Directors, the Foundation will seek those resources from individuals, corporations, foundations, and

other organizations. Additionally, the Foundation will provide faithful stewardship of the resources and special collections which it owns, and of the funds which the Foundation raises or which have been entrusted to it. The Foundation will also ensure efficient and appropriate expenditure of funds in keeping with the goals and mission of the Free Library, as well as the expressed wishes of donors. Finally, the Foundation will, from time to time, manage and administer those programs whose funding is raised through the Foundation, in concert with the Board of Trustees of The Free Library. (http://www.library.phila.gov/about/role.htm)

An example of the type and scale of a major library foundation project is the Free Library of Philadelphia Foundation's "Campaign for a New Central Library." The campaign aims to raise funds for a major renovation and expansion of the Free Library's main branch, at an estimated total cost of $175 million (Free Library of Philadelphia, 2007). As a part of the campaign, the Free Library of Philadelphia Foundation received an anonymous private donation of $15 million, given in 2007 with the restriction that an additional $15 million in matching funds must be raised in order to receive the full amount. Although it is not a large enough donation to cover the whole cost of the project, this single, large private donation goes a long way toward achieving that goal. And without private donations such as this, the project could not be completed.

Another benefit of a library foundation is increased appeal to donors wary of giving money to government agencies. Many donors, especially individuals, feel more secure donating to a private foundation than to the libraries themselves, as they worry that donations to libraries might be added to general government coffers, whereas donations to private non-profit organizations are more likely to be in the manner the donor intends (Boese and Brannon, 2001). Edwin S. Clay, director of the Fairfax County Public Library system, has stressed that "Foundation money enhances and enriches, and is not [intended] to replace or serve in lieu of public money" (Clay, as quoted in Boese and Brannon, 2001, p. 212). Regardless of the benefits of library foundations, at this point they are still relatively rare in US public libraries.

There are a few public libraries, such as the Providence Public Library, which are heavily funded through endowment funds, and which can therefore be considered quasi-public. In its online appeal for donations, the Providence Public Library explains that: "We are one of the few major libraries in the United States that is a private not-for-profit institution governed by a Board of Directors, giving us the flexibility to respond to community need rapidly and effectively" (http://www.provlib.org/about/support/default.html). For fiscal year 2005, it received $38.16 per capita in city, state, and federal funding combined, and $32.22 other (individual, foundation, and corporate) revenue per capita (National Center for Education Statistics, 2005). That is, non-government funding accounted for nearly half (45.8%) of the budget.

## 3. Government Grants

A number of the items reviewed discussed programs funded by government grants. In addition to overseeing the distribution of federal library funds to the states, IMLS also oversees the selection and administration of competitive grants for all types of libraries in the United States, including public libraries. Within the part of its budget dedicated to grant support, IMLS provides more federal grant funding for library-related research than has ever before been available, as well as large grants for other types of programs and services related to libraries, with a strong emphasis on information technology and on programs that can be replicated in other institutions and in other communities.

IMLS grant initiatives related to libraries include National Leadership Grants, which fund new and ongoing library projects and programs as well as library-related research projects; National Awards for Museum and Library Service, which are given to honor outstanding extant programs; smaller scale planning grants; grants to library administrative agencies to distribute federally mandated state library funds; the Laura Bush 21st Century Librarians program, which provides funds for educating students to become future library school educators; the Native American Library Services initiative, and the Native Hawaiian Library Services program (http://www.imls.gov/applicants/name.shtm).

As an example of a grant project related to public libraries, Dr. Lynn Westbrook of the University of Texas at Austin's School of Information received a grant for $407,780 under IMLSs 2007 Laura Bush 21st Century Librarian program. The project will create a community-wide cooperation model for recruiting library support staff into library and information science master's degree programs. Project partners include eight public and academic libraries around Texas, each of which will provide students for the program. Each student will receive free tuition, a small living stipend, and a laptop computer. The goals of the project are to increase the number of professional librarians in the field and to create a series of library management workshops for the library community, developed jointly by university faculty members and local library managers (University of Texas at Austin, 2007).

## 4. Corporate and Foundation Grants

The literature also included numerous descriptions of programs funded by corporate and foundation sources. While not as significant as donations from individuals, corporate grants and donations are still an important source of alternative funding for public libraries, and it appears that corporate support for public libraries is increasing across the country. Unlike many individual donors, corporate donors typically expect to receive something in return for their contributions. Often this "return" comes in the form of putting donors' names on publicity materials for funded programs. Corporate funding thus has the combined effect of providing additional funds for libraries while serving as corporate public relations material.

For example, the Target Foundation makes grants from local Target stores to community organizations, in order to "support programs that promote a love of reading and encourage children, from birth through age nine, to read together with their families" (http://sites.target.com/site/en/corporate/page. jsp?contentId = PRD03-001818). These awards have included many grants to public libraries to support small-scale projects such as story times and other literacy programs. For one such grant, in 2006 the Friends of the Lincoln Township (Michigan) Public Library received a $3000 Target Grant to sponsor the library's Every Child Ready to Read @ your library program. The funds were used to purchase materials from the Public Library Association (PLA) and from ALAs Association for Library Service to Children (ALSC) (http://www.lincolnpublic.lib.mi.us/about_friends.htm).

Target's competitor Wal-Mart has also entered the library funding business by making large donations to public libraries in its home state of Arkansas. In 2004, Wal-Mart donated $1 million to the public library in Bentonville and $300,000 to the Rogers and Fayetteville public libraries (Oatman, 2005).

On a still larger scale, the non-profit Gates Foundation has put huge amounts of private foundation funding into public library support, both in the United States and around the world. The Gates Foundation (known originally as the Gates Library Foundation) first started providing public library funding in 1997 with an initial $200 million commitment to purchase computer hardware and Internet connectivity for public libraries in impoverished communities (Hoerner, 2004, p. 2). The original program focused on libraries in communities with at least 10% of the residents living below the official poverty level. For each library selected, four project components were provided: (1) computer hardware and software for between one and six computers; (2) Internet connectivity, including initial installation and setup costs; (3) technology training for library staff, with visiting trainers provided by the Gates Foundation; and (4) technical support, mainly through telephone support and a dedicated web site (Hoerner, 2004, pp. 3–4).

While some librarians and library researchers lauded the Gates Foundation's efforts, others worried that the one-time donations would soon leave libraries with outdated computer hardware. Indeed, the original program left libraries to face the question of program sustainability on their own. Still others have suggested that the donations of funds dedicated to computer technology served to advance the interests of Microsoft, the corporate source of Gates Foundation funding, and that low-income libraries would have been better served with unspecified donations that they could have used to support their most pressing financial needs, whether or not those needs included technology purchases (Sanford Berman, as quoted in Goldberg, 1998). As Stevenson (2007) argued, "in as much as Microsoft products continue to be at the center of Gates' philanthropy to bridge the digital divide, it is the commercial software industry that benefits most, not the intended recipients of the program, the digitally divided" (n.p.).

Many critics of the Gates Foundation program have suggested that if philanthropy were the only true motivator, the project would focus more on enabling library users to take advantage of free/open source software, instead of supplying products that create an need for the use of proprietary commercial software and software updates. Emphasizing free/open source software would also decrease libraries' dependency on private funding for the sustainability of their computer resources. Stevenson (2007) has further argued that "Given the emphasis on Microsoft products within Gates' library philanthropy, the value of the program for growing Microsoft's market share cannot be ignored—this particularly in light of the increasing popularity of open source software worldwide" (n.p.).

Regardless of these objections, the project's initial reach was widespread, serving more than 1000 libraries. After the first round of donations was completed, the Gates Foundation formed the US Libraries Initiative (http://www.gatesfoundation.org/UnitedStates/USLibraryProgram/default.htm)    to continue the work of the original program. Possibly in response to some of the initial criticisms, the Initiative now aims to support and update Internet technologies in domestic libraries, as opposed to making one-time technology donations and expecting libraries to achieve sustainability on their own. Ongoing programs include matching grants for replacing and adding new public library computers, and a new, 5-year program for helping libraries in low-income communities update computer hardware. This second phase of the US Libraries Initiative, called "Keeping Communities Connected: The Net Step" will spend an initial $30 million to replace aging computer hardware in libraries in 18 states, and then spend still more in the remaining states over the 5-year period (Oder, 2007a).

## D. Minor Alternative Funding Sources: Professional Association Awards

The final category of alternative funding represented in the literature was professional association awards and grants. These types of awards are limited in number and are typically for small amounts, making them a minor source of public library alternative funding. As they are funded by associations of information professionals and others interested in promoting librarianship, they generally raise fewer objections than funding from private sources.

The most common types of professional association awards are literature or other library materials awards, and scholarships for librarians or library school students to attend professional association meetings. For example, the PLA, in cooperation with Baker & Taylor, annually presents the Baker & Taylor Entertainment Audio Music/Video Product Award. The purpose of the award is to "to promote the development of a circulating audio music/video product collection in public libraries and increase the exposure of the format within the community" (http://pla.org/ala/pla/plaawards/bakertayloraudio.cfm). The award pays $2500 to the winning public library for the purchase of audio, music, or video products ordered through Baker & Taylor.

## IV. Results: A Case Study of the West Chester Public Library's Alternative Funding

To add depth to this broad picture of alternative funding for public libraries, and for deeper investigation into the second research question ("From what sources do libraries solicit funds, and how do they use them?"), the next step in the research process entailed a case study of the West Chester Public Library, located in West Chester, Pennsylvania. It was selected due to its usually high reliance on non-tax funding.

Begun in 1815 as a subscription library, 18 years before the first tax-supported US library, the West Chester Public Library was originally funded entirely through private (subscription) funds. It was reorganized as a free, tax-supported institution in 1898 (Sundwall, 2007, p. 1) at a time when tax-supported public libraries were becoming common throughout the United States. For most of the 20th century, the library relied exclusively on tax funds for materials and operations. In response to declining state and local funding, library director Victoria Dow has made the pursuit of non-tax funds a major focus of her tenure. In 2007, tax funds comprised only about 45% of the library's roughly $600,000 annual budget, with alternative funding filling in the remaining 55% (2006 Income and Expenditures, 2007, p. 5).

The bulk of state funding, roughly 90%, goes to purchasing materials. The remainder is grouped together as "operating funds." Most donations and other alternative monies are added to the operating funds. As a result of actively seeking alternative funding, the library's operating funds have greatly expanded over the past few years, enabling it to offer more programs and services to the public than it could with just tax support.

With roughly 45,000 items in the collection, three full-time, and nine part-time staff, the West Chester Public Library is a medium-sized public library and a part of the Chester County Library System. It is an independent entity, as opposed to a part of the local government. The library can therefore accept tax-free donations and does not need a library foundation to do so on its behalf. Fundraising is the prime responsibility of the Board of Trustees and of the library director. Each Board member is expected to generate funds, either personally or by seeking funding. The Board also runs a major gift campaign, for which the members personally approach potential major donors. Both the director and the Board spend time cultivating potential major donors by sending library newsletters with personal notes to potential donors, by inviting potential donors to visit the library, and by providing special perks such as VIP seating for featured library events. In addition, the Board has contracted a part-time development officer whose main responsibilities include developing and maintaining funding contacts, writing grants, and developing and overseeing fundraising programs. Other library staff members also help with specific projects.

The West Chester Public Library's alterative funding efforts can be divided into four categories: fines and fees, individual donations, corporate sponsorships, and grants. Each of these funding categories is described in the following sections.

## A. Fines and Fees

Many public libraries that are part of local government systems are required to return revenue from fines and fees to government coffers. As an independent entity, the West Chester Public Library can put its revenue from fines and fees back into its own operating budget. Each year the library collects around $40,000 in library fines and fees, making a significant addition to the budget. For 2006, fines and fees totaled just over $42,000 (2006 Income and Expenditures, 2007, p. 5).

Standard overdue penalties and related charges account for some of the total fines and fees revenue, but fees for services are the major revenue source within this category. Most significantly, circulation fees for DVDs and audio books make up the bulk of the fees charged. In future years this might change as the film and audio collection evolves to compete with NetFlix, movie downloads, and other new and emerging digital services (Victoria Dow, personal communication, September 12, 2007).

## B. Individual Donations

The library's largest source of alternative funding is individual donations. Each September the staff coordinates an Annual Appeal, for which letters are sent to possible donors. There are two different appeal letters. The first is a personalized letter that is sent to a list of known past donors and to others who have expressed interest in giving in the past but have never donated. Most of the larger donations come from this part of the appeal. The second, more generic, letter is sent to people in the library card holder database. The staff considers a one- to two-percent response from the second list to be a successful endeavor (Victoria Dow, personal communication, September 12, 2007). In addition to the annual appeal, there is also a large button labeled "Donations!" displayed prominently on the upper left of the library homepage (http://www.wcpubliclibrary.org/), and a request for donations in the library's quarterly newsletter to encourage library users to contribute.

## C. Corporate Sponsorships

While not as considerable as individual donations, corporate donations do bring in roughly 20% of the library's alternative funds. As corporations typically expect something in return for their donations, the library puts corporate logos on public relations materials, provides VIP seating at corporate-funded events, and mentions donors in the newsletters (Victoria Dow, personal communication, September 12, 2007).

Past experience has shown that special events are the least efficient way to raise money due to the staff time and expense involved in planning, so the library focuses on just one big fundraising event each year. The annual Literary Heroes Breakfast (http://www.literacyheroes.com/) gives awards to community members who support local literacy efforts. Now in its third year, past winners have included reading tutors, English-language tutors, book discussion leaders, and local teachers.

Multiple corporations and institutions sponsor the Literary Heroes Breakfast. Each major sponsor pays $5000 and in return receives a list of nominees for consideration in one of the award categories. The sponsor then forms a committee to select a winner in their category, and a representative from the organization presents the award at the event. Sponsors include two banks, a local television news channel, the local newspaper, a pharmaceutical company, a florist, and many others. With its combined focus on literacy and fundraising, the event generates funds for the library while simultaneously furthering the library's literacy-related mission.

## D. Government, Corporate, and Foundation Grants

The library also applies for government, corporate, and foundation grants. In the area of government grants, the director favors state and municipal grants over federal grants due to the increased likelihood of funding success (Victoria Dow, personal communication, September 12, 2007). However, the library did secure a federal grant for its 2005 building renovation, and several state-funded Department of Community and Economic Development grants as well. When seeking state government grants for specific programs, the director and the Board first approach legislators to ask for support and to test the likelihood of receiving funding. The library has also received small grants from the local municipal parks and recreation fund for a number of smaller projects.

The West Chester Public Library also applies for foundation grants from large regional foundations and from smaller local foundations and service organizations. These funds are very competitive and are harder to obtain than state and local grants. Applying for these programs begins with a phone call or a letter of inquiry to a program administrator to investigate the fundability of an idea, as funder's interest is a crucial component of grant success.

For example, in response to growth in the local Spanish-speaking population, the library obtained a $10,000 grant from the Claneil Foundation (http://claneilfoundation.org/mission.php) to update and enlarge its Spanish-language materials collection. The Claneil Foundation is a private Foundation located in Plymouth Meeting, Pennsylvania. Its mission is to:

> create healthy communities by supporting organizations that:
> - make a difference in the lives of individuals, families, and the institutions that support them;
> - develop an informed, educated, and engaged citizenry; and
> - increase the understanding and appreciation of natural, built, and cultural assets. (http://claneilfoundation.org/mission.php)

The intent of the library's new Spanish-language materials collection is to welcome the growing Spanish-speaking population to the library and to make them feel like part of the library community (New Spanish Language Collection, 2007, p. 1). The new collection includes adult fiction, magazines, medical information, and English-Language Learner (ELL) materials. The funds were also used to add materials to a pre-existing, but small, children's Spanish-language materials collection and to support programs associated with the new collections, such as story times in Spanish and staff training in basic Spanish words and phrases. The new collection, which kicked off with an open house in September 2006, has led to a significant increase in the number of Spanish-speaking families using the library (p. 1).

## E. Looking to the Future

The West Chester Public Library's movement toward alternative funding reflects the broader national public library trend toward increasing reliance on non-tax revenues. The library will likely continue its fundraising efforts as long as they prove profitable, and the staff and Board will likely continue to explore new avenues for alterative funding in future years (Victoria Dow, personal communication, September 12, 2007). For example, a new planned giving program is in progress. The brochure for the new program has already been printed, and the staff plans to send it to financial planners and others who help people plan wills and bequests.

# V. The Arguments for and Against Alternative Funding for Public Libraries

Combining the broad picture of library funding that resulted from the literature review with the in-depth picture of alternative funds use that resulted from the case study, the potential effects of an increased reliance on non-tax funds become clear. These potential effects are also the major arguments in the ongoing debate over the use of alternative funding, and they are the focus of research question 3 ("What are the major arguments for and against alternative funding for public libraries?"). Major arguments against alternative funding include sustainability, reduced tax support, loss of objectivity, and the commercialization of public spaces. Chief among the arguments in favor of alternative funding are program diversification, community involvement, and increased visibility.

## A. Arguments Against Alternative Funding: Sustainability

On one hand, even small awards such as the Baker & Taylor Entertainment Audio Music/Video Product Award can be a major boost to a small library's budget, in this case, to a materials budget. On the other hand, sustainability is a serious problem with these types of funds. An award such as this is a one-time payment. As the materials begin to age, the library might not have the funds to replace or update them, meaning that the quality of materials provided will likely decline after the initial award period unless additional funds can be raised. A couple of years after the initial library grants, the Gates Foundation came to realize how difficult it was for libraries, especially libraries located in impoverished communities, to secure the necessary funds for hardware and software maintenance and renewal (Stevenson, 2007). The

Gates Foundation example shows that often libraries cannot achieve sustainability of projects started with grant funds or with individual donations.

## B. Arguments Against Alternative Funding: Reduced Tax Support

Many opponents of alternative funding ask questions such as, "Is there a danger that focusing heavily on alterative funds will encourage local government leaders to cut tax support?" and "Will the library be seen as capable of self-support due to its success in raising funds?" These alternative funding opponents assert that not only is tax support the traditional form of public library support, it is the *appropriate* form:

> The public library, used directly by more people than police, fire departments, or schools, must maintain its claim as an essential public service to survive. It informs all ages, and that information is as essential to modern living and citizenship as formal schooling. When you allow the public library to depend on private money, you suggest that it is unworthy of that essential tax support that has paid 90 percent of its budget since libraries were founded. (Berry, 2002, p. 8)

These opponents of alternative funding argue that working toward increased tax support

> is where our energy should be directed, not toward courting donors and collaborators, but rather on insisting that public libraries really are what we have been calling them: bulwarks of democracy—common, neutral, but diverse spaces that deserve full and public funding without resorting to compromising partnerships and fiscal gimmicks like fines and fees. (Sanford Berman, as quoted in Goldberg, 1998, p. 43)

## C. Arguments Against Alternative Funding: Loss of Objectivity

Those who view the loss of library objectivity as an argument against alternative funding ask questions such as, "Will the increasing appearance of corporate and foundation logos and names on library materials be seen as endorsement of private interests?" "As private funds are used to purchase more of the materials collections, will donors object to materials that conflict with their beliefs and goals?" "Will community members see the library as losing its objectivity, and as no longer representing the community's varied interests?"

Another aspect of the loss of objectivity argument involves objections to putting private monies into the public sphere. For example, while more than one million dollars that Wal-Mart has donated to Arkansas public libraries will enable those libraries to provide bigger and better services than they could otherwise, the donations are not free of corporate strings. The new

"Wal-Mart Story Time Room" in the Blair Library in Fayetteville can be seen as not only corporate philanthropy, but also as corporate advertising.

This objection also refers to possible conflicts between the missions and philosophies of libraries and corporations. For example, in naming the new facility the Wal-Mart Story Time Room, is the library endorsing Wal-Mart and its products, services, and business practices? And while most people would object to library sponsorship from a tobacco or alcohol producer, what about sponsorship from other businesses, such as fast food companies? Does sponsorship from McDonald's suggest that the library endorses eating fast food? Many opponents of alternative funding answer "yes" to these questions and warn that the dangers of loss of objectivity outweigh any benefits of increased budgets.

## D. Arguments Against Alternative Funding: Commercialization of Public Spaces

Closely related to loss of objectivity is the idea of the commercialization of public spaces. Public libraries as public spaces have traditionally been free of advertising and commercial ventures. Placing company logos and names in corporate-funded library areas can be seen as the commercialization of public library spaces. Buschman (2003, 2005) has argued that using private money to fund public libraries signifies the "dismantling of the democratic public sphere" (Buschman, 2005, p. 1). He has suggested that "libraries embody an essential element of democracy: a place where the ideal of unfettered communication and investigation exists in rudimentary form, allowing for critical and rational discussion of the issues of the day" (Buschman, 2005, pp. 9–10), and that private funding diminishes libraries' worth as places for free, open, unbiased discussion spaces.

However, many proponents of alternative funding acknowledge the possible commercialization of public spaces and argue that increased library budgets are worth the risks. Engelfried and Reynolds (2002) wrote that "Corporate sponsorship in public libraries is a scary thing. As public institutions dedicated to free, equal, and untainted access to our services, we get justifiably nervous about alliances with profit-oriented businesses" (p. 49). The authors explain that despite these worries, they supported corporate and foundation sponsorship of Oregon's 2000 Statewide Summer Reading Program. Program sponsors included Wells Fargo Foundation, Oregon Public Broadcasting, and Washington Mutual Bank. The authors attribute much of the success of the program, including the doubling of participation, to the sponsorship, which enabled the Oregon Library Association to send "promotional materials to libraries at no cost, gave libraries grants to hire guest performers, and launched a statewide advertising campaign" (p. 49). While they did find that "some libraries were still hesitant to participate in a program with sponsors' names on the materials," the authors concluded that on balance, the sponsorship, and the program it supported, was a success (p. 50).

## E. Arguments in Favor of Alternative Funding: Program Diversification

The major argument in favor of alternative funding for public libraries is that the funding boost that alternative funds provide can enable libraries to expand their services to include worthwhile programs that they otherwise could not afford. The Literacy Heroes Breakfast is an example of one such program that both benefits the community (by supporting literacy) and the library (by generating funds). Private contributors are also often more open to funding innovative new programs than are governments and tax payers. For example, it is extremely unlikely that the West Chester Public Library could have built the new Spanish-language materials collection without supplementary funding.

A more extreme case is the Salinas (CA) Public Library. In 2004, city residents voted down two proposed library funding measures, and the city council responded with a plan to close the city's public libraries (Salinas Tax Measures Fail, 2004). The combination of a grassroots funding campaign, support and fundraising efforts from the mayor, and corporate and foundation grants prevented the closure of the libraries (Eberhart, 2005).

## F. Arguments in Favor of Alternative Funding: Community Involvement

In addition to increased purchasing power and program diversification, those who argue in favor of using private funding for public libraries often cite increased community involvement as a major benefit. Individuals, companies, and organizations who donate funds to the library are likely to be more interested in the library's operations and well-being, and they might be more inclined to use its services. In this way, alternative funds might lead to increased library support from those who work for or patronize corporate funders. For example, if Coors Brewing Company employees volunteer at the Denver Public Library annual book fair, they help contribute to the library and its community while also raising the public image of the company.

## G. Arguments in Favor of Alternative Funding: Increased Visibility

The increased purchasing power that alternative funds enable can also improve the visibility and reputation of the library. Few library budgets funded just by taxes have sufficient resources for running large marketing and public relations campaigns, but such programs can be made possible with the use of alternative funds. Corporations can be important public library allies and collaborators, important both for their economic power and for the increased library visibility that their marketing and public relations expertise can engender. As Woodsworth (1996) wrote, "It's time for us to develop meaningful alliances and partnerships with the corporate sector. We have to do more than say, 'If you give, I'll take'" (p. 40). For example, shoppers at a Fayetteville Wal-Mart might see a press release about the Wal-Mart library grants, and they might decide to visit their local library as a result, providing free advertising for the library to non-user populations.

## VI. Conclusion

The basic argument against alternative funding for libraries lies in the belief that the public should support its libraries through tax funds at levels sufficient enough to provide high-quality services, and that library staffs should focus on trying to improve tax support. This side of the debate claims that public libraries are a "public good" that benefits everyone in a community (Hennen, 2004). Funding equity is also a key issue. Seeking alternative funding normally takes a great deal of dedicated staff or volunteer time. Consequently small libraries, with smaller staffs and smaller potential volunteer pools, can be disadvantaged in the search for non-tax funds, as can libraries located in impoverished areas with lower tax bases.

The other side of the debate argues that in order for public libraries to best serve the information needs of their communities, they need greater financial support than tax sources alone can provide. As such, "corporate partnerships [are] a practical approach to managing a library" and to making up for budget deficiencies (Linda Mielke, as quoted in Goldberg, 1998, p. 43). Seeking alternative funding is therefore crucial for improving public library services, and private donors are viewed as allies in the effort to improve public library services.

It seems clear that the West Chester Public Library, and many others like it that have been successful at raising alternative funds, could not offer the same level of services without these additional monies. What is less clear is how the influence of alternative funding will change the direction of public library services in years to come. It is possible that the arguments surrounding alternative funding for public libraries might continue for many years as libraries continue to explore and define the role of private funding for their daily operations.

## Acknowledgment

The author wishes to thank Victoria Dow of the West Chester Public Library for her assistance in helping to prepare the case study section of this manuscript.

## References

2006 Income and Expenditures (2007). *The Story* 2(2), 5. Available online at: http://www.wcpubliclibrary.org/index.php?option = com_content&task = view&id = 20&Itemid = 33

Agosto, D. E. (2005). The digital divide and public libraries: A first-hand view. *Progressive Librarian: A Journal for Critical Studies & Progressive Politics in Librarianship* 25, 23–27.

American Library Association (2007). *Federal funding.* Accessed on September 1, 2007, from: http://www.ala.org/ala/washoff/woissues/washfunding/funding.cfm

Berry, J. N. (2002). Don't let government off the hook. *Library Journal* 127(8), 8.

Boese, K. C., and Brannon, P. (2001). Interpreting the present to ensure a future: An interview of financial success at the Fairfax county public library. *The Bottom Line: Managing Library Finances* 14, 219–226.

Burger, L., and Garrison, N. (2006). Construction funding 101. *American Libraries* 37(4), 63–65.

Buschman, J. (2003). *Dismantling the public sphere: Situating and sustaining librarianship in the age of the new public philosophy.* Libraries Unlimited, Westport, CT.

Buschman, J. (2005). Libraries and the decline of public purposes. *Public Library Quarterly* 24, 1–12.

California's $14-million library budget cut came as a surprise (2007). Accessed on September 3, 2007, from: http://www.ala.org/ala/alonline/currentnews/newsarchive/2007/august2007/califbudgetcut.cfm

Coffman, S. (2004). Saving ourselves: Plural funding for public libraries. *American Libraries* 35, 37–39.

Coffman, S. (2006). Building a new foundation: Library funding. *Searcher* 14(1), 26–34.

Craft, M. A. (1998). Public library ventures: Risks, rubs and revenue. *The Bottom Line: Managing Library Finances* 11, 140–145.

Davis, D. M. (2006). The status of public library funding 2003–2005: Impact of local operating revenue fluctuations. *Public Library Quarterly* 25, 5–26.

Dempsey, B. (2004). Cashing in on service. *Library Journal* 129(18), 38–41.

Eberhart, G. M. (2005). Salinas mayor launches campaign to keep libraries open. *American Libraries* 36(3), 12–13.

Engelfried, S., and Reynolds, A. (2002). Sponsorship 101: How partnerships can expand summer reading. *American Libraries* 33(2), 49–50.

Free Library of Philadelphia (2007). *Free Library Announces Major Campaign Gifts.* Accessed on August 24, 2007, from: http://libwww.library.phila.gov/PressRel/Pressrel.cfm?id = 404

Goldberg, B. (1998). What price partnerships? *American Libraries* 29(2), 43–46.

Goldberg, B. (2004). New Jersey town reacts to library Internet fees. *American Libraries* 35(5), 19.

Gorman, G. E., and Clayton, P. (2005). *Qualitative research for the information professional: A practical handbook*, 2nd ed., Facet, London.

Hennen, T. J. (2004). Restore our destiny: Full—not plural—funding. *American Libraries* 35(7), 43–45.

Hoerner, D. (2004). Public libraries, public access computing, and the Bill & Melinda Gates foundation. In *Encyclopedia of Library and Information Science*, 2nd ed., pp. 1–6, Marcel Dekker, New York.

Hoffert, B. (2006). Budgets rebound. *Library Journal* 131(3), 38–40.

Holt, G. E. (2005). Getting beyond the pain: Understanding and dealing with declining library funding. *The Bottom Line* 18(4), 185–190.

Johannsen, C. G. (2004). Managing fee-based public library services: Values and practices. *Library Management* 25, 307–315.

Kniffel, L. (1997). Fees fight. *American Libraries* 28(7), 49–51.

Martin, R. S. (1993). *Carnegie denied: Communities rejecting Carnegie library construction grants, 1898–1925*. Greenwood Press, Westport, CT.

Molyneux, R. E. (2006). Recent funding trends. *American Libraries* 37(3), 29.

National Center for Education Statistics (2005). *Library statistics program: Compare public libraries*. Available at: http://nces.ed.gov/surveys/libraries/compare/Focus LibrarySearchResult.asp

National Center for Education Statistics (2007). *E.D. TAB: Public libraries in the United States: Fiscal year 2004*. Available online at: http://nces.ed.gov/pubsearch/pubsinfo.asp?pubid = 2006349

New Spanish Language Collection (2007). *The Story* 2(2), 1. Available online at: http://www.wcpubliclibrary.org/newsletters/WCPLSpg07news.pdf

Nicely, D. D. (2002). Private funding for capital projects. *The Bottom Line: Managing Library Finances* 15, 163–166.

Oatman, E. (2005). Wal-Mart gives libraries $1.6 million. *School Library Journal* 51(9), 16.

Oder, N. (2007a). Gates offers new grant program. *Library Journal* 132(3), 16.

Oder, N. (2007b). Keeping pace. *Library Journal* 132(1), 55.

Salinas tax measures fail: Libraries will shut down (2004). *American Libraries* 35(11), 18–19.

Seavey, C. A. (2003). The American public library during the great depression. *Library Review* 52, 373–378.

Sessa, F. B. (2003). Public libraries, history. In *Encyclopedia of library and information science*, pp. 2379–2392, Marcel Dekker, New York.

Shoham, S. (1998). Fees in public libraries. *Public Library Quarterly* 17, 39–48.

Stevenson, S. (2007). Public libraries, public access computing, FOSS and CI: There are alternatives to private philanthropy. *First Monday* 12(5). Accessed on September 23, 2007 from: http://www.firstmonday.org/issues/issue12_5/stevenson/index.html

Sundwall, H. (2007). *The Story* 2(2), 1–2. Available online at: http://www.wcpublic library.org/index.php?option = com_content&task = view&id = 20&Itemid = 33

United States Census Bureau (2007). *American FactFinder.* Available online at: http://factfinder.census.gov/servlet/SAFFFacts?_sse = on

University of Texas at Austin (2007). *School of information awarded $1.3 million from the federal Institute of Museum and Library Services.* Accessed on August 14, 2007 from http://www.utexas.edu/opa/news/2007/07/information10.html

Woodsworth, A. (1996). Libraries & corporate partners. *Library Journal* 121(13), 40.

Zach, L. (2006). Using a multiple-case studies design to investigate the information-seeking behavior of arts administrators. *Library Trends* 55, 4–23.

# From Foundation to Federal Funding: The Impact of Grants on Education for Library and Information Science

Linda C. Smith

Graduate School of Library and Information Science, University of Illinois at Urbana-Champaign, Champaign, IL, USA

## I. Introduction

Funding, first from foundations and later also from government agencies, has been a factor in shaping the development of education for library (and information) science in the U.S. for more than 80 years. Educational programs experienced substantial investments in three periods: (1) from the Carnegie Corporation in the 1920s and 1930s; (2) from the U.S. Office of Education in the 1960s and 1970s; and (3) from the Institute of Museum and Library Services in the first decade of the 21st century. This chapter documents the impacts of the first two and argues for the need to analyze the impact of the third. Other, more modest, investments from both foundations and government agencies have had less lasting impact. This chapter identifies the major sources of funding and projects funded, assesses the level and type of impact, and concludes with implications for the future. The focus is on funding for research, development, and resource enhancement in library (and information) science education, not research conducted by library and information science (LIS) faculty on other topics (e.g., as funded by the OCLC/ALISE library and information science research grant program) (Connaway, 2005).

INFLUENCE OF FUNDING ON ADVANCES IN LIBRARIANSHIP
ADVANCES IN LIBRARIANSHIP, VOL. 31
© 2008 by Emerald Group Publishing Limited
ISSN: 0065-2830
DOI: 10.1016/S0065-2830(08)31005-8

## II. Andrew Carnegie and the Carnegie Corporation of New York

Formal education for librarianship began in January, 1887, when Melvil Dewey launched the School of Library Economy at Columbia College (now University) (Davis, 1976). Despite Andrew Carnegie's interest in encouraging communities to invest in the construction of new public libraries, initially he declined to support training of librarians, rejecting a request from Melvil Dewey in 1890 (Vann, 1961, p. 58). In 1903 Carnegie reversed this stance, with an endowment of $100,000 to aid in the educational program for librarians to be offered at Western Reserve University in Cleveland (Vann, 1961, p. 118). Other grants followed: to the Carnegie Library of Pittsburgh for its Training School for Children's Librarians (1903); to the training program at the Carnegie Library of Atlanta (1905); and to the training program at the New York Public Library (1911) (Vann, 1961, p. 120).

In 1911 Carnegie established a foundation, the Carnegie Corporation of New York, to continue his philanthropic work. As additional requests for support were being received from training programs, the Carnegie Corporation chose to investigate the training situation in order to better respond. On March 28, 1919 Charles C. Williamson, then Head of the Division of Economics and Sociology at the New York Public Library, was appointed director of a study on library training for the Carnegie Corporation (Vann, 1961, p. 173). He undertook visits to the 15 existing schools, housed in both universities and public libraries, and did not consider other forms of training. The report was forwarded to the Corporation on March 30, 1922 (Vann, 1961, p. 177), and it was subsequently published as *Training for Library Service* (Williamson, 1923). Davis (1976, p. 120) termed it "a landmark survey, similar in significance to Carnegie studies of the period in other professions," noting that it "had a far-reaching effect on librarianship and its educational institutions." The report focused the attention of librarians in general, and the American Library Association (ALA) in particular, upon the need for educational reform (Vann, 1971).

Williamson (1923, pp. 136–146) presented his recommendations in summary form under 11 headings:

1. Types of library work and training. There was a difference between professional and clerical work in libraries and education, and library schools should train only professionals.
2. The library school curriculum. There was little agreement among the schools as to the relative importance of subjects, and there should be greater standardization. The content of the curriculum and methods of instruction should be dynamic and reflect the most progressive library service.

done more for librarianship in the eyes of nonlibrarians than nearly any other event in recent library history." Carter and Owens (1993) provided data on the number of Title II-B fellowships and traineeships awarded for library career training during the period 1966–1992, with $38,191,659 as the total amount awarded, including 3152 awards for master's, 265 awards for post-master's, and 1239 awards for doctoral study.

In the same period, the U.S. Office of Education Library and Information Sciences Research Branch funded a study to develop a research agenda for library education. Borko (1973, p. 1) summarized the motivation for the study: "[Library schools] wish to change and improve, but what needs to be changed and in what direction? Efforts to create improvements are being hampered by the lack of a comprehensive and integrated body of knowledge which would identify current educational needs and the most effective methods for their achievement. In essence, the research to support innovative educational decision-making is lacking." A multi-step method was employed. Recognized leaders in library education were asked to discuss research needs in 10 specified areas (the aims and content of graduate library education; general vs. specialized library education; the integration of information science and library automation into the library school educational program; relating instructional methodology to teaching in library schools; library school administration; library school faculty and students; relationships of professional associations to library schools and libraries; the library school and requirements for staffing libraries; continuing education for librarians; and research needs relating to the role of the library in the community). Then the Delphi Technique was used to rank proposed projects, resulting in five priority groups: I. Improving and updating the skills of professional librarians; II. Library school educational planning and relevance; III. Administration of the library school and library with regard to specific courses, skills, and programs; IV. Forms of instruction and supportive facilities for maintaining instruction; and V. The role of professional associations and communication among librarians. Borko (1973, pp. 220–221) concluded: "With completion and publication of the research to establish priorities, the work of the editor is concluded. If, however, there is no implementation, the purposes of his effort and that of the contributors will not become realized ... It is up to the concerned professionals in library science education to propose, plan, and execute the specific research projects that would provide information and then to convert our knowledge into a program for improving library education. Without implementation, research planning is a useless exercise. The proposed research must be undertaken and the results transferred into improved curricula for the education of librarians." Despite availability of the study in book form, published by the American Library Association, subsequent citations to the book are relatively few in number, suggesting limited impact in terms of stimulating subsequent research.

## IV. Foundation and Government Funding in the 1970s and 1980s

Studies relevant to library education continued in the 1970s and 1980s under other auspices. The H.W. Wilson Foundation was established in 1952 by Halsey Wilson, founder of the H.W. Wilson Company. This foundation supported a study undertaken by Ralph Conant, a social science researcher, on behalf of the Advisory Committee to the Office for Library Education of the ALA. The hope was that a critical examination might do for library education in the 1980s what the Williamson report had done in the 1920s. Based on site visits to selected schools and a series of interviews with faculty, students, alumni, and employers, Conant (1980, pp. 8–9) made a number of recommendations:

- Reduce the number of accredited graduate programs to better match anticipated demand for graduates.
- Lengthen and enrich the master's program to include thorough coverage of the fundamentals of professional librarianship, a substantial internship or practicum, and a specialization. A national plan should include an allocation of specializations among the graduate schools.
- Limit enrollment to those who have the potential to assume professional positions in the field.
- Improve the quality and relevance of the graduate programs by appointing qualified professionals to their faculties, by encouraging faculty research on contemporary library problems, and by training faculty in effective methods of instruction.
- Involve graduate library schools in continuing education.
- Make the accreditation process an effective instrument of correction and reform by including professional evaluators on accreditation teams.
- Systematize reform by establishing a national forum for library education and giving it the mission of developing a national plan for the education and training of professional librarians.

The response of library educators was quite critical. For example, Darling (1981, p. 99) asserted that "the reader of the report ... will not be able to find suitable justification for the proposed reforms in the chapters of uncritical reporting of opinion that make up the bulk of the book;" Rothstein (1980, pp. 534–535), noting the "poor quality of Conant's research and presentation," lamented that "the Williamson report for the 1980s remains to be written."

In the early 1980s, the U.S. Department of Education funded a project on *New Directions in Library and Information Science Education* (Griffiths and

3. Entrance requirements. Professional library training should be based on a college education and be offered on a strictly graduate basis.

4. The teaching staff and methods of instruction. Many instructors were not qualified to teach graduate students, and quality could be raised by better salaries. More full-time instructors and more textbooks were needed. Field work was one method of instruction and should involve purposeful observation.

5. Library school finances and salaries. Financial support for schools was inadequate, and each school needed an independent budget.

6. The need for more library schools and more students in training. Recruitment of students was hindered by the low salaries and poor working conditions. The primary need was for "a better grade of student and higher standards of instruction," offering scholarships to attract good students to existing schools.

7. The library school and the university. Library schools should be organized as a department of a university to maintain prestige and proper standards.

8. Specialized study. Library service was growing highly specialized. Schools should offer 2-year courses: the first year for general principles and the second for specialization.

9. Training in service. Library workers should seek continued professional growth and improvement. Correspondence studies should be developed.

10. Certification of librarians and standardization of library schools. There were no standards for fitness for library work. A system for voluntary certification of librarians should be developed, and library schools should be held to higher standards through accreditation.

11. The problem of the small library. Special courses should be developed to train librarians for small libraries with limited budgets.

This report stimulated a number of important developments. The Carnegie Corporation initiated a Ten-Year Program in Library Service in 1926 in order to implement some of Williamson's recommendations. An allocation of $4,170,000 was planned: $1,440,000 would support existing schools; $1,385,000 would be for the establishment of a new type of graduate library school; and $1,345,000 would provide support for the ALA (Churchwell, 1975, p. 57). One major project undertaken by ALA to address the lack of standard textbooks noted by Williamson was development by 1930 of a series of textbooks, covering the topics of circulation, reference, cataloging and classification, book selection and order work, library service for children, and the library in the school (Churchwell, 1975, p. 36).

According to Churchwell (1975, p. 58), "the Carnegie Corporation, more than any other agency or reason, quickened interest in the movement to locate library schools on university campuses and greatly facilitated such moves." Support enabled the New York State Library School to merge with the New York Public Library School and move to Columbia; helped to establish college- and university-centered library schools at the University of Denver, Hampton Institute, and the University of North Carolina; and assisted the Atlanta Library Training School to become part of Emory University. (For more on the impact on accreditation and diversity, see

Sections VII and VIII below). Support at this level, particularly during the Depression, sustained a period of orderly development in education for librarianship. Other foundations—the Rockefeller Foundation, the General Education Board, and the Rosenwald Fund—all gave money to advance library education, but the Carnegie Corporation was the chief benefactor (Churchwell, 1975, p. 38). Churchwell concluded: "Since the programs of all library schools were severely restricted by very inadequate financial support, the generous provisions made to them by the Carnegie Corporation through its Ten-Year Program in Library Service may be considered the most powerful force that affected the course of development of education for librarianship between 1919 and 1929" (p. 66).

Achieving the Carnegie Corporation goal of establishing a new type of graduate library school was accomplished in 1926 with the founding of the Graduate Library School at the University of Chicago. This was intended to do for the library profession what the Johns Hopkins Medical School and the Harvard Law School had accomplished in their respective fields (Churchwell, 1975, p. 62). Richardson (1982) described in detail the founding of the school and its subsequent development.

Students were admitted to doctoral study beginning in 1928. In 1940, on the occasion of the 50th anniversary of the University of Chicago and the 12th anniversary of the Graduate Library School (GLS), Dean Louis R. Wilson reflected on the role of GLS in "extending the frontiers of librarianship" and noted its "oneness with the University" with the result that "its investigations and publications receive the full support and publicity of the University and are placed on an equal footing with work in other departments" (Wilson, 1940, p. 16). He further elaborated that "such a program is to be characterized by the same standards and range of scholarship as those which characterize the work of the University as a whole. There is insistence that the subject matter of library science shall be considered as something more extensive than mere present best practice and as something of so great importance as to be able to contribute to the development and enrichment of modern civilization" (Wilson, 1940, p. 19). He laid out an ambitious agenda for the next decade (pp. 19–23): (1) development of a theory or a philosophy of library science; (2) detailed formulation of guiding principles for each subdivision of library science; (3) training students to carry on library activities in accordance with such philosophy and principles, to teach the various branches of library science on this basis, and to carry on investigations to further clarify principles and methods of evaluating library practice or to solve library problems; (4) developing within its students a critical and experimental attitude toward librarianship; (5) publication of results; (6) increasing the educational effectiveness of the library in its various forms; and (7) contributing to a better understanding of the means of communicating ideas through print, radio, and moving picture.

As graduates of the GLS doctoral program moved into positions as directors and faculty members in other schools, they were "instrumental in improving teaching standards through the fresh, more critical and scholarly viewpoints" gained from their study at GLS (Wheeler, 1946, p. 77). While most commentators credit GLS with important contributions to establishing library science on a sounder scientific basis, Houser and Schrader (1978, p. 146) have argued that the initial promise was not realized because during Wilson's tenure as dean of GLS, he "changed the original mission of the School from theory building for a scientific profession of library science to preoccupation with management techniques and skills for the administration of libraries."

In 1936, the Carnegie Corporation again sought an evaluation of library education and engaged Ralph Munn, director of the Carnegie Library of Pittsburgh, to make it. While acknowledging improvements (faculties had been enlarged and improved, newer and better methods of presentation introduced, standards raised, and curricula revised), his report also analyzed then-current criticisms of library education (Munn, 1936, pp. 22–27). One point in particular was that "the library schools are not fully integrated with their universities" (p. 25), now that schools operated by public and state libraries were largely eliminated and schools were established under university or college auspices. Munn (1936, p. 26) expressed concern that "in too many cases ... the connection between library school and university is one of official recognition only; in few cases has the library school become part of the actual fabric of the university. Some university administrations are uninterested and even a bit hostile, but in other instances the library school director has himself sought to erect barriers which separate the school from the general life of the university." This foreshadowed one of the major reasons for library school closings as documented by Marion Paris (1988) 50 years later.

In 1946, a decade after Munn's study, the Carnegie Corporation of New York requested Joseph Wheeler, formerly librarian of Enoch Pratt Free Library in Baltimore, to prepare a report on matters affecting present-day training for librarianship, with special reference to library schools, their faculties, graduates, students, curricula, relations to higher education and to the profession of librarianship. The purpose was both to look back on what had been accomplished since the initial large allocation of funding in 1926 and to explore the future of training for librarianship. The Wheeler report on *Progress & Problems in Education for Librarianship* (1946) reiterated the need for strong library schools, advocated some specialization in training areas by each school, and recommended a concerted program to recruit young people of marked aptitude and ability for the profession.

Finally, Jesse Shera (1972) noted that the origin of his influential book on *The Foundations of Education for Librarianship* was a 1956 grant from the Carnegie Corporation of New York "to undertake a study of library education ... a distillation of [Shera's] own thinking on this important subject" (p. vii). Shera's study was "a result of a theory of librarianship which has been in the process of maturation for more than a quarter century of teaching and administration, first at the University of Chicago, and subsequently at Western Reserve University." Shera went on to explain: "My purpose has been to explore the role of the library as it contributes to the total communication system in society and the meaning of that role for the library profession, and having determined the requirements of that role to identify those which are appropriately met by graduate professional education" (p. vii). Furthermore, "I have attempted to give education for librarianship a more meaningful theoretical and interdisciplinary perspective than has characterized it in the past" (p. viii). In this he was shaped by his experience at GLS, from which he earned his Ph.D. degree in 1944.

## III. U.S. Office of Education and Title II-B Funding

The next major investment in library education came from the federal government rather than foundations. Under Title II-B of the Higher Education Act of 1965, substantial support was provided in the form of both fellowships for students and support to schools to defray the cost of courses of training in librarianship. Holmstrom and El-Khawas (1971) provided an overview of the first four years of the program. While awards were made for all levels of study, 270 of the more than 1500 fellowship awards made in the first four years went to doctoral students. Many individuals who would never have entered such programs were able to do so, creating a cadre of future faculty that led to a shift toward library school faculties with a larger proportion of individuals holding doctoral degrees. Holmstrom and El-Khawas (1971, p. 215) cited the opinion of Russell Bidlack from the University of Michigan describing another positive outcome for the schools that participated: "The existence of these fine fellowships, finer in some respects than those existing in almost every other field, has given library schools visibility on their own campuses which they had not enjoyed previously, and has given the students holding these fellowships a new status among other graduate students. The fact that library education was given this kind of recognition by the Congress in the Higher Education Act has done more for librarianship in the eyes of nonlibrarians than nearly any other event in recent library history." Carter and Owens (1993) provided data on the number of Title II-B fellowships and traineeships awarded for library career training during the period 1966–1992, with $38,191,659 as the total amount awarded, including 3152 awards for master's, 265 awards for post-master's, and 1239 awards for doctoral study.

In the same period, the U.S. Office of Education Library and Information Sciences Research Branch funded a study to develop a research agenda for library education. Borko (1973, p. 1) summarized the motivation for the study: "[Library schools] wish to change and improve, but what needs to be changed and in what direction? Efforts to create improvements are being hampered by the lack of a comprehensive and integrated body of knowledge which would identify current educational needs and the most effective methods for their achievement. In essence, the research to support innovative educational decision-making is lacking." A multi-step method was employed. Recognized leaders in library education were asked to discuss research needs in 10 specified areas (the aims and content of graduate library education; general vs. specialized library education; the integration of information science and library automation into the library school educational program; relating instructional methodology to teaching in library schools; library school administration; library school faculty and students; relationships of professional associations to library schools and libraries; the library school and requirements for staffing libraries; continuing education for librarians; and research needs relating to the role of the library in the community). Then the Delphi Technique was used to rank proposed projects, resulting in five priority groups: I. Improving and updating the skills of professional librarians; II. Library school educational planning and relevance; III. Administration of the library school and library with regard to specific courses, skills, and programs; IV. Forms of instruction and supportive facilities for maintaining instruction; and V. The role of professional associations and communication among librarians. Borko (1973, pp. 220–221) concluded: "With completion and publication of the research to establish priorities, the work of the editor is concluded. If, however, there is no implementation, the purposes of his effort and that of the contributors will not become realized ... It is up to the concerned professionals in library science education to propose, plan, and execute the specific research projects that would provide information and then to convert our knowledge into a program for improving library education. Without implementation, research planning is a useless exercise. The proposed research must be undertaken and the results transferred into improved curricula for the education of librarians." Despite availability of the study in book form, published by

the American Library Association, subsequent citations to the book are
relatively few in number, suggesting limited impact in terms of stimulating
subsequent research.

## IV. Foundation and Government Funding in the 1970s and 1980s

Studies relevant to library education continued in the 1970s and 1980s
under other auspices. The H.W. Wilson Foundation was established in 1952
by Halsey Wilson, founder of the H.W. Wilson Company. This foundation
supported a study undertaken by Ralph Conant, a social science researcher,
on behalf of the Advisory Committee to the Office for Library Education of
the ALA. The hope was that a critical examination might do for library
education in the 1980s what the Williamson report had done in the 1920s.
Based on site visits to selected schools and a series of interviews with faculty,
students, alumni, and employers, Conant (1980, pp. 8–9) made a number of
recommendations:

- Reduce the number of accredited graduate programs to better match anticipated demand for
  graduates.
- Lengthen and enrich the master's program to include thorough coverage of the fundamentals of
  professional librarianship, a substantial internship or practicum, and a specialization. A national
  plan should include an allocation of specializations among the graduate schools.
- Limit enrollment to those who have the potential to assume professional positions in the field.
- Improve the quality and relevance of the graduate programs by appointing qualified professionals
  to their faculties, by encouraging faculty research on contemporary library problems, and by
  training faculty in effective methods of instruction.
- Involve graduate library schools in continuing education.
- Make the accreditation process an effective instrument of correction and reform by including
  professional evaluators on accreditation teams.
- Systematize reform by establishing a national forum for library education and giving it the mission
  of developing a national plan for the education and training of professional librarians.

The response of library educators was quite critical. For example, Darling
(1981, p. 99) asserted that "the reader of the report ... will not be able to
find suitable justification for the proposed reforms in the chapters of
uncritical reporting of opinion that make up the bulk of the book;"
Rothstein (1980, pp. 534–535), noting the "poor quality of Conant's
research and presentation," lamented that "the Williamson report for the
1980s remains to be written."

In the early 1980s, the U.S. Department of Education funded a project
on *New Directions in Library and Information Science Education* (Griffiths and

King, 1986) to identify, describe, and validate both current and future competency requirements (knowledge, skills, and attitudes) of information professionals in a variety of different environments (e.g., libraries, museums, archives, records management centers) performing a variety of functions (e.g., reference, acquisitions, exhibit management) at all stages of career development from entry-level through senior administrative level. In assessing the impact of the published study, Cooper and Lunin (1989, p. 313) noted that while the study was "heralded as a work that would have far-reaching consequences and influence on curriculum design in schools of library and information science/studies, the report instead generated controversy and criticism of both its methodology and its findings. Reviewers, for example, noted the lack of cohesion in the large number of competencies identified and lamented the limited amount of new information the investigation brought forth." Dougherty (1987, p. 203) concluded his review of *New Directions* with: "Let us hope that those responsible for directing the course for professional education will think long and hard before launching another initiative to reform education. The last two initiatives, namely the Conant study and now the *New Directions* project, have not been up to the task and in fact their failure will make a third attempt even more difficult and problematic."

Fifteen years after the publication of Borko's *Targets for Research in Library Education*, the U.S. Department of Education once again undertook development of a research agenda for library education in the context of a larger project on *Rethinking the Library in the Information Age* (Matthews, 1988). Robert M. Hayes contributed the section enumerating a research agenda on "Education and Training of Librarians," noting that "strategic planning for library and information science education is critical for establishing university priorities and for making national policy" (Hayes, 1988, p. 43). Observing the changing roles and responsibilities for librarians as a result of the impact of new technologies, Hayes asserted that "education for library and information science must prepare the information professional to handle these responsibilities with excellence, not mediocrity. The purpose of this report is to provide a frame of reference for a research agenda that will support public policy to meet these new requirements" (Hayes, 1988, p. 43). He then enumerated a long list of research questions, organized in the framework of the accreditation standards (goals and objectives, curriculum, faculty, students, resources, governance), explaining that "all of the questions presented as the basis for a research agenda are aimed at maintaining and increasing the personal commitment and intellectual qualification of librarians as centrally important information professionals in our society" (Hayes, 1988, p. 45), with each set of questions intended to identify data needed for policymaking at both a national and institutional level. He highlighted eight questions as being of particular importance (Hayes, 1988, p. 60):

1. How important is the professional librarian to society, and what is the evidence of that importance?
2. What are the proper roles and responsibilities of various academic programs in meeting the needs for professional librarians?
3. What are the appropriate means for measuring the quality of library educational programs?
4. What is and, with the objective of excellence in library education, what should be the effect of societal changes on programmatic goals and objectives?
5. How should specialization be dealt with in first professional degree programs?
6. What is the essential minimum of faculty for first professional degree programs, considering both numbers and qualifications, in the context of excellence in professional preparation?
7. How can the quality of students best be advanced, considering recruitment, admission requirements, and recommended undergraduate preparation?
8. Of the various alternatives for continuing education for the profession, which are the most effective in terms of advancing excellence in the information profession?

As with the Borko study before it, despite a clear articulation of a research agenda for the education and training of librarians, the Hayes report did not serve as a significant stimulus to subsequent research.

## V. Experimentation and Innovation with Foundation Support in the 1990s

The 1990s began with the publication of Stieg's (1992) *Change and Challenge in Library and Information Science Education*, a study completed with support from the Council on Library Resources. She sought to address two questions: "What is the present state of library and information science education and where is it headed? If this is not what we want, what must be changed?" The book provided a thorough discussion of issues and trends in library education, concluding that "change is necessary, but agreement on the form and direction it should take has yet to emerge" (Stieg, 1992, p. 171). Subsequently, the W. K. Kellogg Foundation took the lead in funding a number of projects focused on curriculum transformation, including HRISM, KRISTAL-ED, and KALIPER.

The Human Resources for Information Systems Management (HRISM) program began in 1994 to "test the notion that an infusion of funds would help schools of library and information science transform themselves into agents of change and overhaul their curricula with an eye toward the requirements of the future" (Marcum, 1997, p. 35). Grants were awarded to the University of Michigan, Drexel University, University of Illinois at Urbana-Champaign, and Florida State University, with each grant aimed at testing a different innovative approach, including creating specializations; interconnecting undergraduate, graduate, and continuing education curricula; reaching students at a distance using a variety of online technologies; and developing a new undergraduate program. Marcum (1997, p. 38) concluded that "all four of these schools recognized that library science programs are part of a larger information landscape. Instead of disbanding its existing library science curriculum, each school opted to use new moneys to expand the boundaries of the field and to make a statement about the role that such a school could play." She cautioned that "the schools that have broadened the definition of information studies have been able to do so only by obtaining external funds for making the transition." It remained to be seen whether other schools would make such changes without the stimulus of grant funds.

Following the investment of the W. K. Kellogg Foundation in curricular change at several programs through its mid-1990s HRISM initiative, the Kellogg-ALISE Information Professions and Education Reform (KALIPER) Project (1998–2000) sought to carry out a study of the nature and extent of major curricular change in LIS education, "perhaps the most extensive examination of the LIS curricula since the Williamson Report (1923)" (Pettigrew and Durrance, 2001, p. 170). The study employed a team approach with 20 scholars from different schools, placing the Kellogg-HRISM developments in a broader context. In the hopes of fostering collaborative and continued scholarship in LIS education, the teams included experienced faculty as well as doctoral students and assistant professors. Pettigrew and Durrance asserted that (p. 173): "The KALIPER project represents an unprecedented attempt to document and understand the recent past, current status, and future directions of the LIS field." Stages of the investigation included: (1) a survey of deans and directors about factors that affect curricular change; (2) case studies of 26 schools regarding how their curriculum has changed; (3) curricular analysis and interviews with faculty at seven additional schools to determine whether the projects' preliminary findings reflected their experience; (4) in-depth analysis of curricular changes within such specific areas as archives and records management, school media, distance education, and undergraduate programs; (5) analysis of LIS academic job announcements from 1990–1998 in the ASIS Jobline and *American Libraries*; and (6) analysis of faculty specialization descriptors from ALISE directories. Summary findings identified six trends regarding curricular change, noting that while the majority of schools are undergoing significant change, the areas targeted for change vary from school to school (Pettigrew and Durrance, 2001, pp. 173–179):

1. In addition to libraries as institutions and library-specific operations, LIS curricula are addressing broad-based information environments and information problems.
2. While LIS curricula continue to incorporate perspectives from other disciplines, a distinct core has taken shape that is predominantly user-centered.
3. LIS schools and programs are increasing the investment and infusion of information technology into their curricula.
4. LIS schools and programs are experimenting with the structure of specialization within the curriculum.
5. LIS schools are offering instruction in different formats to provide students with more flexibility.
6. LIS schools and programs are expanding their curricula by offering related degrees at the undergraduate, master's, and doctoral levels.

In an assessment of the KALIPER findings, Sutton (2001, p. 243) noted that trends 3 and 5 most likely reflect "nothing more than the natural evolution of the traditional LIS domain," with the increase in computing and communications technologies affecting what is taught in LIS schools and how teaching and learning take place, while trends 1, 2, 4, and 6 "represent potential systemic changes that substantially alter the boundaries of the playing field." He suggested that the latter four trends can be explained in light of Robert Taylor's (1979) metaphor of the Copernican shift—the shift from a Ptolemaic universe with the library at its center to a Copernican universe with information at its center. Sutton cautioned that the findings are relatively tentative given the study's method; demonstrating links between the changes perceived and their causal factors would require additional, more carefully controlled research. In a more recent assessment, Mezick and Koenig (2008, p. 601) noted that while observers and participants hoped that this study would have a major impact on LIS education, they found relatively few subsequent references to it in the literature. They concluded that "the KALIPER project seems to have been the result of change, not the cause of it. It can be argued that the project served little purpose other than to report on the changes that were already happening." In any case the KALIPER study documented that some of the changes accomplished with external funding at the four programs receiving funding through Kellogg's HRISM program were also occurring at other schools without external grant funding. It is also worth noting that a number of these changes were foreshadowed by the increasing emphasis on information science in library school curricula beginning in the late 1960s (Smith, 1998, p. 124). As early as 1967, Swank observed that "the new content represented by these changes is impressive—the extension of librarianship into new fields of information handling, the intensification of library services, the infusion of new knowledge and techniques from other disciplines, with emerging new specializations" (Swank, 1967, p. 40).

The Kellogg Foundation funded a third initiative with a focus on library and information science education during this period, the Kellogg CRISTAL-ED (Coalition on Reinventing Information Science, Technology, and Library Education) Project (Drabenstott and Atkins, 1996). This was a five-year project to reinvent such education to meet the changing needs of information professionals. Through this project the School of Information and Library Studies (now School of Information) at the University of Michigan sought to facilitate development of a national, multidisciplinary collaborative consortium to define new areas of professional specialization to serve society's needs for information access and use in the age of digital information. Goals of the CRISTAL-ED project included: (1) reinvent the core curriculum for information and library studies; (2) define new specializations; (3) create a distributed community of faculty and practitioners (collaboratory) to deliver the new professional education; and (4) build "living" laboratories in information-intensive organizations to serve citizens, faculty, and students. To garner a wide range of opinions, exchange ideas, and learn from others involved in comparable activities, the University of Michigan established a moderated listserv named CRISTAL-ED in January 1995. Initially the intent of the listserv was to focus on the vision of the new information and library studies education, and then target planning, prototyping, and implementing new core curricula for such education. A record of the discussions from January 1995 through April 1999 is still maintained (http://www.si.umich.edu/cristaled/discussions.html). The listserv had the benefit of opening up the discussion on the future of LIS education to a broader audience, but, as with other studies in this period, it is not clear whether it stimulated changes beyond curriculum development already under way at the University of Michigan and elsewhere "to produce graduates who will create and manage a broad set of knowledge-work environments including but not limited to libraries" (Drabenstott and Atkins, 1996, p. 67).

## VI. Institute of Museum and Library Services

Following the decline in Title II-B funding during the 1970s, no new major federal investments in library and information science education were forthcoming until the establishment of the Institute of Museum and Library Services (IMLS). As specified in the Museum and Library Services Act (MLSA) of 1996 and reauthorized in 2003 (http://www.imls.gov/about/

timeline.shtm), the new agency combined the Institute of Museum Services, which had been in existence since 1976, and the Library Programs Office, which had been part of the Department of Education since 1956. Substantial increases in funding for library and information science education coincided with the four-year term of Robert S. Martin (a former library and information science educator) as director of IMLS from 2001–2005. In addition Laura Bush, as a First Lady holding a master's degree in library science, was supportive of investment in library education.

IMLS launched a new multi-million dollar grant program to recruit and educate the next generation of librarians. The rationale for targeting funds in this way was provided in the news releases announcing the awards (http://www.imls.gov/news/2005/062805b.shtm): "The grants are designed to help offset a current shortage of school library media specialists, library school faculty, and librarians working in underserved communities, as well as a looming shortage of library directors and other senior librarians who are expected to retire in the next 20 years." Analysis of grants awarded as retrieved from the IMLS database (http://www.imls.gov/search.asp) shows a dramatic increase from the period in which education and training grants were made by IMLS under the auspices of the National Leadership Grant program (57 in the period 1998–2004, distributed as follows: 1998 (6), 1999 (12), 2000 (14), 2001 (9), 2002 (8), 2003 (5), 2004 (3)) to the period in which awards were made under the Laura Bush 21st Century Librarian program (171 in the period 2003–2007, distributed as follows: 2003 (27), 2004 (27), 2005 (39), 2006 (35), 2007 (43)). The growth in numbers is matched by a growth in dollars allocated, from over $922,500 in 1998 to almost $28 million in 2007. (As noted earlier, for the entire period from 1966–1992, Title II-B funding for fellowships and traineeships totaled about $38.2 million). IMLS grants are awarded to libraries and professional associations as well as library and information science schools, but the latter are also often partners with other types of organizations named as the lead recipient of the grant. The press release announcing the 2007 awards (http://www.imls.gov/news/2007/061907.shtm) indicated that since 2002, the Laura Bush 21st Century Librarian Program had awarded grants to support 2913 master's degree students, 178 doctoral students, 1166 pre-professional students, and 5629 continuing education students.

The Program Overview for the Laura Bush 21st Century Librarian program describes its scope as: "supports projects to develop faculty and library leaders, to recruit and educate the next generation of librarians, and to conduct research on the library profession, and to support early career research on any area of library and information science by tenure-track, untenured faculty in graduate schools of library and information science.

It also supports projects to attract high school and college students to consider careers in libraries, to build institutional capacity in graduate schools of library and information science, and to assist in the professional development of librarians and library staff" (http://www.imls.gov/applicants/grants/21centuryLibrarian.shtm). The grant program invites proposals in six categories:

(1)  Doctoral programs, to prepare faculty to educate the next generation of library professionals or to develop the next generation of library leaders;

(2)  Master's level programs to educate the next generation of librarians;

(3)  Research (with some specific targeted areas such as establishing baseline data on professional demographics and job availability and evaluating current programs in library education for their capacity to meet identified needs);

(4)  Pre-professional programs (attract promising junior high, high school or college students to consider careers in library and information science through statewide or regional pilot projects);

(5)  Programs to build institutional capacity (develop or enhance curricula with particular areas identified such as expertise in digital assets or data curation); and

(6)  Continuing education (in areas such as improving services to audiences with special needs such as youth at risk, seniors, and those with language, physical or other barriers to service).

A review of the grants awarded indicates that many different schools have received one or more grants, some to the school alone, others to the school in partnership with schools at other institutions, and others to the school in partnership with libraries or library associations. Each funded proposal requires both an evaluation and a dissemination plan. The evaluation is to be framed using outcomes-based planning and evaluation (see the Shaping Outcomes tutorial at http://www.shapingoutcomes.org). Dissemination requires that the results be made accessible to the library and information fields through such means as conference presentations, publications, and web sites. While it is too early to assess the collective impact of the IMLS-funded projects, the emphasis on evaluation and dissemination should provide a mechanism for institutions beyond those receiving the grants to benefit from lessons learned from the programs developed.

## VII. Accreditation

As long as the library profession retains holding a master's degree from an accredited degree program as an important credential for employment, the accreditation standards and process will affect the schools that seek to gain or retain accreditation. These standards and review processes have been shaped by investments from both foundations and government agencies, beginning with funds given to the ALA by the Carnegie Corporation following the Williamson Report. As noted by Roy (1998, p. 11), both the profession and the Carnegie Corporation took the report recommendations seriously. ALA responded in 1924 by creating a permanent agency, the Board of Education for Librarianship (BEL), which would accredit education programs. The BEL adopted Minimum Standards for Library Schools in 1925 as well as accreditation procedures, and the standards were first revised in 1933 (White, 1976, p. 218). New standards for accreditation were adopted by the ALA Council in 1951 as more suitable to the graduate programs carried on in a majority of library schools beginning in the late 1940s (White, 1976, p. 224). In 1955 BEL became the Committee on Accreditation. Asheim (1975, pp. 154–155) explained how a grant from the H. W. Wilson Foundation in 1969 enabled review and revision of the 1951 *Standards for Accreditation*, leading to the adoption of a new set of *Standards* in 1972.

Both the U.S. Department of Education and the H. W. Wilson Foundation contributed to the development of the *Standards for Accreditation of Master's Programs in Library and Information Studies* adopted in 1992. The ALISE/H.W. Wilson Foundation Accreditation Conference, held in September 1984, sought to bring together representatives of the professional societies most concerned about accreditation, to see if the current scope, structure, and financial support were adequate for the future and if not, what alternative organizational structure might be considered (Seavey, 1984). At the conference, Hayes (1984, p. 141) announced that the U. S. Department of Education would fund an 18-month project with the objective of involving a number of the professional societies in a concerted effort to examine and arrive at solutions to the several problems discussed at the conference: structure of accreditation, finance, guidelines for program goals and objectives, guidelines for faculty, guidelines for curriculum, and guidelines for society specific objectives. Bunge (1991) noted that as a result of this project, the ALA Committee on Accreditation concluded that the 1972 standards were in need of revision and the Standards Revision Subcommittee was established in 1988. Dalrymple (1998, p. 93) observed that the 1992 *Standards* place great emphasis on ongoing planning and evaluation and involve assessing the outcomes of educational programs. Prior to implementation of the new standards, the ALA Office for Accreditation obtained funding from the U.S. Department of Education to introduce outcomes assessment into LIS accreditation through seminars and the publication of a resource manual. One aim of these materials was to provide an incentive for LIS programs to create a shared body of knowledge and experience that demonstrates how the process of setting educational objectives can result in observable outcomes. With the increasing availability of online Program Presentations (self-studies) from ALA-accredited programs (linked from http://www.ala.org/ala/aboutala/offices/accreditation/index.cfm), there is now a mechanism for sharing the experience of individual programs more widely.

## VIII. Increasing Diversity

Both foundation and government funding have been important in working toward a goal that has seemed out of reach without this support: improving the representation of African American, Hispanic, and Native American individuals in librarianship. DuMont's (1986) historical review focused on African American librarians in particular. The first school to educate African American librarians, the Hampton _Institute_ Library School, was founded with a grant from the Carnegie Corporation. In the period 1925–1939 it had 183 graduates. Looking for a suitable university home rather than a technical institute to continue such a school, the Carnegie Corporation granted an endowment to Atlanta (now Clark Atlanta) University in 1941. The school became accredited in 1943 and from its beginning was an important supplier of African American librarians for the entire U.S. Three decades later two predominantly African American public universities received foundation support and successfully pursued accreditation status: Alabama A&M in 1975, with support from the W.K. Kellogg Foundation, and North Carolina Central University in 1975, with support from the Carnegie Corporation of New York and the Andrew W. Mellon Foundation. Alabama A&M was accredited as a single-purpose school, emphasizing school library media programs. The only ALA-accredited program remaining in 2008 at a predominantly African American university is that at North Carolina Central University.

Federal government funding has also benefited individuals from diverse backgrounds seeking to pursue a degree in library science. The Title II-B fellowship program became a vehicle for integration of minority students into more schools beginning in 1970 when the regulations were changed to provide that fellowship funds awarded be utilized to equalize opportunities for minorities. DeLoach (1980) examined the effect of Title II-B on minority recruitment for the years 1970–1977, showing a positive impact. DuMont concluded (1986, pp. 243–244) that, for the period through the mid-1980s, "the historical evidence presented here shows that black representation in professional education for librarians has depended on the monumental efforts of a very few white and black library leaders to develop special programs for blacks. They have had to rely on the interest and contributions of foundations and most recently the federal government to provide a full range of opportunities for blacks to study librarianship. The overall effectiveness of the various programs supported by these private and public sources has not been measured. In the end, it seems that the lack of knowledge of effectiveness is also an impediment to equal opportunity."

With first the National Leadership and now the Laura Bush 21st Century Librarian grant funds from IMLS, LIS schools are once again garnering resources to improve recruitment, enrollment, and graduation rates of more diverse students, better matched to the demographics of the U.S. population. For example, the LIS Access Midwest Program (LAMP) (http://www.lisaccess.org) is a recruitment effort involving several academic libraries and LIS schools in the Midwest. Knowledge River at the University of Arizona (http://sirls.arizona.edu/KR/index) focuses on educating Hispanic and Native American librarians. IMLS grants are now also supporting ALA's Spectrum Initiative (Stone, 2007), expanding the number of scholarships available to M.S. students and funding the Spectrum Doctoral Fellowship Program. As noted in the discussion above regarding IMLS grants, it will be important to evaluate these efforts and disseminate the findings to other schools concerned with recruiting and educating a more diverse student population.

## IX. Reflections on the Impact of External Funding

This review of projects and initiatives funded by grants from foundations and federal government agencies suggests that outcomes have been variable. Certainly the consolidation of library education in college and university settings was accelerated by the Williamson Report, as was the emphasis on accreditation of such schools by the ALA. The Graduate Library School established with Carnegie Corporation support at the University of Chicago raised the profile of research in library science and, through its graduates who took faculty positions elsewhere, influenced education at other schools. The Title II-B fellowship funding supported preparation of faculty at a time when schools were seeking to shift the balance of faculty to include more with doctoral-level preparation. Finally, professional ranks have included more African American librarians than would have been the case without foundation and federal support.

As discussed in this chapter, several educational surveys have been funded by both foundations and federal government agencies, with the Williamson Report being the most notable in its impact. In writing of the educational survey as an instrument of reform, Blauch (1955, pp. 12–13) said:

"The survey is a means that has been widely used to stimulate improvement in education for the professions ... When the survey is conducted by competent surveyors, it usually becomes a landmark in the history of education in the particular field. It provides a basis for self-criticism and evaluation by the professional schools, informs the profession about the status and service of its educational institutions, and sometimes establishes new ideals and goals for cooperative action through the association concerned with the particular field".

It seems that to date only the Williamson Report has achieved "landmark" status, though other surveys discussed in this chapter served as useful reflections on developments and trends for the period in which they were conducted. Likewise funded and published research agendas for library education have had limited impact. In contrast, the manpower studies used to justify major funding for the Laura Bush 21st Century Librarian program have had a significant impact in terms of the rapid infusion of funding into library schools to remedy the perceived and anticipated shortages. For example, the press release announcing the 2005 Laura Bush 21st Century Librarian grants (http://www.imls.gov/news/2005/062805b.shtm) justified the initiative by noting that: in May 2000, *Library Journal* reported that 40% of America's library directors plan to retire in 9 years or less; in July 2000, the *Monthly Labor Review* reported that in 1998 57% of professional librarians were 45 or older; and in March 2002, *American Libraries* showed that based on 1990 Census data almost 58% of professional librarians will reach age 65 between 2005 and 2019.

As is true in basic research, the agendas of external funding agencies, whether foundation or government, can initiate changes in educational programs that might not otherwise occur, or might not occur as rapidly. This can be seen most recently in the areas highlighted for building institutional capacity under the Laura Bush 21st Century Librarian program (http://www.imls.gov/applicants/grants/21centuryLibrarian.shtm):

- Develop or enhance curricula within graduate schools of library and information science. In particular:
  - Develop or enhance courses or programs of study for library, museum, and archives professionals in the creation, management, preservation, presentation, and use of digital assets.
  - Develop or enhance courses or programs of study related to the development of critical thinking skills, such as organization leadership and research methods.
  - Broaden the library and information science curriculum by incorporating perspectives from other disciplines and fields of scholarship, such as public policy, ethics, American studies, urban planning, mass communication, and instructional design.

- Develop projects or programs in data curation as training programs for graduate students in library and information science. Data curation includes the authentication, archiving, management, preservation, retrieval and representation of high-quality digital data for use and re-use over time.

While such events as the closing of the Graduate Library School by the University of Chicago in 1991 and Clark Atlanta's School of Library and Information Studies in 2005 (Oder, 2003) can be viewed as steps backward, undoing investments made by the Carnegie Corporation, the trends outlined in the KALIPER report and the likely progress resulting from the Laura Bush 21st Century Librarian program investments in building capacity as well as student support for pursuit of LIS education at all levels are encouraging steps forward. The support of doctoral students in particular is an important source of new faculty, as the earlier generation of faculty funded by Title II-B for doctoral study is now retiring.

## X. Implications for the Future of Library and Information Science Education

Roy (1998, pp. 12–13) concluded her brief history of librarian education in the U.S. with the following observation: "The first fifty years of librarian education are best characterized as a time that introduced, yet did not resolve, a series of questions shared by other developing social service disciplines. These questions concerned who the student should be; what should or could be taught; who should be the educators and to whom should the educators report; where should the education be found; how should education be accomplished; and to what end should such education strive." While schools seek accreditation of their master's programs under a common set of standards, the first paragraph of the Mission, Goals, and Objectives section of the *Standards for Accreditation* makes clear the expectation that the answers to Roy's questions are answered at the institution level (http://www.ala.org/ala/educationcareers/education/accreditedprograms/standards/standards.cfm): "A school's mission and program goals are pursued, and its program objectives achieved, through implementation of a broad-based planning process that involves the constituency that a program seeks to serve. Consistent with the values of the parent institution and the culture and mission of the school, program goals and objectives foster quality education."

Going forward, it is interesting to speculate whether external funding, coupled with creative use of new technologies, will stimulate a new era of collaboration in course and program design in library and information science education.

As early as 1990, a Council on Library Resources report on "Library Schools in Research Universities", funded by the W.K. Kellogg Foundation, observed that (Council on Library Resources, 1990, p. 55) "if the library schools of research universities are to take the lead in recasting library education and building an influential and credible research program, an all-out collaboration of the strongest schools is required to enhance and reinforce even the most ambitious institutional efforts. Consolidation of strengths offers the only realistic prospect for success in making fundamental, long-term improvement in professional education. An opportunity exists to invigorate the profession, but it will require great effort by first-rate institutions and individuals—faculty and academic officers alike—with a personal commitment to librarianship in all its forms." A decade later, Sutton (2001, pp. 243–244) in his commentary on the KALIPER study observed that "in the past, LIS educational institutions have generally served geographically constrained constituencies in the form of local students and local institutions (primarily libraries). As a result LIS schools have served as comprehensive institutions covering as many bases as their geographic regions required and their resources could accommodate. With increasingly available expertise available through alternative modes of delivery, LIS schools might be less compelled to be all things to all people and to evolve as 'centers of excellence' in particular specializations."

The proposal process for IMLS Laura Bush 21st Century Librarian grants encourages multi-institutional collaborations and has already stimulated some innovative partnerships in support of library and information science education. Two examples, WISE and IPL, are cited here to suggest what may emerge from these efforts.

The Web-Based Information Science Education (WISE) consortium (http://www.wiseeducation.org) seeks to increase access to and improve the quality of online education in library and information science. Led by Syracuse University and the University of Illinois at Urbana-Champaign, a building institutional capacity grant enabled WISE to grow from the initial three to 13 institutions in three countries (U.S., Canada, New Zealand). Schools participate in sharing online courses, enabling students at one school to gain access to a course offered by another school and not available as part of the degree program at his or her home institution. Initial evaluation findings reported by Montague and Pluzhenskaia (2007) revealed that students were generally satisfied with online education experiences both within the consortium and in other online education contexts. Course sharing across this many schools enables students to access learning opportunities (spanning the LIS curriculum spectrum) unavailable through a single program, including such courses as theological librarianship, designing the public library of the future, publishing for the profession, and information visualization.

In the other project, a building institutional capacity grant will enable Drexel University College of Information Science and Technology, in collaboration with the University of Michigan, Florida State University, and the University of Pittsburgh, to transform the Internet Public Library (IPL) (http://www.ipl.org) into a fully featured virtual learning laboratory for digital reference. Enhancements that will result from this grant include digital reference learning objects available to faculty in all ALA-accredited LIS programs; a laboratory with access to new technologies used to offer digital reference service; and a collaborative learning community for faculty, students, and working librarians.

Just as IMLS grants have been a factor in encouraging collaboration among LIS programs housed in different universities, such grants may also serve to foster closer collaboration between practitioners and educators in recruitment of students and design and delivery of programs. In particular graduate schools of library and information science or school library media certification programs are eligible to apply for funds to educate students at the master's level only if they apply in a partnership that includes libraries, library consortia, or library associations. While practitioners (Williamson, Munn, Wheeler) played an important role in the Carnegie Corporation-funded reviews of library education, many of the subsequent studies and grant-funded activities discussed in this chapter were led largely by educators themselves. These new IMLS grant-funded partnerships offer an opportunity to explore new forms of practitioner/educator collaboration to strengthen library and information science education.

While many libraries have benefited from collaborative activity for years, collaborations among schools and among schools and libraries or library associations must move forward despite differences in institutional culture, priorities, resources, and mission. External funding serves as a stimulus, but sustainability (like evaluation and dissemination, this is a criterion for receipt of IMLS funding) will require finding workable collaborative models that can continue once external funding ceases.

This chapter has focused on funding for research, development, and resource enhancement in library (and information) science education rather than research conducted by library and information science faculty on other topics. The latter continues to receive increasing emphasis and funding from both foundation and government sources. As this chapter demonstrates, significant foundation and government funding for LIS education per se has been episodic, making prediction of likely future trends in funding difficult. This makes it critical that mechanisms be found to analyze and synthesize the outcomes of the projects funded through the Laura Bush 21st Century Librarian Program, so that lessons learned can be disseminated to benefit educational programs beyond those directly involved in the specific projects.

In their discussion of KALIPER project findings, Pettigrew and Durrance (2001, p. 179) concluded that common instigators (and sometimes inhibitors) of change included: (1) the demands of students, employers, graduates, and professional associations for graduate competencies; (2) the growth and expense of supporting emerging technology; (3) internal campus relationships and positioning; (4) availability and/or presence of faculty with new subject expertise; (5) competition from other LIS programs; and (6) the availability of financial support for innovation. While financial support from foundation and government sources is only one of these factors, there can be no doubt that it has played a significant role in the development of library and information science education in the U.S. for more than 80 years.

## References

Asheim, L. (1975). Trends in library education—United States. *Advances in Librarianship* 5, 147–201.

Blauch, L. E. (1955). *Education for the Professions*. U.S. Office of Education, Washington, DC.

Borko, H. (ed.) (1973). *Targets for Research in Library Education*. American Library Association, Chicago, IL.

Bunge, C. A. (1991). Accreditation standards revision: Does it matter? *Wilson Library Bulletin* 65, 65–66.

Carter, Y. B., and Owens, J. E. (1993). *Library Career Training Program: Abstracts of Funded Projects 1992, Title II-B, Higher Education Act*. U.S. Department of Education, Washington, DC.

Churchwell, C. D. (1975). *The Shaping of American Library Education*. American Library Association, Chicago, IL.

Conant, R. W. (1980). *The Conant Report: A Study of the Education of Librarians*. MIT Press, Cambridge, MA.

Connaway, L. S. (2005). A research funding opportunity for library and information science faculty: The OCLC/ALISE library and information science research grant program. *Journal of Education for Library and Information Science* 46(3), 258–265.

Cooper, M., and Lunin, L. F. (1989). Education and training of the information professional. *Annual Review of Information Science and Technology* 24, 295–341.

Council on Library Resources (1990). *Program Reports. I. A Review of the CLR Research Program, 1986–1990. II. Library Schools in Research Universities*. Council on Library Resources, Washington, DC.

Dalrymple, P. W. (1998). Current trends in accreditation of library and information science programs. In *Library and Information Studies Education in the United States* (L. Roy and B. E. Sheldon, eds.), pp. 81–100, Mansell, London.

Darling, R. L. (1981). A comment on the final Conant report. *Journal of Education for Librarianship* 22(1&2), 98–99.

Davis, D. G., Jr. (1976). Education for librarianship. *Library Trends* 25(1), 113–133.

DeLoach, M. L. (1980). *The Higher Education Act of 1965, Title II-B: The Fellowships/ Traineeships for Training in Library and Information Science Program: Its Impact on Minority Recruitment in Library and Information Science Education*. Ph.D. dissertation, University of Pittsburgh.

Dougherty, R. M. (1987). Review of new directions in library and information science education. *Journal of Education for Library and Information Science* 27(3), 201–203.

Drabenstott, K. M., and Atkins, D. (1996). The Kellogg CRISTAL-ED project: Creating a model program to support libraries in the digital age. *Advances in Librarianship* 20, 47–68.

DuMont, R. D. (1986). The educating of black librarians: An historical perspective. *Journal of Education for Library and Information Science* 26(4), 233–249.

Griffiths, J-M., and King, D. W. (1986). *New Directions in Library and Information Science Education*. Knowledge Industry Publications, White Plains, NY.

Hayes, R. M. (1984). The American Library Association—U.S. Department of Education grant. *Journal of Education for Library and Information Science* 25(2), 141–144.

Hayes, R. M. (1988). Education and training of librarians. In *Rethinking the Library in the Information Age*, vol. II, pp. 43–74, Office of Library Programs, Office of Educational Research and Improvement, U.S. Department of Education, Washington, DC.

Holmstrom, E. I., and El-Khawas, E. (1971). An overview of the first four years of the Title II-B fellowship program. *College & Research Libraries* 32(3), 205–216.

Houser, L., and Schrader, A. M. (1978). *The Search for a Scientific Profession: Library Science Education in the U.S. and Canada*. Scarecrow Press, Metuchen, NJ.

Marcum, D. B. (1997). Transforming the curriculum; transforming the profession. *American Libraries* 28(1), 35–36. 38.

Matthews, A. J. (ed.) (1988). *Rethinking the Library in the Information Age*, 3 vols. Office of Library Programs, Office of Educational Research and Improvement, U.S. Department of Education, Washington, DC.

Mezick, E. M., and Koenig, M. E. D. (2008). Education for information science. *Annual Review of Information Science and Technology* 42, 593–624.

Montague, R.-A., and Pluzhenskaia, M. (2007). Web-based Information Science Education (WISE): Collaboration to explore and expand quality in LIS online education. *Journal of Education for Library and Information Science* 48(1), 36–51.

Munn, R. (1936). *Conditions and Trends in Education for Librarianship*. Carnegie Corporation of New York, New York.

Oder, N. (2003). Clark Atlanta university to close 62-year-old LIS school. *Library Journal* 128(19), 16.

Paris, M. (1988). *Library School Closings: Four Case Studies*. Scarecrow Press, Metuchen, NJ.

Pettigrew, K. E., and Durrance, J. C. (2001). KALIPER: Introduction and overview of results. *Journal of Education for Library and Information Science* 42(3), 170–180.

Richardson, J., Jr. (1982). *The Spirit of Inquiry: The Graduate Library School at Chicago, 1921–1951*. American Library Association, Chicago, IL.

Rothstein, S. (1980). Review of the Conant report: A study of the education of librarians. *College & Research Libraries* 41(6), 532–535.

Roy, L. (1998). Personality, tradition and library spirit: A brief history of librarian education. In *Library and Information Studies Education in the United States* (L. Roy and B. E. Sheldon, eds.), pp. 1–15, Mansell, London.

Seavey, C. A. (ed.), (1984). The ALISE/H.W. Wilson Foundation Accreditation Conference, September 16–18. *Journal of Education for Library and Information Science* 25(2), 63–162.

Shera, J. H. (1972). *The Foundations of Education for Librarianship*. Becker and Hayes, New York.

Smith, L. C. (1998). Defining the role of information science. In *Library and Information Studies Education in the United States* (L. Roy and B. E. Sheldon, eds.), pp. 119–139, Mansell, London.

Stieg, M. F. (1992). *Change and Challenge in Library and Information Science Education*. American Library Association, Chicago, IL.

Stone, A. (2007). Spectrum turns 10: ALA's diversity recruitment program marks its first decade. *American Libraries* 38(2), 42–43.

Sutton, S. A. (2001). Trends, trend projections, and crystal ball gazing. *Journal of Education for Library and Information Science* 42(3), 241–247.

Swank, R. C. (1967). Documentation and information science in the core library school curriculum. *Special Libraries* 58, 40–44.

Taylor, R. S. (1979). Reminiscing about the future: Professional education and the information environment. *Library Journal* 104(16), 1871–1875.

Vann, S. K. (1961). *Training for Librarianship Before 1923: Education for Librarianship Prior to the Publication of Williamson's Report on Training for Library Service*. American Library Association, Chicago, IL.

Vann, S. K. (1971). *The Williamson Reports; A Study*. Scarecrow Press, Metuchen, NJ.

Wheeler, J. L. (1946). *Progress & Problems in Education for Librarianship*. Carnegie Corporation of New York, New York.

White, C. M. (1976). *A Historical Introduction to Library Education: Problems and Progress to 1951*. Scarecrow Press, Metuchen, NJ.

Williamson, C. C. (1923). *Training for Library Service: A Report Prepared for the Carnegie Corporation of New York*. Updike, Boston.

Wilson, L. R. (1940). The objectives of the graduate library school in extending the frontiers of librarianship. In *New Frontiers of Librarianship*, pp. 13–26, Graduate Library School, University of Chicago, Chicago, IL.

# Index